O9-ABF-680

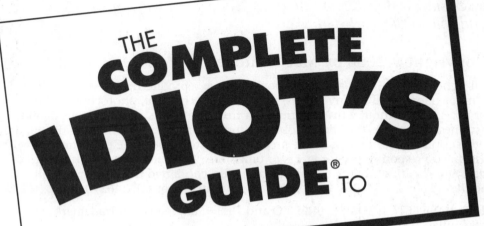

THE COMPLETE IDIOT'S GUIDE® TO

Business Etiquette

by Mary Mitchell
with John Corr

ALLSTON BRANCH LIBRARY

alpha
books

Macmillan USA, Inc.
201 West 103rd Street
Indianapolis, IN 46290

A Pearson Education Company

For Letitia Baldridge, whose foresight and vision led to the very first book on business etiquette. Without her leading the way, this book would not and could not be written.

Copyright © 2000 by Mary Mitchell

All rights reserved. No part of this book shall be reproduced, stored in a retrieval system, or transmitted by any means, electronic, mechanical, photocopying, recording, or otherwise, without written permission from the publisher. No patent liability is assumed with respect to the use of the information contained herein. Although every precaution has been taken in the preparation of this book, the publisher and author assume no responsibility for errors or omissions. Neither is any liability assumed for damages resulting from the use of information contained herein. For information, address Alpha Books, 201 West 103rd Street, Indianapolis, IN 46290.

THE COMPLETE IDIOT'S GUIDE TO and Design are registered trademarks of Macmillan USA, Inc.

International Standard Book Number: 0-02-863615-5
Library of Congress Catalog Card Number: Available upon request

02 01 00   8 7 6 5 4 3 2 1

Interpretation of the printing code: The rightmost number of the first series of numbers is the year of the book's printing; the rightmost number of the second series of numbers is the number of the book's printing. For example, a printing code of 00-1 shows that the first printing occurred in 2000.

Printed in the United States of America

Note: This publication contains the opinions and ideas of its author. It is intended to provide helpful and informative material on the subject matter covered. It is sold with the understanding that the author and publisher are not engaged in rendering professional services in the book. If the reader requires personal assistance or advice, a competent professional should be consulted.

The author and publisher specifically disclaim any responsibility for any liability, loss or risk, personal or otherwise, which is incurred as a consequence, directly or indirectly, of the use and application of any of the contents of this book.

AL BR
HF5389
.M57
2000x

Alpha Development Team

Publisher
Marie Butler-Knight

Editorial Director
Gary M. Krebs

Product Manager
Phil Kitchel

Associate Managing Editor
Cari Shaw Fischer

Acquisitions Editor
Randy Ladenheim-Gil

Development Editor
Joan D. Paterson

Production Team

Production Editor
Michael Thomas

Copy Editor
Cliff Shubs

Illustrator
Jody P. Schaeffer

Cover Designers
Mike Freeland
Kevin Spear

Book Designers
Scott Cook and Amy Adams of DesignLab

Indexer
Chris Wilcox

Layout/Proofreading
Michael J. Poor/Terri Edwards

Contents at a Glance

Contents

Part 2: In the Arena   47

5   A Fact of Office Life: Meetings   49

Part 5: Beyond the Office   217

Foreword

As one of the world's foremost accounting firms, we have had to become sensitive to changes in the international business culture. In doing so, we have found that the most dynamic and pervasive characteristic of the changes happening all around us is the growing appreciation of the importance of courtesy, civility, and kindness in our dealings with our clients, the public, and one another.

A great deal of our employee training is devoted to the development of "people skills." It is becoming increasingly clear that, if you want to swim in the ever-shifting waters of the modern business culture, you must have good business manners.

This is particularly true when dealing with our friends and associates from different cultures. Nevertheless, I believed that good business manners are every bit as important in our everyday dealings with our closest colleagues, our most familiar clients, and others that we meet, however casually, on the job and off.

Accordingly, a comprehensive, sensible, and authoritative guide to correct business manners, such as this one, is an important and valuable work.

Kenneth Daly

Partner-in-Charge
Financial Risk Management
Assurance Services

Introduction

Shifting attitudes and the bubbling stew of old and new behavioral rules and expectations in the business arena can scare you to death, whether you are just entering it or whether you have 20 years of experience under your belt. Business behavior these days is dramatically influenced by new pressures, new complexities, and new sensitivities. And still, many old rules and rituals remain in place and must be observed.

The so-called corporate culture has changed radically in a few short years, and even a degree from the Harvard Business School isn't enough to ensure that you will be able to deal effectively and successfully with the tidal wave of change brought about by the electronic revolution, the shrinking of the globe, the new role of women, the Americans with Disabilities Act, and more.

In business, having good—or even just acceptable—manners these days means so much more than knowing what fork to use, although that is one of the areas covered in this book. It means knowing how to address people, how to introduce them, and how to greet them. It means knowing how to dress for all occasions, how to entertain, and how to converse, correspond, and respond to compliments and criticism. It means being able to handle difficult people and situations with confidence and grace. It means being able to deal with people from different cultures without unknowingly offending them.

People will judge you, perhaps harshly, on your business manners. Poor manners or etiquette ignorance can derail an otherwise promising career. This is neither fair nor unfair; it is simply the reality.

The idea behind this book is to provide the information that will enable you to move about in the business arena with confidence and face daunting situations armed with the knowledge that, whatever the outcome, you have behaved properly through it all.

Everything you need to know about the world of etiquette in the world of business is here in this book, in chapters organized to make that information easy to find, easy to understand, and easy to remember.

Special Features

Four extra items are presented apart from the text. You will see these as boxed notes, and they will help you learn about business etiquette.

Memo to Myself

These boxes contain advice on how to handle various business situations.

Business Blunders

These boxes help you avoid saying or doing the wrong thing in a business setting.

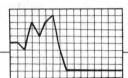

The Bottom Line

These boxes spell out the way it is, getting to the most fundamental facts in any situation.

From the File Drawer

In these longer sidebars you'll find historical information about etiquette and fascinating quotations about how to behave.

Acknowledgements

During the process of writing this book, I was blessed with the generosity of friends and colleagues who willingly shared their expertise and information to help with my project. Heartfelt thanks goes to Marjorie Matthews Corr, Doris Allen-Kirchner, Julian Krinsky, Thea Lammers, Annette Law, Sarah Packer, Dan Rudasill, Jean Valente, Eileen Weinstein, Janet Weiss, Gardi Ipema Wilks, and Kathy Windsor.

Trademarks

All terms mentioned in this book that are known to be or are suspected of being trademarks or service marks have been appropriately capitalized. Alpha Books and Macmillan USA, Inc. cannot attest to the accuracy of this information. Use of a term in this book should not be regarded as affecting the validity of any trademark or service mark.

Part 1

First Things

The world of business and social etiquette, or simply good manners, has been evolving and changing as long as people have lived together in communities. That process continues today.

In this first part of our book, we look at the rules and conventions by which people tend to judge us and explore how those rules came to be what they are. We examine the evolution of business etiquette and how it applies to day-to-day life in the workplace.

As part of "First Things," we look at the way people expect to be greeted and the protocols that apply to the business of introducing people to one another—and introducing ourselves.

This part also includes a chapter on job interviews; Chapter 4, "The Job Interview," should help address many of the concerns and critical issues surrounding how we present ourselves and how we behave during these interviews. After all, these same concerns apply to daily life in the business world as well.

Chapter 1

A Brief History of Etiquette in the United States

In This Chapter

➤ How the rules of behavior evolved

➤ Americans mold their own manners

➤ The literature of civility

➤ Manners at the millennium

Etiquette began back in prehistoric man's time, when old Uncle Orf shared a hunk of mammoth meat with Og the Ugly and was, in turn, invited to sleep that night in Og's damp and dingy cave. Etiquette was then, and is now, based on kindness and the idea that we must have rules of behavior to reduce incidents of head-bashing and their accompanying social tensions. So, Og the Ugly did not eat another person's mammoth meat unless he was invited to do so; likewise, while in Og's cave, Uncle Orf did not sleep on Og's fur pallet without permission.

With those prehistoric conventions in mind, let's take a look at how etiquette grew to what it now is today—this time, by examining more hard-and-fast facts.

Evolution

The history of etiquette got what might be called a growth spurt about 11,000 years ago, when agriculture changed the way humankind lived. People with crops stayed in one place. Communities were formed. People took up social roles that went beyond those who hunted and those who cooked. Head-bashing was on the way out. Cooperation and tolerance were on the way in.

Memo to Myself

Even primitive people learn that life is easier and that things get done more efficiently when behavior is modified out of consideration for others.

Then …

Etiquette is still nothing more than good manners, which is consideration of others based on kindness and respect. It is this foundation of kindness and respect that gives etiquette its authority. As social circumstances changed, etiquette evolved—and it probably reached its most exaggerated and florid expression in Western civilization as medieval chivalry. In fact, many contemporary etiquette rules and practices can trace their roots to the code of behavior known as chivalry. For example, chivalry called for protection of the weak and respect for rank and achievement.

Chivalry

Historian Joseph Strayer traces the emergence of chivalry to the twelfth century in the Aquitaine region of southern France, although it may have had roots even further back with the Moors of Spain.

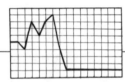

The Bottom Line

In general, access to education in the twelfth century was limited to some nobles and the clergy.

A new sort of upper-class society, comprised principally of royalty, nobles, and clergy and with a new sort of social code, began to emerge in Aquitaine, and this social evolution spread slowly throughout the rest of Western Europe. The new code made important changes in society, imposing some restrictions on brute power and acting as a restraint for bad temper and homicidal passion.

By the end of the twelfth century, chivalry meant honor, loyalty, protection of the weak, and respect for a worthy opponent. The concept of the "gentleman" also took hold.

A true gentleman was expected to demonstrate more than physical prowess. Although society did not place a great deal of emphasis on education until the Renaissance, a gentleman was nevertheless expected to have some knowledge of music, poetry, and history. What's more, he was expected to know how to behave at social gatherings and how to demonstrate respect for superiors, women, the clergy, and the elderly. Suddenly the need for rules to govern this behavior became much more evident.

Courtly Love

Behavior for both sexes was influenced by the idea of courtly love, although these romantic notions were applied almost exclusively to relations outside of matrimony. Marriage remained for some time a business affair, with decisions made on the basis of power and dowries.

However, Strayer believes that the concept of courtly love, the doting love poetry of the time, and the veneration of Mary, the mother of Jesus, proved powerful influences in raising the status of women in general. With this increase in status, women began to be treated with more respect. Marrying for love, once considered a quaint or even daffy notion, began to be accepted more generally.

Even if the social restrictions and traditions that began to evolve from the twelfth century had not begun with the idea of chivalry, they would have come into existence by other means. If society is to function, it must have rules—and if a society is to function smoothly, it must have manners.

Although the basic reasons for rules governing social behavior were the same everywhere, different practices and customs evolved in different places. For instance, accepted funeral attire is white in China and black in the West. This evolutionary journey took a distinctly and characteristically robust road in the United States.

New World Pioneers

Social customs in the United States could not help but depart dramatically from the customs of the Old World. For one thing, most of the early settlers were farmers, peasants, and people who had been cut off from the social attitudes and customs of the "best" European society.

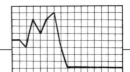

The Bottom Line

The distinctive style of American manners evolved because pioneers wanted to and were able to break from the Old World social structures and traditions.

Those European peasants who settled the United States generally were despised and exploited in their homelands—they made the perilous journey across the wide and fearsome ocean to a strange land because they hated the social rigor of European society and had no intention of recreating it in their new land. In short, they wanted a better life for themselves and for their children.

Besides, there was little time for the contemplation of social graces in the New World—there was a wilderness to conquer. Crops had to be planted and reaped. Towns had to be built, and unknown mountains and valley had to be explored. And the struggle to tame the wilderness was constantly renewed as American civilization marched westward into the unknown.

But every civilization must create its own system of courtesy and manners, and although the evolving American system was somewhat influenced by Old World traditions, it was ultimately shaped by New World circumstances.

One of the most significant of these circumstances was the scarcity of women. In Europe, women were continually in the majority and were both the creators and the guardians of the traditions of courtesy. In the New World, though, women were not only a minority, but they were so scarce and their civilizing influence so valued that men tended to treat them with a consideration that approached reverence. Not only were women respected and protected, but men also competed for their attention with exaggerated and sometimes comical politeness.

Early Manners

Even in the most rough and ready situations in pioneer times, certain minimal standards of civility were in force—and sometimes these standards carried the force of law. Early documents reveal that those accused of lying, cursing, slandering, or flirting faced legal penalties, and these rules were created and enforced by government or the clergy.

Although the new American society lacked the ostentatious refinements of chivalry, the concepts of honor, courage, and respect were part of the fabric of life.

From the File Drawer

Early American guides to proper behavior tended to be rather basic:

"Pick not thy teeth at the table syttyinge nor use at thy meate over much splyttyng."—Francis Seager, *The School of Vertue*, 1557.

"Never use your knife to convey your food to your mouth, under any circumstances; it is unnecessary and glaringly vulgar. Feed yourself with a fork or spoon, nothing else. A knife is only for cutting."—Anonymous, *Hints on Etiquette*, 1836.

A much-reprinted eighteenth-century guide for children advised: "Spit not, cough not, nor blow thy nose at the table, if it may be avoided."

No less a personage than George Washington felt the need to write and publish a "Guide to Civility." This guide, too, concerned itself with the basics. It advised, for example, that adults at the dinner table should refrain from using the tablecloth to clean their teeth.

Moving Up

These back-to-basics behavior guides were later found to be, if not hilarious, at least insufficient. As leisure and wealth increased in the New World, people began looking about for more advanced and comprehensive guidance in the matter of manners.

The Southern plantation owners (and their ladies), plumply pleased with their productive fields and their slave-driven prosperity, and the thriving merchants and tradesmen of the Northern port cities (and their ladies, within the limits of their social freedom, that is) began creating a system of social decorum and even elegance to reflect their new wealth and power.

In these circumstances, Washington's "Guide to Civility" and Ben Franklin's aphorisms ("Fish and visitors stink after three days") would not suffice. More elaborate and refined rules were needed.

So, the new American wealthy and wannabes looked back to England for guidance. What they found were etiquette books in English that were, for the most part, translations, adaptations, and outright plagiarism of French works on the subject.

Since the age of chivalry, the French had been the chief experts and exporters of instruction and advice in matters of manners. (You'll recall that chivalry traces its roots to Aquitaine, France, as mentioned previously.) Those traditions passed along from France, through England, and to the

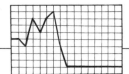

The Bottom Line

The idea of social decorum and mutual respect did not extend to women or to those in bondage, however. Although treated with deference, these people were expected to remain "in their places."

United States actually had *their* origins in the medieval and Renaissance court etiquette of Western Europe. In that society, the sophisticated and civilized gentleman was expected to be not only upright and correct, but also brave, pious, and just. Women were expected to be modest, meek, chaste, and compassionate.

Moving On

So, the bookshelves of Americans of "a better class" became heavy with English books that espoused niceties of dress, deportment, and language that were, at best, inappropriate and, at worse, antithetical to the American way of thinking and doing things.

As the new nation moved into the nineteenth century, many of these Old World social traditions and practices were discarded like a garment too tight for the vigorous, broad-shouldered American.

When England was beaten again in the War of 1812, the United States stirred and stretched as never before, extending its reach to the Rio Grande and the Pacific Ocean. Railroads and waterways such as the Erie Canal carried people into the interior and carried agricultural products back to the East. Towns sprang up, and those towns became cities. Industry huffed and puffed its way across the land.

In 1828, the son of a destitute immigrant, Andrew Jackson, moved into a White House previously occupied by the Harvard-educated Adamses and powerful Virginia land owners. With him came a new idea that ordinary people could make themselves into whatever they wanted to be. More specifically, the new president was living proof that you didn't have to be born a gentleman to be a gentleman.

The New Advisers

Once again, this new semiegalitarian society cast about for its own sort of etiquette. From about 1930 until the Civil War, Americans turned away from imported books of etiquette and began buying up home-grown guides to proper behavior. Unlike the imported books, which emphasized probity, valor and modesty, the American guides presented etiquette as a set of rules to be learned. These Yanks did not have the time or the inclination to be lectured about character, chivalry, and morality; they wanted to learn the rules they needed to know to move comfortably in society.

From the File Drawer

Author Nathaniel Willis wrote in 1851: "We should be glad to see a distinctively American school of good manners, in which all useless etiquette were thrown aside, but every politeness adopted or invented which could promote sensible and easy exchanges of good will and sensibility."

This was a new way of thinking about the value of good manners, and it was quite different from the observation of the English nobleman Lord Chatham in the eighteenth century: "Politeness is benevolence in trifles."

These new books also departed from the imported literature in their overall attitude about how women should behave. Most notably, the guides embodied a distinct shift from the idea that women should be meek, pliant, and weak. At least one advised bluntly that "crying is not longer fashionable."

> The tone of these works was generally less preachy—and was sometimes tongue-in-cheek: "Always keep callers waiting, till they have had time to notice the outlay of money in your parlors."

The Americans' departure from European norms became ever more evident. After the Civil War, the new "American nobility" decided that the proper expression of its wealth and power was to outstrip the moribund "parchment nobility" of the Old World.

This ushered in the era of the Robber Barons, the railroad and steel magnates and the merchant princes. During this period, men such as Andrew Carnegie, John D. Rockefeller, and Cornelius Vanderbilt rose up as leaders of this new nobility and were called "The Four Hundred" in newspapers and magazines. These new plutocrats—some from the most humble beginnings—burst upon the social scene with a sometimes absurd orgy of conspicuous consumption; in the process, they rewrote some of the old mannerly traditions—particularly those mitigating against gross public extravagance—and resurrected some others.

From the File Drawer

This new era was a phenomenon viewed by many with distaste and by some with alarm. E. L. Godkin, journalist, wrote in 1895:

"We are about to renew on this soil, at the end of the 19th Century, the extravagances and follies of the later Roman Empire and of the age of Louis XIV."

Another observer decried the fact that "the sham aristocracy indulges in mushroom manners." Mushrooms, of course, are large but of little consequence.

Abundant Guidance

Ordinary Americans watched the gluttonous flamboyance of the new aristocracy with avid interest, following the flourishes of these almost mythical figures in magazines and newspaper society columns. The desire to learn the rules of "society" and the manners of the "swells" became, if anything, more acute and widespread. Etiquette books flowed into bookstores. Magazines (particularly women's magazines) and newspapers ran "deportment" columns. Even advice to what used to be called "the lovelorn" now contained advice on proper behavior.

However, some backlash arose to all this concern with deportment. Some critics called it "punctilious" and complained about the new devotion to "artificial refinement." To these critics, the *Appleton's Journal* gave the following arch reply in 1871:

"Is it not better to carry punctiliousness a little too far than continually to be sinning against those minor morals on which the pleasure of intercourse so much depends."

And there was no shortage of punctiliousness:

➤ When bowing, only the head was to be bent, and a mere lowering of the eyelids was insufficient and rather rude.

➤ When crossing the street, a lady was to "gracefully raise her dress a little above her ankle."

➤ Formal calls were to last no longer than 15 minutes.

➤ Men were not to smoke in the presence of women, and women were not to smoke at all.

The etiquette of the ballroom was complex and severe. The dining room was a bewildering complexity of goblets, plates and silverware.

Following are some examples of ballroom etiquette:

> "Soup should be eaten with a table spoon, not a dessert spoon. It would be out of place to use a dessert spoon which, as the name implies, is intended for eating fruit tarts, custards, pudding or any sweet not substantial enough to be eaten with a fork." —Manners and Rules of Good Society, 1912.

> "The unmentionable but most necessary disguise of the 'human form divine' is one that never varies in this country, and therefore I must lay down the rule: For all evening wear—dark cloth trousers … tail coat and waistcoat, stiff, tight and comfortless. The plainer the manner in which you wear your misery, the better." —Habits of Good Society, 1859.

The Decline of Opulence

The severity and complexity of all this etiquette began to loosen around the turn of the century. Wealth began to lose its novelty and glamour, and many of the wealthiest families pulled back from ostentatious behavior. The accelerated pace of life began to mitigate against extravagantly ceremonious occasions. Women also became more socially and financially secure and began to develop interests outside the usual social scene.

After World War I, this move away from trivial elegance became more pronounced. The automobile provided freedom of movement. Movies and radio programs celebrated the virtues of the ordinary folk. Finally, the Great Depression seemed to wash away the last of the old society's customs and values.

Naturally, etiquette advice changed along with the times. Emily Post and, to a greater extent, Lillian Eichler offered advice that was less accusatory and more practical and straightforward than the etiquette doyennes of previous eras had delivered.

A consensus seemed to arise that appropriate behavior need not be a complex and severe business, but it could be simpler, more spontaneous, and more genuine. World War II reinforced this perception: The American hero was the grimy guy in the foxhole, the sturdy defense worker on the night shift. Rosy the Riveter became the new and universal symbol of the new status and independence of the American woman.

Postwar Manners In the post-Civil War United States, the extravagant dress and social customs of the rich were both severely criticized and also much copied. In fact, well into the 1950s, concern for correct behavior took the form of fitting in and dressing right. Advice columns and publications remained popular but became more chatty than instructional; they seemed aimed at helping people become "part of the crowd."

Then came the 1960s, the era of denim and disobedience, hippies and the drug culture, long hair and longer dresses. A widespread suspicion arose that having good manners somehow prevented people from "being real." Letitia Baldrige, the renowned arbiter of taste and protocol, was Jacqueline Kennedy's chief of staff at the White House.

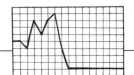

The Bottom Line

Even during the rebellious 1960s, experts on etiquette emerged and were consulted, if not honored.

In 1980, Letitia Baldrige wrote *The Complete Guide to Executive Manners*, the first book devoted solely to corporate manners. This book was an outgrowth of newspaper columns and magazines articles that Baldrige had written, calling for an end to chivalry in the workplace. She was the first to take the position that women were not going to be able to make major decisions in the boardroom if they allowed themselves to be pampered and protected as the weaker sex.

Into the Millennium

From the 1970s and through the 1990s, the most significant changes in attitudes toward good manners have occurred most dramatically in areas of race relations, technology ("Netiquette"), the appreciation of varying cultures, and respect for those with disabilities. The 1990s, in particular, has seen an upsurge in interest in the forms and traditions of good manners, especially in the professional and business worlds. It is becoming even more apparent that "people skills" are as important as—or more important than—technical skills. (Of course, the phrase "people skills" is just another euphemism for good manners.)

As we look back on all the upheavals, disasters, and wonderful achievements of the American society, we find an abiding and continuing willingness and even eagerness to accept information and advice about behavior. We have called it etiquette, manners, courtesy, and just "behaving yourself"—whatever its name, etiquette has been and remains a reflection of the desire of an essentially good natured and vital people to exist harmoniously with those around them.

Memo to Myself

These days, good manners are expected to include an appreciation of the diverse cultures and customs we increasingly encounter on our shrinking planet.

The Least You Need to Know

➤ Although the rules of courtesy vary from place to place and from one era to another, they are based on a desire to live peacefully and happily with one another.

➤ In the United States, as elsewhere, the rules of etiquette change with the times.

➤ There is and always has been a distinct style of American etiquette.

➤ Common sense and friendliness go a long way, but even the most sensible and friendly person can benefit by learning the rules of etiquette that have evolved over the ages.

Etiquette in the Business World

Business manners and social manners evolved along parallel paths in the United States. However, through all the years, all the social trauma, and all the changes in attitude, one characteristic of business etiquette remained in place: Behavior in the business world is based on rank. This is because, although social etiquette has evolved greatly, etiquette that governs society is loosely based on the principles established during the age of chivalry. Business etiquette is based on the rules and traditions of military life.

This was true both before the discovery of the New World and after. There were, however, important differences. In Europe, rank within the business world was rigid. Workers were generally assigned to roles consistent with their "station in life," and it was enormously difficult to advance through the ranks.

In the United States, class lines were not as clear as in the Old World, and a rough-and-ready equality was the norm. The nation was growing fast and changing daily. Often a worker would fulfill many roles, sometimes just assuming them as the situation demanded. Obviously, it was much easier for people to move through the ranks in the American business world. However, this did not substantially diminish the concept of military rank within business establishments or the power of rank within these establishments.

Moving through the ranks these days requires something more than a rough-and-ready willingness to work. In doing research for his book, *Malloy's Live for Success*, author John Malloy found that almost every executive he interviewed considered social skills as a critically important prerequisite to success in the business world. These included practicing good table manners, knowing how to introduce people, being able to carry on a polite conversation, and having a firm grasp on the basic rules of courteous behavior.

Rough Stuff

Being polite is sometimes not enough in the tough and competitive world of business. You must also be prepared to handle crisis situations, personality clashes, criticism, and the other problems that invariably arise when humans gather in one place to get work done.

Memo to Myself

Little things mean a lot in close working situations, particularly little things such as drumming fingernails, humming tunes, and slamming down telephones.

Survival and success in the business world require a knowledge of how to deliver and how to receive both criticism and compliments. As you make your way up the ladder, you will be receiving both; at one rung or another of that same ladder, you will be handing out both. We know it is easy to mishandle these situations for one main reason: They're quite frequently mishandled.

How to Handle Criticism

Unless you and the people you work with are nicer than Santa and smarter than Einstein, you will be giving or receiving criticism during your business career. Expect it, accept it, and respond in a reasonable manner. Following are some tips for dispensing criticism.

Giving Criticism

➤ **Keep it private.** Never criticize someone in front of others.

➤ **Keep it impersonal.** Don't say what the person did was "dumb" or "wrong." Talk about behavior, not personality—and no name-calling.

➤ **Be specific.** Saying that the whole meeting was a mess is not a criticism; it is a complaint. Say instead that the participants should have been notified earlier, that there should have been an overhead projector in the room, and that there should have been a complete, printed agenda.

➤ **Avoid bloodshed.** The purpose of criticism should be to improve performance, not to destroy confidence. Use moderate language and a calm tone of voice. One way to soften the criticism is to begin with a compliment. "You are usually so efficient that I was surprised by the lack of an agenda and an overhead projector. And, really, the participants should have been notified earlier."

In short, kindness and consideration should be at the root of criticism.

Receiving Criticism

It sounds hard to do, but try this: Think of incoming criticism as an opportunity, not a calamity.

➤ Don't duck or run for cover. If you fouled up, take it on the chin. Don't trot out excuses or try to switch the blame. Make it clear that you accept responsibility, that you are sorry, and that you want to fix things and make sure it never happens again.

You might say something like this: "I'm sorry about the foul-up. I can see that I have to think ahead and stay on top of the details."

➤ If it gets personal, don't respond in the same way. Say that you are sorry. You can add something like, "I'm sorry that this has upset you," and give the other person some time (and space) to cool down.

➤ If the criticism is unjustified, you have a perfect right to say so—but be cool. If the other person is not cool at all, put off discussing the matter for the time being.

You might say something like this: "Actually, I was out of the office with a client when that happened. Maybe we should get together later and work this out."

How to Handle Compliments

Compliments and criticism are two sides of the same coin. Both can evoke a strong response, and both can reveal a lot about the character of the people involved.

Giving Compliments

Before you compliment somebody, think over the following points:

➤ Be sincere. Don't compliment someone because you are trying to make a friend or boost morale. False compliments are too transparent. If you don't mean it, don't say it.

➤ Be specific. This is an example of a well-given compliment: "That was an excellent report on upgrading our internal messaging system." On the other hand, this compliment isn't so well-given: "You seem really plugged in on the technology issues."

➤ Be timely. If a compliment is warranted, give it right away. Its value fades with time.

➤ Don't make comparisons. A compliment is usually diminished if you compare it with some other achievement, unless that other achievement is truly terrific—then it sounds insincere.

When somebody deserves to be complimented, don't wait, don't compare, and be honest.

Receiving Compliments

When someone compliments you, that person is not necessarily looking for a response. Yet, people often feel that they must respond at length, which is always a mistake.

➤ Just say "Thank you."

➤ Don't get modest and say something like: "Oh, it was nothing."

➤ Don't say that you could have done even better with more time or more support.

➤ Don't unilaterally upgrade the compliment: "Good? It was better than good. It was terrific."

A simple "Thank you" is usually enough, and its brevity is always appreciated.

How to Handle Conflict

Unpleasant situations often can arise in the work environment, so it's best to be ready. These conflicts take various forms and can happen at any time. Having good manners doesn't mean that you have to attempt to avoid or back away from conflict. On the contrary: Sometimes the only possible and reasonable response is a tough response.

Sexual Harassment

If you're the subject of sexual harassment, react strongly and immediately. Deliver a tough put-down on the spot, and go directly to the senior officer in your company or your department head to report the incident and demand action. The put-down can take many forms, such as these:

"I didn't realize how pathetic you are until this minute. You really are a silly little jerk."

"What a stupid remark. Don't you know you're making a fool of yourself?"

If you take the matter to senior management, give yourself time to calm down and organize your thoughts. If there has been a pattern of offensive behavior, you may want to write out details, including any warning you may have given to the offender.

If you decide that a warning is the correct response, make it strong:

"If you ever say or do anything like this again, I'm going to raise so much hell around here that you will never live it down."

Inappropriate Questions

People sometimes ask stupid and insulting questions, such as "How come you don't have any children?" or "How much do you make, anyway?"

Don't get mad, and don't lecture the jerk on good manners. You can simply ignore the question and go about your business, which in itself sends a clear message of disapproval. You can look the person in the eye for a long moment and say, "I'm not going to answer that."

Another response that puts the questioner on the spot is, "Why do you ask?" You're effectively putting the ball back in the other person's court and dodging a response altogether.

Cosmetic Surgery

If you have had a cosmetic procedure done, it's okay to talk about it. In fact, if you look radically different, broaching the subject will make things easier for those around you. If you think a coworker or friend has had cosmetic surgery, just say something like, "You look wonderful today."

If the other person then says that he has had surgery, ask, "Are you pleased with the results?"

Don't second-guess anyone's decision in this area. Don't tell someone that cosmetic surgery is a "crazy" idea—and don't volunteer the names of others who have had the surgery.

Jokes and Slurs

If someone is telling a dirty joke, you can say, "I don't want to hear this," and move away. If it's too late for that, look the comedian in the eye and say, "I don't think that's funny."

If someone makes an offensive remark or an ethnic slur, you can say, "That remark was out of line" or "If you feel that way, you should keep it to yourself."

Personal Attacks

If someone who is not present is being attacked—particularly if that person is a friend—you can't let it pass without responding. Of course, you certainly don't want to respond by launching your own personal attack on the speaker. Try something like this:

> "I don't think that's true."

> "I don't think that's the way it happened. Even if it is, I'm sure Jane had a good reason for reacting as she did."

If the other person ask what the reason could be, say, "I don't know. Why don't you ask Jane?"

Office Visits

An excellent way to get a quick fix on a person's manners is to watch her behavior while visiting or receiving visitors. People have made judgments about one another in these circumstances probably as far back as the time when home was a cave.

Receiving Visitors

You are as much the host in your office as you are at home. The general rule for receiving visitors is that you should get up, come around your desk, greet the visitors with a handshake, and get them seated before returning to your chair.

If you get the word that a visitor is at the reception area, the general rule is to go there, greet the visitor, and lead him back to the office. If he has a coat, hang it up, or hand it to a receptionist or an assistant to hang up. Don't stand around chatting about the weather in the reception area; get back to the office promptly. The time for opening pleasantries is when you are both seated.

If the visitor is someone who stops by frequently, it may not be necessary to get up to greet him. But you must at least stop what you are doing—no matter how busy you think you are—say hello, and wait for the person to tell you the reason for the visit.

Getting Rid of Pests

If the visitor is someone who has gotten into the annoying habit of stopping by for some idle chat, you can break the habit by saying something like this:

> "I'm sorry, Tom, but I don't have time to see you right now. Can you come back at *(consult your appointment calendar)* 4:30?"

You may have to do this only once or twice before the frequent visitor gets the idea.

If the frequent visitor is a senior executive, you should at least rise when he enters until you are told, "Don't get up."

Paying Visits

Like the host, the visitor has certain definite responsibilities, particularly when visiting a colleague without an appointment. Certainly, the rules for such business visits are not like those that apply to visiting someone's home. However, any unplanned visit represents an interruption. Even when the visit has been scheduled in advance, the visitor must show respect for the host's time and "personal space."

Business Blunders

When visiting, don't carry your coat around. Hang it someplace or drape it over something. On rainy days, don't be a drip—get rid of the boots and umbrella right away.

Rules for Visitors

When you are visiting someone in the workplace, remember that you are entering that person's space just as surely as you are when you visit someone at home. Consider the following guidelines.

➤ Don't enter if you can see that the person is on the telephone or is with someone.

➤ If the person is alone, ask, "Are you free right now?"

➤ If it's going to be a short visit, don't sit down. If it's going to be a longer visit, say so: "Do you have time to go over the numbers on the Caltech project? I want to be sure we're on the same page before we go into the meeting."

➤ Never touch anything on someone's desk, even if it happens to belong to you. Don't even turn around a family picture to get a better look.

➤ If you have a coat, ask where you can hang it. If there is no place to hang it, drape your coat over a chair. Don't carry it around or put it on your lap.

➤ If you are late, apologize and explain—briefly.

➤ Wait to be told where to sit. If the host does not tell you where to sit and remains seated, take what seems to be the most appropriate chair. Don't remain standing at the desk—you are not in the principal's office.

➤ Don't talk to the top of the person's head. Wait for the person to look at you before you speak.

➤ Don't spread out. Keep papers on your lap, not on the other person's desk or on the floor. Put your briefcase or purse on the floor beside you.

Keeping these rules in mind might mean that you can leave after a visit feeling fairly certain that you will be welcome the next time you visit.

Home Sweet Cubicle

Don't be a cubicle-crasher. For those who must work in one of those cubicle complexes, privacy becomes all the more precious because there is so little of it. Be considerate:

Memo to Myself

Treat everyone's cubicle space as if it were an office with a door.

➤ Don't be a partition-hanger. Avoid peering over or, worse, draping yourself over the top of the cubicle wall to speak with the occupant.

➤ If the person is on the telephone or is with someone, come back later.

➤ Stand at the entrance and ask if the person has time to speak with you. If it's something that can be answered or resolved quickly, it might be easier to deal with it without entering the cubicle space.

➤ If you go in, don't touch anything.

Cubicle life is intrinsically bothersome; don't make it worse with inconsiderate behavior.

Asking for a Raise

If you believe that you deserve a raise, go ahead and ask for it. Don't beat around the bush. Say something like this:

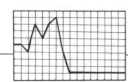

The Bottom Line

One tactic you might consider is to ask for benefits or privileges rather than a cash raise. Examples include a company car, a company credit card, or increased medical benefits. Sometimes these can be more beneficial than cash.

"I've been taking a look at the department goals and how my performance relates to it. I'd like to discuss my compensation."

Do not link your request to your personal needs. You deserve more compensation in the light of what you do and how it benefits the company. Build your case in dollars. Prepare for this by building a record of doing first-rate work and doing a bit more than is expected. One way of building that record is to let the boss know about your accomplishments through a brief note:

"We got the Williams shipment out well ahead of deadline for the third time this year, and the client expresses his appreciation."

Your message should be modest, enthusiastic, and, above all, brief. Remember that raises are seldom based on performance charts, but rather on personal evaluations. Even companies that have tight salary budgets can be flexible. So, if you believe you deserve it, ask for it.

The Smoking Dilemma

Don't let your reputation—or your career—go up in smoke. In times past, a cigarette was a symbol of sophistication. Now, smoking symbolizes addiction and weakness. If your building is a nonsmoking building, and you are one of the people huddled at the entrances to smoke in good weather and bad, you will have to accept the fact that you may be stigmatized as one of the weak ones by people passing in and out.

In addition, because of the now-documented threat of secondhand smoke, some non-smokers consider the presence of tobacco smoke in the air an actual assault on their health. Smokers sometimes encounter downright belligerent reactions.

Even if smoking is permitted in your building, follow these guidelines:

➤ Never smoke in a room where there are no ashtrays.

➤ Smoke only in designated areas

➤ If you smoke in your office, remember that the lingering stink of stale smoke will be offensive to some visitors.

➤ Don't say, "Do you mind if I smoke?" If the other person says she does mind, it creates an uncomfortable situation. On the other hand, the person may say she doesn't mind and yet still be resentful.

➤ At lunch, it is best to refrain, even when you're sitting in the smoking section. If you absolutely must light up, wait until everyone has finished eating, and never use a plate or saucer as an ashtray.

Following these simple guidelines will help to ease the situation.

Dance of the Doors

Somehow, the wish to be "mannerly" causes people to behave irrationally when it comes to doors. They dash ahead of others so that they can be the one to open the door, and they stand there holding the door and beaming until everyone in sight has passed through. They also insist on holding the door open for the next person, even if that person is a good distance away, thereby forcing that person to skip along faster than he or she might want to. It's annoying and so unnecessary.

Memo to Myself

Always thank a person who holds the door for you, even if you wish she hadn't.

Door Dogma

Just remember the basic dogma of doors: Nobody appointed you doorman. Regardless of gender, if you are the first of a group to reach the door, open it and go through it, holding it just long enough to make sure that it doesn't slam into the person following you. If you are alone, glance back to make sure nobody will be hit when you release the door, and keep moving.

Every Rule Has an Exception

An exception to the door dogma is when someone coming along is carrying a package or a child. In this case, wait and hold the door open. Another exception occurs when you are hosting others or showing them around. In these circumstances, it's a good idea to open the door for your guests and motion them to precede you. If it's a revolving door, you go through first and wait for the others on the opposite side.

Men no longer hold doors open for women just because they are women. Some women resent such "courtly" gestures.

In the presence of a senior executive or an honored guest, it's a good idea to let that person reach the door first and go through it.

Elevator Downers

As with doors, a lot of unnecessary and annoying displays of "good manners" occur in connection with elevators.

Basic rule #1: Do not maneuver around so that someone else can be the first one on or off.

➤ If you are among the first to enter on the ground floor and will be getting off at one of the lower floors, stand in the corner near the door and let others fill in the space behind you.

➤ If you are in the front and are getting off at a higher floor, step out at intervening stops, hold your hand on the door to prevent it from closing, and reboard after others have gotten off.

➤ If you are at the control panel, press the hold button to keep the doors open until everyone is aboard; then ask people to call out their floors so that you can press the floor buttons for them.

Basic rule #2: Just stand there. Save conversations and witticisms. Don't remove hats, coats, or gloves because you may bump others or cause them to think you will.

Gift Gaffes

Gift-giving at the office is an area that calls for caution and cool judgment. Consider two basic rules:

1. Extravagance is bad manners and bad strategy. This may make the recipient feel that an equally expensive gift is expected in return, and it sets a standard that you may not wish to keep up in the future.

2. It's better to keep the gift-giving out of the office, when possible. These occasions—particularly around holidays—can turn into popularity contests, resulting in hurt feelings or resentment. Besides, all work stops during un-wrapping, thanking, chatting, and so forth.

When You're the Boss

Every time you give gifts to employees at holidays or on other special occasions, you are setting a benchmark. Whatever the value of this year's gifts, employees may expect it to be matched or exceeded in future years, provided that business continues to be good. If you give a token gift this year after giving a substantial gift last year, it can cause disappointment and confusion—and possibly a rumor that the company is going through hard times or that the boss is unhappy with just about everyone. A ceiling of $25 dollars is a good guideline, particularly because this is the limit the government puts on such expenditures for them to be tax-deductible.

Of course, there are exceptions. If an employee has been with the company for a long time, or if a personal relationship has developed (as it sometimes does with administrative assistants or other close aides), you might want to spend up to $100. More extravagant gifts may be given on significant anniversaries, such at 10 or 20 years of faithful service. In any case, it's a good idea to keep a record of who got what and when.

When You're the Employee

No matter what the boss does, the employee is under no obligation to give gifts to superiors. In fact, this could be a very bad idea. You could be labeled as an apple-polisher. Or, the boss could be very annoyed at what he sees as an unwelcome effort to push your relationship into an area he is not comfortable with. The safest time to give the boss a gift is when something good—something unexpected—happens, such as a promotion. Then it should take the form of cookies or brownies, or some flowers from your garden.

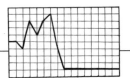

The Bottom Line

If the gift for the boss is more than cookies, it should come from a group. When in doubt, less extravagant is better than more extravagant.

If the gift is to take other forms, the recipient should feel that some thought went into the selection of the gift. This might involve speaking with the recipients' secretary or spouse to inquire about hobbies or tastes in books, music, and food.

The gift should be nicely wrapped and presented in person and should be accompanied by a handwritten note. Even if it is just a few words, a handwritten note is infinitely better than a gift-shop card with printed platitudes.

Wedding Bells

If a colleague or important customer gets married, it is appropriate to send a wedding gift, even if you are not invited to the wedding. If the person deals with a group in your company, a group present may be appropriate. In any case, the gift should not be expensive, perhaps in the $25 range.

Business Blunders

Registering is for weddings *only*. You may not, for example, send out a birth announcement with a "registered at" note.

Then Come Babies

For a client or colleague, the same rules apply as for a wedding. A typical ceiling price would be about $50, and people should all chip in.

If you're the boss, you should acknowledge the birth of a child to a manager with a gift. It's a good idea to have a standard gift, something such as a fine edition of a children's classic, for all children. Some CEOs send a personal, signed letter to the child, predicting a happy and successful life.

Gift-Giving Guidelines

These guidelines will help you through the gift-giving mine fields:

➤ Joke gifts are funny only for a moment, if that long. It's best to stay away from them.

➤ Be careful about gifts of flowers, particularly red roses. These may be seen as having romantic implications. Green plants are safer and more durable. I also have some reservations about sending flowers to hospital rooms because they may not get taken away when they begin to fade. Sick people don't need reminders of the transitory nature of living things.

➤ Never send a gift of alcohol to a person's office. Most companies prohibit alcohol consumption on the job, and the mere presence of booze on somebody's desk looks unprofessional.

➤ Never send a gift to the office of a reporter or editor as thanks for good publicity. This looks too much like a payoff, and it's embarrassing. A thank-you note is quite enough, and it should express thanks for accuracy, thoroughness, and/or good writing, not "publicity."

Receive gifts graciously. Whatever the gift—and however inappropriate or trivial it may seem—it represents some thought and effort on the part of the giver. Respond with warmth to the thought and the effort, even if you can't muster much enthusiasm for the gift itself.

Instituting Awards

If your company decides to institute an awards program, and you are the boss (or the one designated to set up the program), the first thing to do is strive for a consensus on the program's name and purpose. If it's an employee award program, try to get employee input in designing it. Make sure employees know about the criteria for picking a winner and exactly what employees must do to qualify. Make sure winners get as much media exposure, both internally and externally, as possible. Videotape the event.

Decide whether the awards are to be given at specific intervals or on an ad hoc basis.

If you are honoring some prominent person outside the company, make sure that there is sufficient staff to provide transportation and tend to other details. Have copies of the awardee's biography for the emcee of the event and the media.

The Least You Need to Know

➤ Acceptable business behavior changes with changing times but has always been based on rank within the business establishment.

➤ Be prepared for conflict and criticism as well as compliments.

➤ The worst mistake you can make about sexual harassment is committing it. The second worst is enduring it; react immediately and strongly.

➤ Respect other people's office space.

➤ Extravagance is bad manners and bad strategy where gifts are concerned.

Chapter 3

Greetings and Introductions

In This Chapter

➤ Why we need to consider basics

➤ A firm formula for introductions

➤ Navigating through business social functions

➤ Getting the names and titles right

➤ Business card etiquette

Few areas exist in which the rules of business etiquette are more clearly drawn than those governing our behavior when we meet, greet, and introduce people. People want their presence to be acknowledged, and they want to be greeted properly. That said, there are also few situations in which disregarding the rules is more damaging to your reputation—and perhaps your career.

Rising to the Occasion

A simple, proper greeting involves more than is immediately apparent. Let's go over the basics:

1. You should always rise when greeting someone, and you should usually rise when someone new joins the group. (At one time women remained seated when a new person joined a group, but that time is long gone.) There are a few exceptions to this rule: At a very large gathering, only those nearest the new arrivals

rise to greet them. Also, don't rise when it would obviously be inconvenient—if you are wedged behind a table or have things on your lap, for example. In these circumstances, a partial rise or leaning forward is enough to acknowledge an arrival or an introduction.

2. In an office, you should not only rise, but also come around your desk to greet people, unless the person is a colleague or a staff member who visits frequently. Always rise and go to meet a senior executive, no matter how often he visits, if you know what's good for you.

3. Make eye contact and smile.

4. Always shake the hand extended in friendship.

May I Introduce ...

Definite rules govern introductions, and the first and most important one is to make them. It is a most egregious breach of etiquette to allow someone to stand around unacknowledged. In fact, it is better to botch someone's name or even misidentify him than to ignore him.

Memo to Myself

For a proper introduction, say "May I introduce to you ... ," and not "May I introduce you to ...."

First Things

The next most important rule is the "who's first?" rule. In strictly social situations, the person mentioned first—the one being "presented"—is often given preference because of age, sex, or position within the family. That's because social etiquette had its beginnings in chivalry. Business etiquette, however, is based on rank, not age and gender. In business settings, the person of greater authority or importance is mentioned first:

> Mr./Ms Greater Authority, may I present Mr./Ms. Lesser Authority.

However, there's an exception to this rule: The highest-ranking person in your company does not outrank your client. In this case, you mention the client first:

> "Jim Sullivan, I would like to introduce Cora Brady, our chief executive officer."

When introducing persons of equal rank, you may want to hark back to the old chivalry guidelines, giving preference to older people, but it certainly isn't necessary.

Here's Looking at You

Look at the people you are introducing as you introduce them. Look first at the person of greater authority or importance, and then turn and speak to the person of lesser rank.

Names Are Not Enough

Always provide more than the name and title in your introduction. Supplying a nugget of information along with the name and title can serve as a conversation-starter and makes both parties more comfortable. It can also serve as a warning:

"Tom is the auditor looking into the McGonigle matter."

"Margaret is a lawyer with the MicroDyno Corporation."

And always, always let people know when they are being introduced to a member of the media so that they will be aware that they could be speaking "on the record."

Finally, don't dash through introductions. Taking your time makes people feel important—and makes you look savvy.

Introducing Yourself

Sometimes good manners require us to introduce ourselves. Don't be shy—go ahead and introduce yourself in these circumstances:

➤ When you find yourself among persons you don't know at a business or social gathering.

➤ When the person who was expected to make the introductions fails to do so or overlooks you.

➤ When you are seated next to someone at a meal.

➤ When it becomes obvious that someone you have met previously is having trouble placing you. Say something like this:

"Hello, I'm Gail Worthy. We met last spring at the Web page workshop in Dallas."

The nugget rule also applies when introducing yourself. Consider the following example:

"Hello. I'm Brad Coglin. I'm here with the oversight team from ComTech."

This introduction is friendly and a conversation-starter. But go lightly on the details. The others don't need to know up front what your specific functions are or how long you've been on the job or how far you traveled to get there.

Introduce yourself with your first and last name. Do not give yourself an honorific, such as "mister" or "doctor" or "professor." You can say, "Hello, I'm Carter Phelps, a dentist from Seattle." That will signal the other person to respond by calling you Dr. Phelps. And then you may (or may not) say, "Please call me Carter."

Introducing yourself by what you do rather than by your title helps to jump-start conversation. For example, instead of introducing myself by saying, "I'm president of Uncommon Courtesies," I might say, "I write a syndicated column about manners and go all over the world teaching interpersonal skills to corporate employees."

Then What Do I Say?

As important as making introductions is, knowing how to respond when being introduced is equally important.

Informal Responses

No matter how casual the context, a simple "Hi" or "Hello" is not enough. Use the person's name and, if you can, add something, keeping it brief and friendly:

"Hello, Mr. Eckhart. I enjoyed hearing your talk this morning."

Formal Responses

The response to a formal introduction is "How do you do?", followed by the other person's name. (Formal or informal, you should not use the other person's first name until invited to do so.) And remember that "How do you do?" is not a literal question. The response to "How do you do?" is "How do you do?".

Shaking Hands

It's amazing that so little thought is given to the handshake, as it is such a universal practice and so important to our perception of one another. For such an important gesture, the handshake is so often done so badly.

Take a look at the 10 commandments of the handshake:

1. It is firm but painless.
2. It comes with a smile and eye contact.
3. It starts and stops crisply.
4. It lasts no longer than 2 or 3 seconds and is comprised of no more than two or three pumps.
5. It does not continue through an entire introduction. Wait until the introduction is finished before extending your hand.

6. Always be ready to shake hands. That means remembering to leave your right hand free of food, drinks, papers, and other items.

7. Always, always shake with your right hand. If you're carrying something, switch hands or put the object down somewhere before shaking.

8. Don't wear rings on your right hand—they could get squeezed into your skin during a firm handshake, causing you to wince or squirm.

9. Never use the handshake to "drag" the person to the next introduction.

10. If your hand is clammy, give it a swift swipe on your clothing before reaching out to shake.

From the File Drawer

The custom of shaking hands goes back centuries to a time when lawlessness was so commonplace that meeting a stranger—particularly when traveling—could mean danger. As a result, a man encountering someone he did not recognize would automatically reach for his dagger or sword. The stranger would do likewise. When both realized this was a peaceful meeting, they would extend their right hands, without weapons, as a token of friendship.

Handshake Technique

Looking for a foolproof way of avoiding the knuckle-cruncher and the limp-fish "finger" handshakes? Both are bad news in a business context, as is the infamous two-handed shake.

The secret to avoiding getting—or giving—a cruncher or a "finger" shake is to get your hand all the way into the other person's hand so that the web between your thumb and index finger makes contact with that of the other person, locking thumb to thumb.

Extend your hand open, with fingers together. Plant your feet firmly so that you don't rock. Make eye contact. I have noticed that women sometimes make the mistake of standing too close while shaking hands with a taller man. This causes the woman to lean or rock backward to make eye contact. When this happens, the perception is that they are backing away from authority. It's better to stop a little short and then step in or lean in a bit.

Begin with your fingers together and your thumb up.

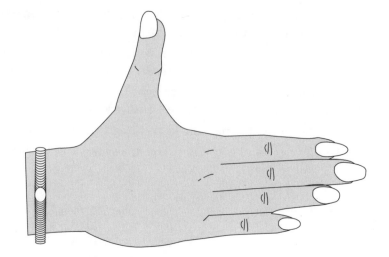

Shake hands web-to-web, with a firm but not crushing grip.

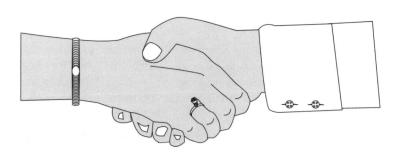

Never offer only your fingertips, causing a weak, limp handshake.

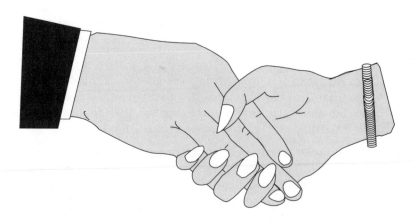

When Do I Shake Hands?

Be sure to shake hands in these circumstances:

➤ When another person offers his or her hand

➤ When you meet someone

➤ When you greet guests, or when you greet the host or hostess

➤ When you renew an acquaintance

➤ When you say goodbye

Touching Is Taboo

Really, the only appropriate physical contact in the business world is the handshake. Otherwise, touching in the workplace—including draping your arm on someone's shoulder or patting another person on the back—is inappropriate, even if the person is of the same gender and even if the person is your friend (or you think he is). Hugs and kisses are out of the question, even at business social functions. Of course, it is acceptable at such functions to give your spouse a perfunctory welcoming kiss, if you happen to be getting along that day.

Business Blunders

Except for the handshake, touching is taboo in the business arena. This includes back-slapping and bicep-grasping.

Party Introductions

Be sure to consider additional factors as well when it comes to meeting and greeting people at business social functions. These include the level of informality, the venue, and the reason for the event. The ideal situation is for the designated host to meet and greet each of the guests. However, this is not always possible. The host may not know the guests by name, for example, and will either appoint a substitute greeter or have more knowledgeable persons join him in the receiving line.

What Is a Substitute Greeter?

The job of the substitute greeter is to introduce the guest to the host and others and to integrate that guest into the room. The substitute greets the guest with a handshake:

"Hello. I'm Helen Thornton. Thanks for coming."

She learns who the guest is and then says something like this:

"Come along and meet our president, Harvey Powell." (At a social gathering, first and last names are appropriate.) Then:

"Harvey Powell, this is Gilbert Smith, the architect on the Fairview Project." Then;

"Mr. Smith, you might want to chat with Ted Wayne, who is going to be working closely with the project." Or;

"The bar and the buffet are just over this way."

It is probably not possible—and certainly not necessary—to introduce the newcomer to everyone at the party. Introduce him to the closest person or group, saying his name first and then naming others in the group or asking them to introduce themselves.

Memo to Myself

Unless a woman specifically asks to be addressed as Miss or Mrs., she should be addressed as—and introduced as—Ms. (pronounced *Mizz*). In a business context, it's "Mrs. Susan Kelly," not "Mrs. Edward Kelly."

The Name Game

The wish to be acknowledged is universal, and doing so properly is one of the basic pillars of good manners. This means addressing people by their correct name and title.

In the business arena, where rank is so important, getting the title right is as vital as getting the name right. Titles signify rank and, for many, symbolize the effort, energy, and talent required to achieve that rank. Be warned: It is more than just an annoyance when you refer to the senior vice president as the vice president or call an administrative assistant a secretary.

Memorizing names and titles on your company's executive tree is time well spent. It is also important to keep tuned in to transfers and promotions. A note of congratulations on a promotion is a worthwhile investment in good will.

Getting It Right

They may not show it, but people wince inwardly when you mispronounce their names, even those with names that lend themselves to error. In fact, those with difficult names are particularly pleased when people make the effort to know and use the correct pronunciation. When in doubt, ask:

Business Blunders

Never, never make a joke about a person's name, even if that person is not present. These jokes are not funny, and they have an almost magical way of getting back to the person whose name is being ridiculed.

> "Sorry, but I'm not sure how to pronounce your name correctly. Can you help me out?"

If someone is introduced to you and you miss the name or are unsure of the pronunciation, ask apologetically but immediately for the name to be repeated.

On the other hand, if your name is difficult to pronounce, it is a generous and gracious gesture to step in and help someone who is making an honest effort to get it right. Don't make a big deal out of it. Smile and say something like this:

> "It's a tough one, isn't it?"

Then pronounce the name clearly. Your rescue operation will be appreciated and remembered.

Into the Abyss

All of us have experienced that tiny twinge of panic when we find that a name has utterly disappeared from our memory bank. Remember that it happens to everybody, and don't make a fuss about it:

> "Please tell me your name. I seem to have a mental vapor lock."

This immediately focuses on the solution, and not the embarrassing problem. If you remember anything about the person, this is a mitigating circumstance and should be used.

> "I remember your interesting remarks at the software seminar."

Memo to Myself

Here's a good way to remember names: When someone is introduced, immediately repeat the name silently and use it in the conversation at the first possible moment.

Anyone who has ever forgotten a name—and that probably includes all of humankind—will be sympathetic to your predicament, as you should be if you suspect that someone has forgotten your name. Smile, put out your hand, and say your name.

The Ritual of Business Cards

The exchange of business cards is often, but not always, part of the greeting ritual in the business world. This card is more than a piece of paper with words and numbers on it; it is an important part of your personal presence and a part of how others in the business world perceive you.

Unfortunately, however, there seems to be a widespread and profound ignorance of the etiquette of business cards.

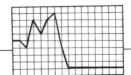

The Bottom Line

Giving your business card to anyone who will take it is a bad idea. You may soon come to regret supplying a stranger with your name, business address, and telephone number.

What?

The card should contain basic information: your name, the company name, postal and e-mail addresses, telephone and fax numbers, and Web site address, if you have one. For most businesses, it is better to avoid typographic flourishes beyond the company logo.

Why?

The card is to be used to convey basic but vital information about you. It should be appended to a document, photograph, or other material you wish to circulate.

You also can enclose a business card with a gift or flowers. You can write a note on the card, crossing out the last name if you are pals.

Memo to Myself

Present your business card with the type side up. When someone hands you a card, look at it and then look at the giver to connect the card with a face. Then put the card away.

When?

This is where people make the most serious mistakes when it comes to business cards. The most frequent abuse is "papering the house." Just because you have 20 cards in your pocket—and 500 more in a drawer somewhere—doesn't mean you should be scattering them around.

➤ Do not thrust your card on anyone, particularly someone senior to you. Wait until you are asked.

➤ When in a group, do not pass out your cards to everyone, like a homework assignment. This gives the impression that you are trying to sell something.

➤ Your card should never surface during a meal, whether it's at a burger joint or at the White House. Obviously, if you are on the selling side and the buying side asks for a card, provide it.

➤ Never present a soiled, damaged, or out-of-date card. If you do not have a presentable card with you and the situation calls for presenting a card, briefly explain, apologize, and write out the information on a clean piece of paper.

➤ Be discreet and unobtrusive about giving someone your card at a social function. Think of it as a private exchange between two individuals.

You should have your cards with you at all times in case you are specifically asked for one. If a circumstance arises in which you believe that it is important and appropriate for the other person to have your card, ask: "May I give you my card?" and not, "Here's my card."

What's Your Style?

Yes, it is important for you to know and remember this chapter's rules for greeting and introducing people and presenting yourself to others. But it is equally important—or perhaps even more important—for you to think of the style of your greetings.

1. Your style should be friendly, open, and generous.
2. No greeting should be so formal that it is without warmth.

One way to develop a gracious greeting style is to remember when you are preparing to meet someone that there is a shared humanity between you. Tell yourself that this is a person you will enjoy meeting, a person who could become your friend. When your smile and your voice reflect sincerity and generosity, others will detect these qualities instantly and respond.

The Least You Need to Know

➤ The most important thing about introductions is to make them.

➤ Mention the most important person first.

➤ Don't hesitate to introduce yourself, but don't overdo it.

➤ Avoid the knuckle-cruncher, limp fish, and two-handed handshakes.

➤ Get the name right, and get the right title to go with it.

➤ Present business cards properly and only when appropriate.

Chapter 4

The Job Interview

In this Chapter

➤ How to prepare and what to expect

➤ Looking out for how you look

➤ Making that good first impression

➤ Strategies for the video interview

➤ What to do after the interview

In few situations will your manners, your etiquette awareness, and your poise be observed more carefully and critically than during the job interview. We included this chapter in the first part of the book because the issues and attitudes that are involved with getting ready for and participating in the job interview go to the heart of so much of what we think of as good business manners. This chapter also emphasizes a point that comes up again and again when we discuss crucial social and business encounters:

Poise is a child of confidence, and confidence is a child of preparedness.

Opportunities Unlimited

Don't think of your job interview as a test; think of it as an opportunity. Remind yourself that it is the interviewer's job to hire people. The company needs someone, or it wouldn't be interviewing, and the interviewer is hoping that you are one of the people the company is looking for.

Do Your Research

Find out everything you can about the company. Read any reports and brochures you can find. Find out if the company has a Web page. Try to contact someone who works there to get her impression of the kind of person the company wants. Before you walk in the door, make sure you know the correct pronunciation and spelling of the company name, what it does, how large it is, and whether it is a national, international, or regional enterprise.

Every company has its own personality. Try to ascertain its general reputation, the sort of work environment you can expect, its attitude toward minorities and women, and how its salary and benefit packages compare with similar companies.

From the File Drawer

One major accounting firm for which I worked insisted that men wear suits and ties. Women were not permitted to wear pants. The following year, the company went to a dress-down Friday code, and women were permitted to wear pantsuits. The following year, the company went to a business casual policy. Now men do not wear jackets, and women may wear pants anytime.

Where to Look

These source materials may be helpful, providing basic information about companies or corporations you may be considering joining. Your local library is the place to look for them.

➤ Moody's manuals

➤ *F & S Index of Corporations and Businesses*

➤ *Standard and Poor's Register*

➤ *McRae's Bluebook*

➤ Fitch Corporation manuals

Make sure you are using current editions.

Scoping It Out

Make a pre-interview visit. Find out how long it takes to reach the building, where to park, and, if possible, exactly how to reach the office of the person you will be seeing. This will reduce your anxiety level on the day of the actual interview and thus boost your confidence. It will also give you a general impression of how people dress.

What Do I Wear?

Find out if the company has a dress code. If necessary, just call Human Resources and ask. In any case, use common sense. At some places, khakis and loafers are fine. At others, suits and neckties are expected. When in doubt, dress *more* conservatively rather than *less* conservatively for the job interview. Avoid extravagant jewelry, tight trousers, and short skirts.

If the company has a casual Friday policy and your interview is on a Friday, ignore the policy—there is no such thing as a "casual" job interview. Men also should not wear hats. Younger men seem to think that baseball caps are suitable for all occasions; they are not, of course, and they are particularly inappropriate for a job interview, even if the job in question is second baseman. (See Chapter 6, "Business Attire and Accessories.")

Making an Entrance

Seize this, your only chance to make a good first impression. Present yourself to the receptionist or secretary, say that you have an appointment with Ms. Jones, and immediately ask where you can put your topcoat/raincoat/umbrella. Dispose of your coat even if there is no receptionist and you are greeted upon entering by Ms. Jones herself; you don't want to sit through an interview with your coat on your lap.

Business Blunders

Never walk into another person's office and just sit down. Wait until you are asked to take a seat; if you have any doubt, don't hesitate to say, "Where would you like me to sit?"

If Ms. Jones comes out to the reception area to fetch you, stand up, make eye contact, and be prepared to shake hands. (For more on proper hand-shake form, see Chapter 3, "Greetings and Introductions.") Follow her to her office; if she stands aside to allow you to enter first, do so without hesitation.

If simply directed to the office, pause at the door until invited to enter, and then enter purposefully. Don't sit until asked to do so. Sit straight and all the way back. Put your briefcase or purse, if any, on the floor beside your chair; put your files, if any, on your lap.

Breaking the Ice

Be prepared to answer an ice-breaker question that is designed to get the conversation started.

"Did you have any trouble finding the building?"

"Did you get caught in the rain?"

"Is this your first visit to Charleston?"

Ms. Jones may begin with questions she already knows the answers to or can easily find on your résumé. That's because she is really assessing your personality and getting a sense of your appreciation of business manners.

Remember these points about responding to ice-breaker questions:

➤ Answer concisely.

➤ Never interrupt.

➤ If the interviewer pauses, don't jump in to fill the gap.

➤ Listen carefully, and look at the interviewer when you speak, not at your hands or the ceiling.

➤ If the question is even slightly difficult or sensitive, pause a moment before answering, as any thoughtful, serious person would.

Memo to Myself

It might make you feel more confident to do a mock interview with a friend before the actual job interview. You could even have another friend videotape it so that you can critique yourself afterward.

Make up your mind that you will answer all questions frankly and fully. A trained interviewer will immediately spot any effort to fudge or deceive. It is more than likely that you will be asked why you left your last employer. Be truthful, but avoid focusing on past personality conflicts. Where possible, turn negatives into positives. Instead of saying that you were being passed over for promotions, say that you are looking for more of a challenge or more opportunity.

After the ice-breaker and routine questions about your background, experience, and education, you'll be asked the "essay" questions. Don't hesitate to sell yourself. Be prepared to talk about your achievements and awards at school or on the job. Also be ready to talk about your interests and hobbies.

Will You Pass the Screening Interview?

Your first interview with a company may well be a screening interview. Its purpose could be to screen out applicants who are clearly unsuitable. This interviewer wants to know the basics:

1. Do you have sufficient language skills?

2. Are you willing to relocate?

3. Do you have the required educational background?

But don't think you can be careless or casual about this interview. Show up on time. Dress conservatively. Listen carefully, and don't volunteer information that you haven't been asked for unless you believe that the information is very important. You want to come across as alert and friendly, but not chatty.

Memo to Myself

Let the interviewer run the show. Don't try to manipulate the direction of the conversation. You want a balance between acting like a robot on one hand and seeming to interview the interviewer on the other. There are questions that can help to establish rapport, such as, "What are you looking for in a candidate?" or "Could you tell me what my typical day would be like?"

Trial by Telephone

Sometimes these interviews are done by telephone. If so, make sure that you have all the material you will need close at hand. Remember that a smile can be heard over the telephone; put some energy into your voice. If you are not prepared with materials and whatever else you may need, it is better to get the name and number of the interviewer and return the call promptly. Above all, make sure that you have energy in your voice.

Business Blunders

During a job interview, never criticize your former employer; this creates the impression that you are disloyal and a malcontent.

Teleconferencing

You may be asked to go to an office and sit in front of a camera for your screening interview. This can be disconcerting, but here are some tips for carrying it off with confidence.

➤ If possible, ask for a preliminary telephone conversation with the interviewer to establish some rapport. You can say that you have never done such an interview and are a little curious about what to expect. If nothing else, this will generate a little sympathetic conversation.

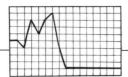

The Bottom Line

Clothes that you consider sexually attractive are generally all wrong for the job interview. There's a big difference between being attractive and being provocative. Sit in front of a mirror to check skirt length. When in doubt, don't wear it.

➤ Arrive a little early, and familiarize yourself with the equipment. It may be possible to adjust the volume, brightness, focus, and other camera functions with a remote. Once the interview begins, however, make no further adjustments.

➤ Don't let the camera rattle you. Remind yourself that, for the recruiter, this is just another routine screening interview. Don't think of it as an audition. Think of it as a conversation. Treat the camera as if it is the recruiter, and look at it when you speak. If there happens to be a monitor, ignore it. If you look at the monitor instead of the camera, it will appear that you are speaking to someone other than the interviewer.

➤ The voice may be out of sync with the picture because of transmission lags. Don't let it throw you.

Above all, remember that the interviewer is looking for the same things as in a person-to-person interview.

Pros and Amateurs

If the company is a large one, your interviewer is likely to have wide experience in hiring. Then again, you may encounter an inexperienced interviewer, such as the owner of a small company. Let's look at both scenarios.

Memo to Myself

Go easy on cologne or perfume. If the interviewer is allergic or sensitive to aromas, the interview will be cut short.

The Pro

This interview will follow a predictable course right up to, but often not including, the end. It will begin with questions about the material in your resumé, and you will be asked to elaborate on past experience or activities and courses at school. Then the "essay" questions start:

"What are your long-range (and/or short-term) goals?"

"Why are you interested in joining this company?"

"Tell me about yourself."

Respond with active, positive language. Stay away from responses that contain negatives:

"I'm not good with math or science, so I'm drawn more to the creative side."

Also avoid vague responses:

"I guess my goal is to get this job and see how things work out."

"I've heard the company has pretty good benefits."

Be positive:

"I'm committed to learning, and I'm prepared to do what it takes to be successful.

"I'm eager to get started on a career in (whatever). This is what I've always wanted to do."

Don't think of these questions as something to get through, but as opportunities to make points for yourself.

The Amateur

During this interview, be prepared for some vague and seemingly irrelevant questions. This person may be feeling as if he's fishing in unknown waters and casting a broad net. He knows what kind of person he wants to hire, but he may not know the kinds of questions that let him know whether he has found that person. So, he may be asking questions just to keep the conversation going until some inner bell chimes and his intuition kicks in.

What he is looking for, whether he knows it or not, is honesty, energy, intelligence, and personality. Keep your answers to the point. Don't slouch or look around aimlessly while this is going on. Use positive language, and resist the temptation to ramble on.

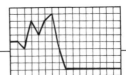

The Bottom Line

Never touch anything on another person's desk. This is a serious breach of good manners and an invasion of privacy. It is similar to visiting someone's home and handling that person's possessions without permission.

Writing a Thank-You Note Is Not a Choice

Yes, a thank-you note is not only appropriate but also essential. The note must be handwritten and must be sent promptly and directly to the interviewer. In addition to thanking the interviewer for his or her time, the note should, if possible, refer to something that occurred during the interview. No, a telephone call will not do. Neither will e-mail.

Here is an example of the sort of thank-you note you can send:

Dear Ms. Jones:

Thank you for seeing me on Thursday to discuss the opening in the Marketing Department at TransFletch Industries. It was a pleasure to meet you, and I enjoyed learning more about the company, particularly its plans for expansion in the Charleston area.

I hope to hear from you soon.

Sincerely,

Carl Murdock

The rules for the job interview are specific and unforgiving, yet they are based on common sense.

If you approach the interview as a valuable learning experience and an opportunity, you will project the most favorable impression. Remember that the event is important to the interviewer as well as to you. Keep calm. Be friendly without being pushy. Be cordial without being distant. Be positive. Be honest. And be yourself.

The Least You Need to Know

➤ The job interview is an opportunity, not a test.

➤ Remember that the interviewer wants to hire someone and is hoping you are the one.

➤ Be prepared.

➤ Don't try to dodge questions.

➤ Dress more conservatively than casually.

➤ Don't be shy about your achievements and interests, but don't repeat yourself; the interviewer heard you the first time.

Part 2

In the Arena

Your everyday habits, gestures, and attitudes in the workplace can make or break your reputation as a thoughtful, civil, and considerate person, as well as a significant player in the business arena.

This part of the book deals with your behavior in the office, at meetings, and in any other setting where work gets done, where people interact, and where inconsiderate behavior can prove most annoying—and most damaging.

Other chapters deal with your appearance: dress, wardrobe, and grooming. After all, how you look on the job every day starts with good grooming, so we've rounded up some advice from experts. Knowing how to dress correctly for various circumstances and in different business venues reflects on your good manners; here you'll learn how to build a wardrobe that will give you the flexibility to respond to all demands and, in the process, reflect not only your concern for good manners but also your good sense.

Finally, we'll look at the rules for crafting correspondence that reflects your good sense every bit as vividly as your attire. Here you'll find information that will help you correspond correctly—and with confidence—in every circumstance.

Chapter 5

A Fact of Office Life: Meetings

In This Chapter

➤ Little things mean a lot

➤ Behavior with your boss, your peers, your staff

➤ Etiquette strategies for the at-home office

➤ Crucial rules for the business meeting

➤ Pitfalls of outside directorships

Bad manners in the workplace are like an itch you can't quite reach: It starts out being annoying, and the annoyance worsens as time passes. When you spend the entire day with the same people, little breaches of the basic tenets of good manners tend to become infuriating, and oafish behavior gets to be downright intolerable. Add to this the fact that we are constantly being judged on the job, and the importance of correct office behavior becomes even more crucial.

In general, common sense, consideration, respect for others, and a willingness to please will serve you well in most situations. But special circumstances inherent in the dynamics of any workplace call for special tactics and techniques. These include the relationship between you and your boss, between you and your peers, and between you and your staff.

Treat Your Superiors Right

The nature of your relationship with the boss must be determined by the boss, and he or she will set the limits to which you can go within that relationship.

Don't Push It

Don't try pushing the envelope to expand those limits just because you think that will make you more comfortable. For example, never invite yourself to any event your boss is attending, and never assume that you can just show up. If you have any doubt, say: "Will you be wanting me to go with you to the opening?" or "Will you be needing me there?".

Rank and File

Never forget that relationships in American business are based on rank, and rank must always be acknowledged and observed. Don't assume that you and the boss are now pals because you have been invited to lunch or a golf outing. Yes, you must go along with the style set by the boss, but only to a degree. Don't lose sight of the central reality. Whether you call the boss "Ms. Simpson" or "Margaret," she is still the boss.

Your Peers

Always remember: The person who is your equal today could be your boss tomorrow. When dealing with colleagues, let the relationship develop at its own pace. Don't assume that a certain level of familiarity or even intimacy exists between you because you do the same kind of work, have the same kind of problems, and share the same facilities and resources.

Business Blunder

Don't take the boss's seat or the one next to it.

A good way to establish an uncomfortable relationship that may last quite a while is to make an unwelcome, too familiar gesture or suggestion and have it coldly rejected by the other person.

At first contact with a coworker, put out your hand, smile, and say "Nice to meet you." You have to make a judgment call here. If the office culture is casual and relaxed, you can say "Nice to meet you, Greg." If you are working in a more conservative culture, say, "Nice to meet you, Mr. Williams," with the expectation that the other person will reply, "Call me Greg, please."

If Williams is new to your office, ask if there is anything you can do to help him get settled. Also let him know where you can be found if he has questions or if he needs help.

This is also a good time to add something positive about the tone of the workplace: "You know, we have a pretty good softball team, if that's the kind of thing that interests you."

Your Staff

You want your staff to respect you, so you must treat those who work for you with respect. Remember that, as the boss, anything you say and do may be taken more seriously than you intended. An unintended slight might be interpreted as a rebuke.

When setting the tone for your relationship with your staff, remember that when in doubt, more formal is better than less formal. Always greet staff members pleasantly. Dictatorship is not a productive management style. Say, "Will you please get that report on the Kennedy project?" rather than, "Bring me the Kennedy report."

Remember that establishing and maintaining a pleasant and mutually respectful relationship with your staff is good strategy as well as good manners. Hostility on the part of your staff can have an enormous negative impact on your ability to perform efficiently.

Acknowledging Others

Always acknowledge the staff's presence. Suppose you are talking with your assistant when a third person (perhaps a client) joins you. It is up to you to make the introductions, and you should introduce them according to the way they will be addressing each other in the future. For example, if you wish your assistant to address the client as Mr. Thomas, you say:

> "Mr. Thomas, this is my assistant, Mr. Patterson."

You use the assistant's surname in this situation, even if you use his first name at other times.

Getting Names Right

It is particularly important when first meeting someone who will work for you to let that person know how you wish to be addressed.

> "Hello, Ms. Cotter. I'm John Driscoll." (Never give yourself an honorific.)

If this doesn't work, and if Ms. Cotter calls you by your first name, you must correct that immediately.

> "Ms. Cotter, I think it will work better if we address each other by our surnames."

It should go without saying that, whatever form of address you use, you never, ever refer to anyone as "honey," "handsome," "girl," "boy," or any other such term. If you don't know the person's correct name, learn it and remember it.

51

Odd Job Detail

You are straying into dangerous territory when you ask your support staff to perform personal errands. They could very well resent it, creating an underlying atmosphere of hostility. They could also complain about it to a more senior executive, which will reflect unfavorably on your professionalism and good judgment. And, performing non-work-related tasks for you can lead to staff members assuming a level of familiarity that you will find inappropriate and uncomfortable. On the whole, stick to business.

Workload Requirements

Be careful not to exceed a reasonable workload for your subordinates. If you are asking them to undertake more than the usual amount of work, acknowledge this and offer something in the way of compensation. If you are sharing a secretary, consult with your associate so that you both can be sure that you are not piling on more work than the secretary can handle. Resist, with all your might, the temptation to compete to see who can claim the larger portion of the secretary's time.

Rules for Your Home Office

If you are planning to establish a home office, you must also establish some rules.

First, the office is for business only, not a place for family members to store things or a place to go when they want privacy. (Or, as in my case, when someone is looking for stamps, paper clips, or telephone numbers from the Rolodex.)

The home office should be off-limits to small children. The office telephone should be for business only. You might want to install a mute button on the phone, which allows you to hear but prevents those listening from hearing distracting noises such as barking dogs or squabbling kids.

Carefully explain your work schedule to your children, and post it in the house. When children intrude, refer to the schedule and repeat the home office rules.

Some tips can make the job easier:

➤ Be equipped with voice mail or an efficient answering system, fax, printer, and anything else you might need.

➤ If the home office is too small for client meetings, find a conference room or a quiet restaurant for meetings. Pick up the tab for restaurant meetings.

➤ Your stationery and business cards need to be as professional-looking as any Fortune 500 company's.

➤ Shut off your telephone and fax ringers when you don't want to be disturbed.

➤ Let people know up front that you work out of your home so that it doesn't come as a surprise.

➤ If you have house guests, let them know about the home office and about your work schedule.

➤ Don't neglect diet and exercise. Compensate for the fact that you are moving around less.

➤ If your office telephone is for work only, answer it as you would answer your extension in the workplace. As much as possible, greet business visitors to your home as you would visitors at the workplace.

The Business Meeting

Don't listen to Dilbert. Meetings—and your meeting manners—are vitally important. Those who think of meetings as little more than an interruption of their work, a kind of droning purgatory in which nothing worthwhile gets done, are not only mistaken, but they are preparing themselves for failure.

Memo to Myself

Business meeting etiquette is like stage lighting: You notice it only when it's bad.

Remember that the critically important thing about meetings is that, besides sharing information, people learn about their coworkers and make judgments about them.

Think of the meeting as an opportunity to present yourself in a favorable light. Resolve that you will avoid the breaches of business manners that are so common and so damaging.

Business Meeting Basics

Remember the four crucial rules about meetings:

1. Be ready.
2. Pay attention to entering and seating.
3. Don't play games.
4. Say it right.

We will look at each of these areas in the next sections.

Prepare, Prepare, Prepare

Arrive ready to work, equipped with your agenda, papers, notebook, and pens. Keep what you think you will need in front of you so that you won't keep people waiting while you fish around for things in your briefcase. (Your briefcase and purse should be on the floor beside your chair, never on the conference table.)

Show up on time or a little early. Hurrying in at the last minute or a few minutes late does not convey the message that you are a busy, dynamic person—only that you are disorganized. Showing up late also is insulting to those who made the effort to arrive on time. When you arrive late, others in the room will feel some resentment toward you, consciously or otherwise. If you are late, apologize and give the reason.

> "Sorry I'm late. Mr. Sullivan said he wanted to see me right away, and you know that when he says right away, he means right away."

If you can, find out who will be attending the meeting. Also find out the purpose of the meeting, and focus your preparations on that.

Decide what you have to say about the issue at hand, and mentally practice your remarks.

Familiarize yourself with *Roberts Rules of Order*. You can find this universally recognized guide to meeting procedure at any library. Only the most formal of meetings will be organized in accordance with this guide, but there is a chance that you will someday be attending a meeting at which someone will ask, "How should we proceed with this?"

And you will hear yourself saying, "Well, according to *Roberts Rules of Order* ... ".

Make Your Entrance

Enter decisively. You may pause briefly to spot key persons and allow others to see you, but do not stand in the doorway. While still standing, shake hands and call people by their names. Introduce yourself to those you don't know. If you are seated and are introduced to someone new, stand up, smile, and shake hands. (For more on shaking hands, see Chapter 3, "Greetings and Introductions.")

Memo to Myself

Smile when you greet colleagues at a meeting. This is the universal gesture of good will—and, yes, it does relieve stress.

Depending on the corporate style of your organization, it may be a good idea to use honorifics (Mr., Ms.) when addressing or referring to people during a meeting, even if you are on a first-name basis at other times. As I have said many times in this book, when in doubt, more formal is better than less formal.

Know Where to Sit

If you are not familiar with the seating arrangement, don't just pick a chair and sit. Ask if it's okay to "just sit anywhere." Avoid sitting at either end of the table, if you can. If you know where the chairperson or the senior officer will be sitting, don't take the next chair; it may be reserved for an aide or a secretary.

Don't Fiddle

Leave paper clips unbent, and don't bounce them. Leave rubber bands unstretched and unsnapped. Don't doodle on your note pad. People will start trying to see what you are drawing, calling attention to the fact that you are not paying attention.

Don't chew gum. Don't pop mints or candies into your mouth, unless you are trying to suppress a cough.

Don't ask for coffee or other refreshments unless they are being offered. If there are food and drinks at the meeting, get rid of your plate and cup as soon as is convenient. Your place at the conference table should be kept as clear as possible.

Memo to Myself

Invest in a quality, good-looking writing instrument. People do notice. It's good for your image because people tend to attach importance to symbols. Furthermore, using it will give you pleasure.

Maintain a high level of energy and involvement in the meeting, resisting the temptation to let your mind wander. Meetings are a good place to demonstrate the fact that you are a team player.

Watch Your Body Language

You may be tired, bored, frustrated, or all of the above at a meeting. And that's okay, as long as your posture is not sending out these negative messages.

Sit straight, with both feet on the floor. You can sit straight and still be relaxed, and you can be relaxed and still be attentive. If you do cross your legs, cross them at the ankles. Don't cross your arms in front of you; it communicates resistance (or even hostility) to what is happening or what is being said. Your body language should communicate openness and approachability.

Keep your jacket and tie on unless the chairperson or the senior executive present sheds his and suggests that others follow his example.

Speak Up

Even if you are a newcomer or consider yourself a minor player, you must be prepared to speak at any meeting you attend. Be ready, and avoid giving the "deer in the headlights" reaction. Try to predict the circumstances in which you could be called upon, and work out what you would like to say.

➤ Don't stand up, unless people routinely stand while speaking at such meetings, or unless the chair says something like, "John, stand up and introduce yourself."

➤ Take a second to frame your remarks.

➤ Like a good journalist, put your most important information up front.

➤ Be as brief as possible. Don't ramble, and don't repeat yourself. If you think a particular point should be emphasized by repetition, say so:

"The timeline is so important in this matter that I think I should repeat the details."

➤ Watch your language. Use positive language, and never begin with an apology: "This might not work, but ...."

➤ Avoid confrontational language. Instead of saying, "You're wrong about that," try "I disagree because .... "

➤ When discussing the work or the position of your company, your department, or your management team, use the pronoun "we." If things are going well, this conveys the impression that you are a team player. If things are going badly, it spreads the blame around and takes the focus off you.

Never be shy about speaking up at meetings, but when you do, make sure you have something to say—and say it briefly and with authority.

Handle Conflict

Avoid dogmatic and inflexible statements. Instead, bring up "points to consider," and make suggestions. State your position firmly and clearly, but don't go on pressing it or defending it at length, particularly if the boss says, "Nevertheless, here's what we'll do," or "Let's move on to another topic."

Do not interrupt while others are speaking, no matter how strongly you disagree with what they are saying. Wait your turn, and then make your points.

Present Your Proposal

If you have a particular point or proposal that you want to present and/or have approved at the meeting, what happens *before* the meeting might be more crucial than what happens *at* the meeting.

Prepare a memo outlining your proposal. Start by saying that you are circulating the information in advance to save time at the meeting, and you would appreciate hearing any reactions or objections so that you will be prepared to respond to them at the meeting.

Consider the feedback carefully. If possible, meet with those providing the feedback to have them expand or explain their observations. During your presentation, you might want to credit those who have made cogent contributions.

In the Chair

You never know when you will be asked to chair your first meeting, and it will probably come sooner than you think.

The opportunity to make a favorable or negative impression on your colleagues is multiplied many times when you are in the chair because attention will be focused

on you much of the time. If the meeting is smooth and successful, you will be cred-
ited. If it is not, you will probably be blamed, whether or not it's your fault.

Advance Preparation

When you are in the chair, being well prepared is of utmost importance.

➤ Provide as much advance notice as possible.

➤ Try to pick a time that is convenient for everyone, but accept the fact that this
may not be possible. At the very least, select a time that is most convenient for
the key players. Avoid Friday afternoon and Monday morning, if you can.

➤ If the meeting will be lengthy, plan to provide breaks so that people can make
telephone calls and attend to personal needs. At lengthy meetings, you may
want to provide simple snacks or lunch. The basic rule here is to keep things as
uncomplicated as possible. Avoid anything greasy, such as chips, and provide
low-fat and vegetarian alternatives. Provide decaffeinated as well as "regular"
drinks, and offer pitchers or bottles of water.

➤ Find out in advance if there will be a need for a microphone, lectern, blackboard
or whiteboard, or audiovisual aids. Make sure that each place at the table has
note paper, a pencil, and whatever else might be needed.

Having done all this, you are ready to go forward.

Seating Arrangements

Decide whether you want to sit at the head of the table or in the middle, and decide
whether you want to reserve the chairs on either side of you for important guests or
for those who may be working closely with you during the course of the meeting.

If you desire a specific seating arrangement, it is fine to use place cards. These should
be two-sided, with the name on both sides. Don't use Mr., Ms., or Mrs., but use Dr.
where appropriate.

From the File Drawer

The custom of giving the honored guest or the top aide the chair to the right of the boss
began when kings always had their most trusted ally at their right. This meant that no enemy
could control the king's sword hand. Because the sword was customarily carried on the right
side, the same strategy was used while walking and on horseback. This is the genesis of the
term "right-hand man."

Debate, Discuss, or Argue?

The best and most productive meetings are characterized by an atmosphere of frank, open, and creative discussion. Your job, as chair, involves not only fostering such discussion, but also making sure that it doesn't get out of hand. There is a point at which positive, healthy debate becomes negative, counterproductive conflict.

A useful tactic is to move to another topic until the combatants have cooled down, or to say something like this:

> "Gail and Bob both make good points and express them well. Now, let's try to move toward a consensus. Any ideas?"

Throughout the give-and-take of the meeting, the chair must remain focused on what he or she hopes to accomplish and what information needs to be drawn out and shared.

At the end of the meeting, thank all guests and give credit to those who deserve it. Also, write a precis (a summary of the essential points or statements) of the meeting within 48 hours and distribute it to the participants.

Handling Interruptions

Whenever people get together, potential arises for conflict and other problems. Be prepared.

For example, imagine that you have a meeting bore and time-waster who wants to swap jokes or talk about his golf game. Establish order right away without confronting that person directly.

> "Okay, folks. Let's settle down. We've got a lot to do this afternoon. If we don't get down to business, we'll be here all night."

As another example, let's say that somebody's cellular phone rings. The chair can't have the meeting interrupted while somebody has a telephone conversation.

> "If that's an urgent call, you'd better take it outside. If not, call them back."

Or, consider that the meeting has just started and someone comes in late. Give that person's name, company, and title, and immediately move on.

If people are coming to meet with you and something unforeseen traps you in your office, send someone to explain and apologize, and keep those waiting informed. If you can, leave your office to explain and apologize in person.

The Importance of Agendas

An agenda works as a great tool for keeping the meeting focused and moving. Distribute your agenda, along with any other paperwork, to the participants well in advance so that they have time to look over the meeting's topics.

An agenda should begin with the time and place of the meeting and should state the name of the chairperson. The most important issues should be addressed first, in case the meeting runs out of time. If the meeting is to occur at mealtime, include a line saying something like, "Sandwiches and beverages will be provided."

A good method of helping you to control the pace of the meeting is to write times and topics on the agenda.

Here's a sample agenda:

TO: Marketing and Public Relations Staff

FROM: Kathleen Carter

PURPOSE: Meeting Thursday, Oct. 28, 2–4 P.M.

(If the meeting is at meal time, say 8–10 A.M., specify that food will be available.)

PLACE: Conference room, 10th floor

AGENDA:

1. Review goals and action plan for ComTech project (30 minutes).
   - ➤ Summary by public relations director
   - ➤ Overview of projected media coverage
   - ➤ Marketing report
2. Discuss other upcoming media opportunities (20 minutes).
3. Consider longer-range priorities (20 minutes).
4. Open discussion (20 minutes).
5. Conclusion, summary, and action plan assignments (20 minutes).

Outside Directorships

During the course of your career, you may well find that you are asked to serve on the board of directors of a charitable or community organization. If so, you will find that these meetings have an entirely different feel and character than those you are used to at the office. A whole different brand of meeting etiquette may be necessary.

Take Them Seriously

You must not take these directorships lightly—they are important career opportunities and can be charged with dangers and complexities. Assume that your boss or whoever asked you to accept the appointment has friends or business associates on the same board. In any case, there is an excellent chance that your performance on the board and at its meetings will get back to your home company.

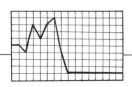

The Bottom Line

Outside directorships should be welcomed. They provide valuable experience dealing with diverse personalities and points of view. These positions will enhance your reputation and build your self-esteem.

We can offer some advice and strategies here, but it will be mainly up to you to learn, through careful and keen observation, the procedures and rules for acceptable behavior on these boards.

For example, you may find yourself on the board of a cultural organization, which is comprised of a diverse set of characters toting some pretty diverse attitudinal baggage. There may be scholars and artists and wealthy dilettantes dabbling in the arts. Others may be representatives of the community that the charitable organization is supposed to be serving. There could be some retired business giants who "know how to get things done."

As you can see, there could be a lot more agendas—mainly unspoken—than the one written for each of these meetings.

Ease into Your Unwritten Agenda

Go slowly at first, being cordial but somewhat reserved. Again, when in doubt, more formal is better than less formal. Make it clear from the start that you belong to no clique and that you won't take sides. At first, say little and listen much until you get a feeling for the group dynamic at work here.

Offer to help the head of the organization with contacts and information, when appropriate. If you can supply something that is lacking, such as computer expertise, do so. Keep notes. Follow up on all promises as promptly as possible.

Be a Cheerleader

Don't be a half-hearted volunteer. Speak up for your outside organization at the office. Talk proudly about the good work it does; if possible, muster some support for the organization from your company. You should buy at least two tickets to your organization's charity benefits and try to interest your company in purchasing a full table as a corporate sponsor. Don't be afraid to be a cheerleader for a good cause.

Fund-Raisers

You may be called upon to organize or help organize a fund-raiser as part of your regular duties or in connection with an outside directorship. Keep these guidelines in mind:

➤ Clear the date on the community calendar to avoid conflicting with another major charity event.

➤ Be careful with the budget, and make sure that your expenses do not exceed—or even approach—the amount you expect to raise.

➤ Try to get your invitations designed professionally (and, if possible, for free).

➤ Mail invitations four weeks in advance.

➤ Keep the speeches short.

➤ Give guests a memento upon departing, and follow up with a letter thanking the donor and suggesting that future contributions would be most welcome.

Even in this age of electronic wizardry and instant communications over great distances, there still are (and perhaps always will be) occasions when people in business get together in a room or around a table and deal with each other within that paradigm called "the meeting." It may sound smart, independent, and cynical to decry these gatherings as a waste of time or corporate theater, but the savvy, career-conscious person sees meetings as opportunities and is very, very careful about his meeting manners.

The Least You Need to Know

➤ The tone and style of your office—and any workplace—is set by top management people, so take your cue from them.

➤ Keep some room for advance and retreat in your relationships; rules and roles change, so your peer today could be your boss tomorrow.

➤ Dilbert notwithstanding, meetings are serious stuff.

➤ Be ready, be careful, and participate fully.

➤ Speak up, but avoid confrontational language, rambling, and repetition.

Chapter 6

Business Attire and Accessories

In This Chapter

➤ How your attire sends a message

➤ Learning situational dressing

➤ Living comfortably with The Code

➤ The meaning of formal, semi–formal, and informal

➤ Concentrating on accessories

People react instantly to how you look, and to a large degree, that means how you dress. Socially inappropriate attire may cause people to feel uneasy and want to distance themselves from you. In the business world, the reaction can be much more harsh and judgmental. People—particularly your superiors—are apt to assume that the quality of your work probably will be no greater than the quality of your appearance.

Some truths are self-evident:

1. There is no such thing as neutral clothing.
2. Everything you put on represents a decision you have made and says something about you.
3. Good manners require appropriate attire.

In the United States, people dress with a great deal more self-expression and with a greater emphasis on ease and comfort than people in other cultures. This, plus the absence of dress codes in schools in the last 25 years, has made it difficult for younger executives to understand the importance of appearance.

Radical dressers do not last long in many organizations. Success breeds success because people like the security of dealing with someone who is a proven commodity. In short, there's something of a code of clothing at work.

Memo to Myself

When in doubt about what to wear, take a look at what the senior executives are wearing. People tend to approve of and relate to others who are like themselves.

The Code

Most companies have a dress code, even those that say they do not. If the code has been officially articulated, you can find out about it by calling Human Resources. In most cases, however, the code is unwritten—and largely unspoken. The best tactic is to speak with people who work there; if you don't know any employees, visit the offices and keep your eyes open.

Once you find out about it, obey the spirit as well as the letter of the code. You don't want people overlooking your excellent qualities because they are wondering why you chose that scarlet blouse.

In some situations, newcomers might get mixed messages. When in doubt, ask, "I'm getting different signals about what people wear here. Am I coming on too casual (or too conservative)?"

One other suggestion is to leaf through business magazines, noting how the people in the pictures are dressed. They may not look like the people in fashion magazines, but they represent business success.

From the File Drawer

In a survey done by image guru John T. Malloy, 72 percent of business people said they thought a woman in a dress could be an effective player in the business arena. However, 93 percent thought she would be more effective if she added a coat.

Different Cloaks for Different Folks

Successful people dress differently for different occasions and different career situations. Wearing the same clothes on a construction site as at a board meeting is like wearing work boots to the ballet.

A young friend of mine applied for a job at a Wall Street financial institution wearing an expensive navy blue suit and Gucci shoes, but with a matching Tweety Bird necktie and braces. His mother thought the outfit was a wonderful expression of his personality, but although he was eminently qualified, he didn't get the job.

On the other hand, it wouldn't be smart to wear a dark, expensive suit and a traditional conservative tie when applying for a writer's job at an ad agency. That outfit might whisper "quality" but shout "too conservative."

So, when making decisions about what to wear, it helps to ask yourself a couple questions:

1. Who am I, and how do I want to be perceived?
2. Where am I, and who are the people I want to impress favorably?

It's a matter of different cloaks for different folks.

Conservative Choices

Let's consider what is appropriate if you are going to work in a law office, a bank, an investment firm, or a government office. These situations require conservative, traditional dress that inspires confidence and conveys authority and competence.

➤ Suits are the uniform of the day.

➤ Accessories are simple and understated: good watches, gold and silver earrings of modest size, pearl and stud earrings. (Men should not wear earrings of any kind.)

➤ Understated jewelry, such as antique pins, can add interest to a conservative suit.

➤ Makeup and hair should be low-key and soft-pedaled. Women must not abandon makeup altogether, however. In the corporate world, women cannot afford to be without, at the very least, lipstick and mascara. The greater danger, of course, lies at the other extreme: makeup so heavy that it looks like war paint.

➤ Women also should avoid the extremes of flats or high heels in favor of low to medium heels.

➤ Skirts must not be tight or shorter than the kneecaps.

➤ Busy prints of any kind do not reflect the quiet confidence you want to project.

➤ Men should not wear necklaces, bracelets, or earrings, and jewelry should be restricted to a good non-digital watch, a wedding ring (if married), and good, understated cufflinks.

Now let's take a look at different levels within the business world, situations in which the standards of dress described here would be inappropriate.

Sales and Marketing Types

Advertising, public relations, and communications firms fit into this category. These are client-intensive industries, and people in them want to send out two messages through the way they dress. They want to show that they have enough pizzazz and style to be interesting, but they also want to show that they still are authoritative and solidly representative of their company.

Understatement works well in this situation. A woman might choose to project a secure sense of style by wearing an unmatched skirt and jacket, especially if the fabric is rich and elegant. But while appearance in this area is different, it is not radically different from the law firm/investment company model. If the first thing about you that strikes a person is your makeup or your accessories, you have gone too far.

Creative Pizzazz

If you are working in an industry such as fashion, publishing, interior design, or cosmetics, you will have to strive for a more fashion-forward and imaginative look. Turtleneck sweaters and unstructured jackets in interesting fabrics can convey creativity as well as style and intelligence.

Color is a good way to establish rapport in some industries; it can help you look approachable and accessible. Often a "shot" of color is more effective than an entire bright orange ensemble, which can be distracting. A skirt with a sweater or scarf or pants with a tunic are reasonable choices. The idea is that people should notice you, not what you are wearing.

Informal Attire

Teaching, counseling, and health care professionals want to project a look that is personal and unintimidating. Attire that expresses personal style and taste is welcome because it reflects a willingness to share one's tastes and values. However, extreme trends and high styles can be intimidating.

Business Blunders

Don't go overboard on casual Friday. "Casual" doesn't mean careless; neither does it mean exotic or provocative.

Casual Friday

A survey by the Society for Human Resource Managers shows that two out of three American companies now allow some form of casual dress on a regular basis. This is good news, but don't be tempted to go overboard on dress-down days.

I found reasonable guidelines in an internal memo circulated throughout one of the largest U.S. corporations. Under the category of "Acceptable Casual Business Wear" were skirts, slacks, pants outfits, or culottes short suits for women. For men, it was slacks with or without a sports jacket, no ties, and comfortable shirts or sweaters. Under "Unacceptable" were jeans, shorts, and sneakers.

Check out what's being done on casual days at your workplace before making major casual wardrobe decisions. When in doubt, err on the side of caution.

Social Functions

When you are invited to a business social function, you may be in doubt about what to wear. If there is a written invitation, it often will specify dress for the occasion in the lower-right corner. If there is no such indication and you have doubts, you can call your host or hostess in advance. If it is an annual event, ask someone who attended previously. Or, you can ask a colleague whose judgment you trust what he or she will be wearing.

If your invitation has a dress notation, it will probably specify "black tie" or "informal." Sometimes "semi-formal" will be used instead of "informal." Let's take a look at each of these dress codes in the next sections.

Black Tie

Black-tie dressing means different things in different parts of the country. In some places, for example, it is acceptable to wear a polka-dot tie with a dinner jacket or tuxedo. (*Dinner jacket* is the correct term. *Tuxedo* is a nickname.) Generally, however, it is safe for men to wear a black bow tie with a black dinner jacket. (Note that tails, a white tie, a morning coat, and so on would not be worn in any business context.)

Wear a white dress shirt. A formal occasion is not the place to make a fashion statement. For example, don't go for a pastel ruffled shirt—you don't want to be mistaken for the maitre d' or the band leader. Stick with black dress shoes and black socks as well.

From the File Drawer

We have Edward VII of England to thank for the dinner jacket. During his short reign (1901–1910), he demanded formal attire less elaborate than the white tie and tails customary at the time. Accordingly, he sometimes wore a formal jacket without tails. Some years later, an American businessman wore this sort of dinner jacket to the Tuxedo Club at Tuxedo Junction, N.Y.—thus the name.

Women have more options in formal wear. These range from a floor-length gown to a dressy suit of a quality fabric such as velvet, brocade, or satin. Women may or may not wear gloves, but they never should shake hands while wearing them. And be careful—at any business-related affair, women should not wear outfits that are too short, too tight, or cut too low in the bodice.

Informal

For informal events, men should wear a dark business suit, a white shirt, and a dark silk tie with a quiet pattern. Women should wear a dressy suit in an evening fabric, a short cocktail dress, or a long skirt and coordinating blouse.

Clothes Talk

One of the most common—and most serious—breaches of etiquette in business and at social events is inappropriate commentary about how other people are dressed. Keep these rules in mind:

➤ At the office, compliment people on their work, not their clothes.

➤ Never ask people where they got their clothes.

➤ Never, ever ask what a person paid for her clothes. If someone asks you, don't tell. Ignore the question or say, "I don't remember," and change the subject.

Some people find such questions intrusive and offensive.

Memo to Myself

If someone compliments you on your clothing or accessories, just say, "Thank you." In fact, this is the best response to a compliment of any sort.

How Do You Handle Compliments?

People compliment one another on their outfits at social functions because the nature of the occasion requires people to dress up and because the constraints of the workplace environment do not apply. If someone compliments you on such an occasion, just say "Thank you," or "I'm glad you like it." Don't do the modesty act and say something like, "Oh, this old thing?" And, remember, it is not necessary to return the compliment if you can't find anything to be complimentary about. A false compliment will ring false, no matter how good an actor you think you are.

Accessories Make a Statement

The statement that your accessories make about you is perhaps more dramatic than the statement made by your dress or suit. Accessories say something about your feeling for flair and your ability to coordinate styles and colors.

For Men

The right accessories can do a lot for how people perceive you. Consider acquiring an alligator or crocodile belt. A starched linen pocket handkerchief adds authority, as do small gold or sterling silver cuff links. Another worthwhile investment might be an elegant dress watch. Stay away from those bulky sports watches, digital watches, and watches with cheap metal bands; don't wear watches with jewels or Mickey Mouse-type icons.

Wear only a wedding band or signet rings. Class rings are passé, and diamond rings should not even be considered. (Tiffany won't even make a man's diamond ring.) In the business world, men should never wear earrings, pinkie rings, bracelets, or necklaces.

Generally, men should always wear a belt with a suit. It should be 1 1/4 to 1 1/2 inches wide and should be the same color as your shoes. Wallets and briefcases should be thin.

For Women

The basic rule is that jewelry should be neither obtrusive nor vulgarly ostentatious. Save your emeralds for the grand ball.

In a business setting, earrings about the size of a quarter work best; they are large enough to be important, yet small enough not to be distracting. Of course, if you are petite, choose something smaller. A good pair of gold earrings or real pearls is a sound investment. However, excellent costume jewelry is available today, and losing an earring is so much less painful when it's not real gold. Dangle earrings, however, do not look professional.

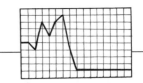

The Bottom Line

Blatant self-mutilation does not reflect a serious, stable personality. One piercing per ear lobe is plenty.

Avoid wearing rings on your right hand. You will feel less dread about getting your fingers crunched or scratching somebody else's hand during the inevitable handshakes that punctuate the business day.

Unless your home office is in the far Yukon, don't wear fur. The message this sends in a business setting is "pretentious," not "successful." Also, you might want to consider the fact that wearing fur may offend those who feel strongly about animal rights.

For Both

When I was younger, I often wore eyeglasses while lecturing, even though I didn't need them, because I thought that people would take me more seriously. You may

Memo to Myself

Good leather gloves with a dull finish are a good investment. It's also a good idea to wear thin gloves so that you don't ruin coats by stuffing heavy gloves into the pockets.

not want to go that far, but it is true that eyeglasses tend to make a person look more authoritative, intense, and serious. Tortoise-shell glasses can be more serviceable than silver or gold because they won't clash with any jewelry, but both gold and silver frames are fine. I recently received an e-mail asking whether a man should wear silver frames with a gold watch to a job interview. The answer is certainly, unless the combination makes him uncomfortable.

Yes, I know you love your faithful old briefcase, but be strong. When it begins to look shabby, retire it to the same closet as your school sweater and your teddy bear. A good briefcase is a very good investment. In fact, it's a good idea to have two: a slim one for meetings and a larger, possibly soft-sided one for carrying material to and from the office. In the slim one, carry only those materials needed for that particular meeting. This projects focus and attention to detail.

Treat Your Feet

You don't often see your shoes, but others do. Shoes are not only a necessity, but they're also an important accessory. As with neckties, buy the best you can afford, and keep them properly cared for. Shabby shoes send a resoundingly negative message.

A buyer for a department store once shared with me a tip she picked up while training for her job: When you meet someone, take a look at her handbag and shoes, and you will know who you are dealing with.

Start out with good-looking shoes, and keep a shoe brush and some fabric-softening sheets in your desk for minor rebuffing.

Shoe Tips

For women, assembling an adequate shoe wardrobe need not break the bank. You need a pair each of black, tan, and navy blue shoes. Pumps with low heels are the most elegant and serviceable, and they are also the most flattering.

Women should never, ever wear running shoes anywhere near the office. Happily, manufacturers these days are producing leather pumps that are good-looking, well-cushioned, and comfortable even for walking long distances or for being on your feet for long periods. Some cities have shoe stores that specialize in especially comfortable, yet stylish, footwear. Follow these recommendations when choosing footwear:

➤ The dressier the shoe, the thinner the sole and the heel.

➤ With lace-up shoes (called Oxfords), the uppers should be of shiny and supple leather.

➤ For men, black wingtips are rather formal and are exactly appropriate for pin-stripe suits and any navy or gray suit.

➤ Classic loafers are entirely appropriate for business, and they go well with every-thing but the most formal blue business suit. Happily, penny loafers no longer contaminate the world. Tasseled loafers have tassels instead of the penny band. They look quite formal in black, but are not suitable for formal wear. (Kilt loafers are similar to tassel loafers, except that they have a fringe of leather instead of the tassel.)

Clothes Make the Man (and the Woman)

It is impossible to overstate the importance of dress in the business world. In a way, how you are dressed has an impact on others even before you meet them: Knowing that you are dressed well influences your carriage and your outlook.

As I pointed out in the beginning of this chapter, there is no such thing as neutral clothing, and there is no business uniform that is right for all settings and all situations. So, give a great deal of thought to what you buy and what you wear. Talk it over with friends whose judgment you trust and with knowledgeable people in the retail world.

Memo to Myself

Before you discard a garment because "it just doesn't do it" for you, try brightening it up with accessories.

What you wear makes a statement about you. Decide what that statement should be, and dress accordingly.

The Least You Need to Know

➤ Your attire must reflect the realities of your career situation, your workplace, your region, and the image you wish to project.

➤ Everything you wear makes a statement about you.

➤ There is a dress code where you work, even if it isn't written anywhere. Find out what is expected, and make your decisions accordingly.

➤ When in doubt, don't be afraid to ask.

Chapter 7

Assembling a Wardrobe

In This Chapter

➤ Assembling a wardrobe that works

➤ The "quality" strategy for professionals

➤ Avoiding The Clothing X Games

➤ Some secrets of great grooming

The real trick to dressing correctly and looking great on the job is being able to do it every day. To do that, a complete and well-planned wardrobe is essential. Building one does not require help from the World Monetary Fund, but it does take some thought and planning.

Two Truths

First, consider these two time-honored truisms about business attire:

1. Quality endures and is recognized everywhere. If you are faced with a decision about whether to buy two good items of dress or one excellent item, go for excellence.

2. Avoid extreme fashions. Trends come and go. You should wear what you believe is best for you and for your career rather than what's hot at any particular time.

You can now begin to think about building your wardrobe with these two factors in mind. When thinking about what you will wear to work every day, consider the elements discussed in the next section.

Guidelines

Read over these things to think about, and ask yourself some questions when you begin thinking about assembling a wardrobe.

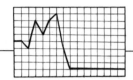

The Bottom Line

When in doubt about what sort of attire is acceptable for the workplace, the conservative choice is generally a better idea than the adventurous choice.

➤ What clothing is appropriate to the particular culture of your workplace? A "coat of many colors" might be fine at the ad agency, but not at Smith Barney. A tweed jacket might be great on campus, but not in some boardrooms.

➤ Your overall style of dress must be based on what you want your attire to say about you and your company. Inventive? Authoritative? Conservative?

➤ Consider regional realities. An outfit that is fine for Boston might be too formal for Los Angeles. Black might be best in New York or Philadelphia, but not for Miami.

➤ What kind of work will you be doing? Will you be visiting people in their homes? Will you be working at construction sites?

When thinking about clothes for work, think also about clothes that don't work in an office setting. Take a look at these examples:

➤ Styles that are too tight or too baggy

➤ Fabrics that are glittery or sheer

➤ Skirts or dresses that are too short or fall to the ankle

➤ Gym, athletic, or sweat clothes

➤ Clothes that swish or flutter

Remember that common sense is the most important ingredient in any wardrobe.

You have a life outside the workplace, of course, and this also must be considered when assembling a wardrobe. You must be ready to meet people comfortably at social and family occasions, some of them a bit dressy, and some of them quite casual.

Let's Get Started

Step number 1—cleaning out the closet—is a tough one. (At least, it is for me.) Begin by making up your mind to be ruthless.

1. First, bag clothes that are clearly out of style. Florid ties, leisure suits, and Nehru jackets are not coming back.

2. Get rid of clothes that no longer fit. Okay, okay—if you really *are* going to lose 15 pounds, keep that cherished suit or dress that is now too small, but don't count it as part of your basic wardrobe until the 15 pounds are well and truly gone. You know, however, that some things will never fit you again. Dump them.

3. Force yourself to part with those all-time favorites. They look familiar and friendly and comfortable to your fond gaze, but they will look tired to those who love them less.

Memo to Myself

You must examine the items in your closet with the cold eye of a corporate downsizer.

Separation Anxiety

After you have finished the decimation process, separate the survivors into three groups:

1. The staples: good suits, shirts, jeans, skirts, black slacks, and turtlenecks.

2. Things that need altering: buttons replaced, hems altered, sleeves shortened, and so forth.

3. Items that you're tired of. There's nothing else wrong with them, but they need help—something that will make you more enthusiastic about them (or at least more tolerant of them). Try adding accessories such as a belt, or try mixing and matching them differently.

In addition to your staples, every wardrobe should include a few choice or "blue chip" items. Make up your mind that you may have to stress the budget to acquire them; it will hurt less if you factor in what I think of as "amortization."

Say you want to buy a $300 jacket that looks and feels great. You might want to wear it three days a week, or 121 days in a year. That's $2.50 a wearing the first year; if the jacket lasts three years, the cost per wearing is 80 cents.

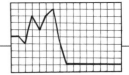

The Bottom Line

Sure, your career comes first, but no wardrobe is complete without casual and party clothes.

Before you make such a purchase, however, consider these guidelines:

➤ The item must be of excellent quality.

➤ It must be of classic design and must be consistent with your personal style.

➤ You should be able to wear it often and with many different outfits.

➤ It should be very complementary and very comfortable.

Quality Checklist

When it comes to quality, fabric is the most important consideration. Once, only natural fabrics—cotton, wool, silk, and linen—were considered "good" fabrics. That is no longer the case. Now many synthetics blend well with natural fabrics for attractive, durable, and less expensive clothing. Remember, however, that the higher the percentage of synthetics, the fewer natural properties the fabric will have. Stay away from 100 percent polyester double knits, twills, and gabardines, as well as simulated leather and phony silks.

Microfibers are exceptionally thin and durable and can be either quite soft or rugged for outdoor wear.

One way to test a fabric is to do a touch comparison with other fabrics, and to crush the fabric in your hand. If the fabric springs back unharmed, it will probably serve you well. Some other things to look for when buying clothing are listed here:

➤ Check seams and linings. The better a garment is made on the inside, the better it will wear.

➤ Buttons should be securely sewn, with a stem between the button and the fabric. They must meet the buttonhole squarely, and colors should match perfectly.

➤ Zippers should be neatly concealed and the same color as the fabric. They should work smoothly and flawlessly.

➤ Jackets should fit squarely. Back vents and collars should lie flat and not pucker. Double-breasted jackets should have inside buttons and buttonholes to hold the line of the garment.

➤ The more supple the leather, the better the quality.

In the long run, it pays to take the time to carefully inspect a garment before you make the decision to purchase it.

Memo to Myself

Buying what's "hot" in the fashion world merry-go-round is not the way to build a wardrobe.

Your Store

Yes, it is important and valuable to look for sales and to comparison-shop, but is also important to build a relationship with a good quality shop and with a professional salesperson in that particular store. This is a person who will help you put together a look that is right for you. This person can also provide you with valuable advice and information and can alert you to upcoming sales.

It is also important to establish a relationship with a good dry cleaning establishment. In addition, a trusty old cobbler can give you important advice about purchasing and preserving leather.

SUIT-able for Men

When selecting a suit, look for four elements: quality, fabric, fit, and proportion. Your suits should not make a fashion statement. If they say anything, it should be "I know what I'm doing."

Be careful about double-breasted suits—it's best to acquire a wardrobe of traditional two-button suits before going into the double-breasted area. Men who are even slightly portly should not even consider a double-breasted suit. It only adds a layer of fabric where you can least afford it—in the middle. In general, men with athletic builds—wide shoulders and narrow waists and hips—look better in double-breasted suits. Fit aside, however, it's a good idea to find out if other men in your office wear double-breasted suits before investing in this style.

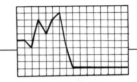

The Bottom Line

In general, double-breasted suits are for wide-shouldered, slim-hipped men. If you are even a bit portly, stay away from them.

Proportion

Shorter men look better with two-button spacing, and taller men can wear four-button spacing with somewhat broader lapels. The waist button of a jacket should come to just below the narrowest part of the torso.

Also keep collars in mind, as they can help balance facial features by giving strength to soft features and softening rigid lines. You will find that straight-point collars balance a round, heavy face, while spread collars offset a long, narrow face.

Pleats

The popularity of pleated trousers these days reflects the fact that they are considered dressier and, at the same time, more comfortable. The classic pleat design has the deeper pleat nearest the fly, with a smaller one nearer the pocket. Cuffs that are about an inch wide give the pant legs just enough weight to help define the pleat and keep contact with the shoe. The trousers should rest on the shoe with just a slight break.

Neckties

If people will remember only one thing about what a man is wearing, it will probably be the necktie. Choose your ties with great care, and buy the best you can afford. Of course, the striped tie is always classic, but we are also seeing more foulards with small, spaced geometric forms, prints, and patterns. Paisley prints are upscale and rich-looking as well. You will find that the most useful colors are dark blue, olive, teal blue, purple, taupe, and all but the most glaring shades of red.

If you wear braces (don't call them suspenders—it's outdated), don't wear a belt. Braces generally should be made of silk with leather fittings and should coordinate with your suit and tie.

SUIT-able for Women

In times past, women had to wear a feminized version of men's business suits to succeed within the corporate culture. Happily, that time has passed. These days, women in business have the option of dressing in more colorful, varied, and feminine ways.

Blazers, collarless jackets, and pantsuits are replacing man-tailored suits in the business arena. Very good quality pantsuits in sober, businesslike colors are acceptable now in most business venues. And, when pantsuits fit correctly, they are more modest, more comfortable, and better looking than skirts, particularly when worn with low-heeled shoes.

Women who are wider in the hips should make sure that the jacket is long enough to completely cover the hips, producing a slimmer line. Very slim-hipped women can get away with a short jacket. Longer lengths flatter taller, long-legged women.

The Message Your Clothing Sends

Your suit can project approachability or rigidity simply by virtue of its fabric and color. For this reason, I seldom wear rigidly constructed suits with both parts matching in color because of the nature of what I teach. The subject of etiquette is intimidating enough by itself, and I want to help modify that by what I wear. When selecting a suit, consider that stiff fabrics such as gabardine convey inflexibility, particularly when they are in dark colors such as black or navy. On the other hand, loosely constructed suits make others feel more at ease. Bright colors also suggest lively thinking.

From the File Drawer

Dress codes now, of course, are considerably more lenient than in the past. In Victorian times, codes were extremely rigid, as is evident in photographs. Women wore lots of clothing that left very little skin visible below the neck. Men wore severe suits and collars that looked almost lethal. Both wore clothing that was generally dark. The change over generations is most pronounced in women's attire. These days, there is plenty of room for self-expression in most work environments.

Skirts

Be careful about skirt length. When deciding on the appropriateness of length, take a long, critical look in a three-way mirror. Then sit down in front of the same mirror. If you have even the slightest doubt, the skirt is too short.

Remember that the most classic skirt lengths do not go out of style, and you can't just whack off 6 inches from a suit skirt because the fashion that year is short skirts. See a good tailor first. Shortening may destroy the proportions of a skirt; sometimes it is better to recycle the skirt at a thrift shop or jazz it up with new accessories.

Generally, the most flattering place to end the hemline is at the slimmest part of the leg. This is usually where the calf meets the knee in a graceful curve. Usually, straight skirts look best when they just cover the knee. Full skirts and pleated skirts look better when they are much longer, perhaps even nearly ankle-length. Here are some pointers to remember about skirts:

➤ Long, slim skirts may seem sophisticated, but they can convey aloofness.

➤ Full, long skirts make a woman look expansive and approachable.

➤ Short, swinging pleated skirts make a woman look more fluid and easy-going.

➤ Long jackets worn over short skirts add an air of professionalism and sophistication.

Collars

Women's collars can also send a variety of messages. For example, asymmetrical and very pointed collars suggest a creative person. Unbuttoned collars speak of flexible open-mindedness. Large, dramatic collars suggest authority, power, and dynamism. On the other hand, those tiny Peter Pan collars do not convey authority. Also avoid floppy and crumbled collars entirely because they suggests a lack of competence. The same is true of collars that are too rigid, pointed, and starched.

Regional Differences

Geography isn't as important as it once was in fashion. However, if you travel as much as I do, you pick up on some regional tendencies.

Northeast: Women tend to follow fashion trends, but resist flounciness and pretty pastels. People look for "easy" clothes that accommodate an active, time-oriented lifestyle. Both men and women are label-conscious and often mix separates.

Southeast: People in this region wear lots of khakis and loafers. They avoid trendy extremes and usually wear light colors. Dresses are more customary than pants in the evening.

Midwest: Common sense and practicality rule here. Trendy clothes and light, airy pieces are out. Women tend to look neat and finished, with careful attention to details such as nails and hair.

Southwest: You can expect to see clothes that make a statement here. People do dress up, and personal styles are evident. Clothing is light, bright, and airy for everyday wear, and it's fancy for parties.

West Coast: In Los Angeles, the key word is comfortable, except perhaps on Oscar night. Clothing is generally simple and fresh-looking. Style goes more formal in San Francisco, though; women tend to overdress more than dress casually.

It *is* possible to have a wardrobe that will look fine no matter what the occasion and will leave us saying, "I don't have anything to wear today." Assembling the right wardrobe takes some thought, planning, and care, but it can be done.

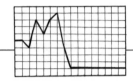

The Bottom Line

Some people can spend as much money as they like on their wardrobe and still not look well dressed. Looking well dressed has more to do with taste and common sense than with money.

Grooming

If you were to ask a roomful of people to list the things that create an instant negative impression, you would get many interesting responses—and perhaps some surprising answers. But although the list of responses might be long and varied, near the top would be something involving grooming:

➤ Lack of cleanliness

➤ Unruly or dirty hair

➤ Too much makeup

➤ Dirty fingernails

Being well groomed is more important than being well dressed in the business world. In fact, a well-groomed appearance can make up for an error in judgment in what you are wearing. But the effect of an elegant, perfectly fitted outfit can be completely negated by poor grooming.

Grooming is also more important than what you say or how well you say it. In fact, the person who is registering the fact that your fingernails are dirty or chipped probably isn't even listening to what you are saying.

So, before you even think about what you will be wearing or what you will be saying, make sure that you have taken care of every detail of good grooming.

1. There's no substitute for scrupulous cleanliness; this is absolutely vital at all times.

2. For men, stubble is unacceptable except under the most extraordinary circumstances. In fact, it's a good idea to keep shaving gear in your desk or briefcase for emergencies. That way, even if you and your management team pull an all-nighter getting a project ready for the morning, you can start the day clean-shaven.

3. Use of deodorants is a must, but avoid heavily scented deodorants and heavy colognes.

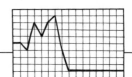

The Bottom Line

The purpose of deodorant is to eliminate smell. Therefore, people should not be able to detect the smell of your deodorant.

Making Up

It's a mistake for women to think that going without makeup altogether somehow makes them look "real" or "natural." It won't—it will make them look washed-out and unfinished. In the business world especially, makeup is a necessary and very important part of the grooming package.

Two basic rules of makeup apply:

1. Less is more.

2. Simpler is better.

The fact that every businesswoman needs some makeup doesn't mean that you must spend long hours in front of a mirror applying and removing layers of paint. Your makeup routine should take no more than 5 or 10 minutes.

Professional Help

Starting out with a basic makeup lesson from a professional is probably a wise investment. Some people say that these professionals want to sell you their own products, and that can be expensive. However, I have found that buying the products actually has saved me money in the long run because I don't find myself at a department store cosmetic counter buying dozens of items I didn't know I needed until I saw them there. Also, having a professional advise you on how to apply the makeup provides a wealth of information, and it comes free at the counter.

Most reputable beauty salons have a professional aesthetician on staff who handles skin care and makeup. Most large cosmetic companies also will occasionally have professionals who do makeovers at stores free of charge.

Your Makeup Kit

Your basic career makeup should include the following:

Business Blunders

The complete absence of makeup is almost as bad as too much makeup.

➤ A bit of foundation to even out face color

➤ Some eye shadow and a bit of eyeliner for definition

➤ Lip liner and lipstick

➤ Powder on the shiny parts of the face (in the center of the forehead, nose, and chin)

➤ A dusting of blush

➤ Some mascara

It's a good idea to start with your eyes. In fact, experts advise designing your eyebrows, eye line, and lip line to match the shape of your eyes. For example, if your eyes are round, give a round shape to your brows and lips. The same goes for almond-shaped eyes. This technique makes the various parts of your face look like they belong together, and the symmetry accentuates the features you were born with.

We return to looking at the eyes when it comes to making decisions about colors for lipstick, eye makeup, and blush.

Brown eyes   Look for colors with brown, orange, or yellow undertones and reds ranging from medium to dark. Avoid mauve or blue undertones.

Blue eyes   Mauve and blue, or mauve and rose undertones go well with blue eyes, as do light pink to fuchsia, pink, and reds.

Hazel or green eyes   Rose and burgundy or brown undertones go well with hazel or green eyes, as do reds with rose, burgundy, or brown undertones.

Black women will look good with makeup of both blue and orange undertones, or deep reds with blue, wine, or brown undertones. Asian eyes are complemented by rose and wine undertones, and reds with blue or wine undertones.

Do some testing. Your best color will seem to give your face a healthy glow and will smooth out your skin and mitigate or eliminate shadows and lines.

Eyebrows

Without eyebrows, the face has no expression, and unruly eyebrows overpower the face and create an unclean impression. With or without makeup, well-groomed eyebrows give the whole face a balanced, clean impression. Waxing brows once a month is the best means of upkeep.

Crowning Glory?

The first and most abiding rule is that your hair must always be clean and well-groomed.

There has always been and will continue to be some ambivalence about the proper length of hair for the business world. I believe that as long as a woman's hair is clean, out of her face, and off her shoulders, she can look professional. That doesn't necessarily mean short hair, however. A colleague of mine with long, flowing chestnut hair wears her hair pulled tightly back in a long braid, and it looks wonderful. Naturally, this is not a style that all of us can adopt with success.

Generally, women look best in a combination of long and short hair—a bit longer here, a bit shorter there. A good cut and a good styling can do things like this for you. And, when you make an appointment with a stylist, the consultation comes with it.

Memo to Myself

When it comes to hair, a good general rule is that it's the size of the face, not the shape of the face, that is most important. For example, a small face will be overwhelmed and overshadowed by a lot of hair. On the other hand, someone with a very large head and face needs a lot of hair for balance.

Face It, Men

Men are faced with some tough decisions about facial hair. On the positive side, facial hair can make a young man look a little older and more serious. It can also disguise a receding chin or lips that are too thin.

On the other hand, facial hair can demand a lot more care and grooming than you might think, and some senior executives may find it offensive or perhaps ostentatious.

If you have a beard to cover scarring, or if you have grown facial hair for what you consider a good, solid reason, then keep it, by all means. If you are in doubt, though, your best and safest bet is to get rid of it.

Personally, I think that handlebar mustaches look silly and that goatees look satanic, and I'm sure there are many who would agree. Still, these looks seem to enjoy periodic comebacks, particularly in the more creative fields. In general, though, it's a good idea to avoid the theatrical when it comes to beards and mustaches. And, no matter what style you chose, facial hair must always look clean and well-tended.

Nails

Your hands are always on display and occasionally are the focus of attention. That's why your nails deserve special attention. It's probably a good idea to invest in at least one good manicure as a learning experience. After that, you should be able to handle

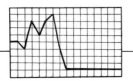

The Bottom Line

If your fingernails make a clacking sound when you use a keyboard, they are much too long and should be trimmed.

the job yourself. This goes for men as well as women. Men who think that getting a manicure is somehow unmasculine should get over that outdated idea.

Take a good look at your nails, with the knowledge that good nails are an indication of good health. Not only must they be kept scrupulously clean, but they also should be shaped with the cuticles pushed back and trimmed. Women must avoid that Morticia Adams look with long red or black claws; gaudy nail colors are not appropriate in a business context. Clear polish is your best bet, and it is also the easiest to maintain: It doesn't chip easily, and when it does, the chips don't show.

Skin

Good grooming means attention to basic skin care. Men and women should regularly cleanse their skin and exfoliate to remove dead skin. I recommend that people cleanse, rinse, and moisturize twice a day and exfoliate weekly. Pharmacies and drug stores stock plenty of good, moderately priced products. Drinking lots of water also is good for the skin, helping to avoid a dehydrated look.

Fitness

Being fit enhances your overall appearance like nothing else. A good, faithful exercise regime will not only improve your posture and carriage, but it also will affect your personality. Fit people tend to feel more focused and confident, and they also look more focused and confident. A national survey showed that a majority of working women interviewed believed that becoming physically fit helped their careers.

Not only does exercise improve your appearance and increase strength and endurance, but it also helps to defuse anger and frustration and gets creative juices flowing. If you are not now engaged in a program of regular exercise, we urge you to start one. You will never regret it.

Memo to Myself

When using perfume, go with a quality product and apply just a little of it. The effect should be subtle.

Style to Instill Confidence

You spend a lot of time in close quarters with lots of people during the work day, and the effect on others of any grooming lapse is apt to be exaggerated. So, no amount of time and effort in this department is wasted. As you can see, good grooming goes beyond being freshly showered and neatly combed—it requires attention to detail.

Grooming can make or break your reputation in the business arena. People will remember bad makeup or dirty fingernails long after they have forgotten whether your necktie complemented your suit color. It's worth any investment in time and money to get yourself looking—and smelling—up to par.

The Least You Need to Know

➤ The real trick in dressing is maintaining a wardrobe that works every day and in every situation.

➤ In building a wardrobe, consider your corporate culture, regional realities, and sport and play activities.

➤ Find shops that work for you, and build relationships with knowledgeable salespeople.

➤ If the question is selecting two good garments or one quality garment, go for quality every time.

➤ Good grooming is more important than dressing right.

➤ Keep fit—feeling great and looking great go together

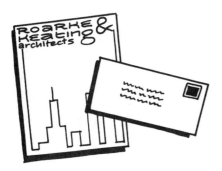

Correspondence

In business, people are writing to each other more than ever. Easy access to e-mail and intersystem messaging means that people are just as apt to write as to telephone. In fact, sending a quick message has some important advantages over calling, not the least of which is dodging the danger of getting involved in a chatty conversation in the middle of a busy day.

But this easy access has some dangers. It could cause us to overlook or transgress the basic rules of correspondence etiquette. It could tempt us to use e-mail in cases where a letter or at least a handwritten note is not only preferable, but necessary.

Writing Letters

In many ways, the pen is mightier than the computer chip, not to mention the cellular phone. A nicely written letter on good stationery has powers no e-mail or computer printout can match.

From the File Drawer

"There is nothing more pleasant than receiving a beautiful letter."

—Amy Vanderbilt

A letter is so much more than an instrument for conveying facts. In a business context, its very appearance makes a statement about your firm. Its style and content also make a statement about you as a person and as a professional.

In more personal circumstances, a letter can be a gift that pleases both the sender and the receiver. It can be more personal than a telephone call and more intimate and touching than even a private conversation.

Do's and Don'ts

Certain customs about how a letter should be organized on the page have evolved over the years and have become accepted and expected almost universally. Think of these as the skeleton of any letter. Once these elements are in place, you will feel free to concentrate on the essential message you wish to convey.

➤ **Address:** If it is not printed at the top of the page, write it in the upper-left corner.

➤ **Date:** This goes under the address in the upper-left or bottom-left corner. In more formal letters, write out the month instead of using numerals.

➤ **Salutation:** The salutation goes flush left. (In informal letters, use the first names of people you know. In all other letters, use honorifics—Mr., Ms.—and the last name.)

➤ **Body:** Leave a space, indent, and begin the body of the letter.

➤ **Complimentary close:** The complimentary close goes to the left, and it may take many forms.

Sincerely is the stalwart standby for most business letters. You can soften that by placing *Yours* in front of *Sincerely* or by using *Yours truly*. If you know the person rather well and wish to be even less formal, try *Best wishes*, or *As ever*. *Cordially*, is considered to be out of date, but I like it and still use it because it is correct and, I think, conveys warmth.

For personal letters, *Fondly* and *Affectionately* are useful. *Love* is a wonderful thing, yet, as in so many aspects of life, it should be offered abundantly but selectively, and seldom in writing.

Gratefully is great for letters of thanks.

Respectfully and *Respectfully yours* are reserved for the clergy.

The Opening

Once you know what the skeleton will look like, it's time to start the body of the letter. Here is where a lot of people have a lot of trouble.

It helps to mentally review and perhaps jot down the main points you want to make. You can begin by referring to previous correspondence or conversations, or by sketching out a situation and then stating the points you want to make about that situation.

If the letter is more personal, you might want to begin with good news: "You will be glad to hear that ...." You can also start by referring to a previous letter or the last time you met. Then just tell the news or say what's on your mind. Never start a letter by apologizing for not writing. You can start by saying, "Things sure have been busy around here" and then go on to give details.

Business Blunders

For letters that you intend to write by hand, use a good fountain pen. Penmanship looks so much better, and this is the sort of detail that is noticed and remembered. Colored ink is okay for casual notes, but for more formal letters and letters of condolence and invitations, use only black ink.

Memo to Myself

The word *you* is a much better way to start a letter than the word *I*.

Style and Structure

Clarity and sincerity are the highest virtues and the noblest goals.

Clarity is wonderfully advanced by having a clear idea of what you want to say in your letter. And this is wonderfully enhanced by making a rough outline and then writing a draft of the letter so that you can scribble, insert, scratch things out, and move things around.

Drafting a letter is also an excellent way to overcome writer's block. When people say, "I never know what to say," what they really mean is, "I don't know how to get started." Get a sheet of paper and get the words flowing—even the wrong words. The right words will come along.

Memo to Myself

Dear Sir or Madam is outdated. If you are writing to a vendor, for example, and you don't know the name of the person, use *To Whom It May Concern* or *Dear Ladies and Gentlemen*. Flattery can't hurt.

Using plain, strong language conveys sincerity. Using simple language will not make you appear simple-minded; some of the most potent ideas in history have been stated in the simplest and most common terms. The other extreme is showing off, using extravagant language, unfamiliar words, or obscure references and images. This kind of showing off is nowhere more obvious and more irritating than in a letter.

A Quick Lesson in Grammar

One error in grammar, spelling, or punctuation can ruin an otherwise excellent letter. Grammatical mistakes have a jarring effect even in the most casual note or quick e-mail. If you have access to spell-check software, use it. If you have even the slightest doubt as to the exact meaning of a word, hit the dictionary.

Here are some of the grammatical errors I see most often:

➤ Leaving the apostrophe out of *it's* when it's a contraction for "it is."

➤ Using *less* instead of *fewer*. The word *less* refers to quantities (such as "less water"), and *fewer* refers to things you can count (such as "fewer marbles"). (Of course, if you mention this error at checkout counters with the sign "10 items or less" the clerk is apt to look at you as if you were speaking Urdo.)

➤ Using the phrase "between you and I." This phrase becomes "you and me" when it follows a preposition, such as *between*, *to*, and *for*.

➤ Using *irregardless* instead of *regardless*.

➤ Using "I, myself" or "you, yourself." (Only use *myself* for emphasis.)

➤ Misusing *imply* and *infer*. The speaker implies; the listener infers.

➤ Misusing *capital* and *capitol*. The *Capitol* is the building; *capital* is everything else.

➤ Perhaps the most common grammatical error is failing to have the number of the noun agree with the verb. Take a look at these examples:

Everyone *is* (not *are*) eligible.

The group of reporters *is* (not *are*) waiting.

Either Tom and Joan *is* qualified.

Both Tom *and* Joan are qualified.

Perhaps the most common punctuation error is failing to put a comma after the end of the first part of a compound sentence, which is two complete sentences hooked together with a conjunction such as *and* or *but*.

For example: "You may stay, but you must not stay later than midnight."

Writing the Thank-You Note

So many of the questions I get when lecturing or by e-mail mention thank-you letters or other means of appropriately expressing gratitude. Three basic rules govern every thank-you letter; if you remember them, you should never again dread sitting down to write the obligatory thank-you.

1. Thank the person for the specific gift, and mention the gift by name.

2. Acknowledge the effort that went into picking, purchasing, wrapping, or making the gift, if that was the case.

3. Report how you have used the gift or how you are looking forward to using the gift in the future.

Business Blunders

Personal notes and letters should not be typed. Resort to typing only if your handwriting truly resembles Chinese algebra. If it does, you can probably improve it with practice—and you should.

Remember that the only true gifts we can give are our time and attention. So distinguish yourself by your "attitude of gratitude," and be sure to thank others when they have helped you, gone out of their way for you, and so forth.

Dear Tamika:

Thank you very much for inviting me to the Chicago management seminar and for arranging for accommodations. Your excellent arrangements made the trip practically effortless, and I appreciate all the trouble you went to. The seminar was extremely informative. The insights and information I picked up there have already been useful and will continue to be as I move into my new area of responsibility.

Gratefully,

Bill Clancy

Of course, the thank-you for a personal gift will differ, but it will follow the same three principles.

> Dear Margaret:
>
> Ralph and I and the two boys want to thank you very much for the handsome Monopoly™ deluxe edition game. I know this game isn't found in most stores, and I truly appreciate all the time and effort you must have spent to find it. The whole family spent last night playing for the first time, and it was a great family experience. I'm sure there will be other equally enjoyable Monopoly™ sessions at our house.
>
> Fondly,
>
> Gladys

Read over these other things to remember when composing your thank-you note, which is, after all, one of etiquette's most enduring and important tasks:

➤ Even if you have thanked someone in person, it is important to follow up with a note. That simple, five-minute act will set you apart from the rest as gracious, refined, and savvy.

➤ When thanking someone for a gift of money, don't mention the amount. The phrase "your generous gift" will do.

➤ No, a printed note from a gift shop is *not* acceptable. Gratitude can not be prepackaged.

➤ No, a telephone call will *not* do.

➤ When refusing a gift, your note should say that you don't feel that you can accept the gift, but thank the person for their thoughtfulness. If accepting such gifts violates your company's policies or your profession's usual standards, say so.

If you have observed all the previous suggestions and have written your note with sincerity, you can send it off with the knowledge that it will be very much appreciated.

Letters of Condolence

When something tragic happens to a colleague or a friend, a letter of condolence is called for. Of course, these letters are very different from thank-you letters, but there is a similarity in that it will help you a great deal if you remember three things. Your letter should do the following:

1. Acknowledge the recipient's loss and suffering, and let him or her know that you sympathize.
2. Convey a sincere desire to help in some way.
3. If there has been a death, the letter should praise the character, accomplishment, and devotion of the deceased.

These letters need not be lengthy, but they should cover all three of the preceding points.

Dear Mrs. Dobrow:

Please accept my deepest sympathy on the loss of your husband, Michael. His passing was a great blow to all of us, and I know that no words of mine can ease your grief.

Michael was my first supervisor when I came to work at Peabody's, and his kindness and guidance helped me to get started there. His wisdom and skill, together with his friendliness and fine sense of humor, made him the most popular "boss" in the company. We will all miss him.

I think you know that Margaret and I live just a few blocks away, and I hope you will call upon us if there is anything either of us can do to help you or your family in the difficult days ahead.

Yours truly,

Nering Huete

Following are some things to remember when writing these notes. You can be sure that these will be appreciated at once and for some time to come.

➤ Condolence letters are often kept in a family archive and may be passed down through generations. They must be handwritten, of course, in black ink on good paper.

➤ Avoid overemphasizing how much you personally feel bereaved. The purpose of the letter is to comfort others, not to make them feel sorry for you.

➤ While the tone of the letter should be sympathetic, it should also be rather formal.

A letter to someone who has just received bad but not tragic news should be sympathetic and should offer support, but it should also end with a note of optimism. You are confident that your friend will rebound, rally, put this behind him, and so forth.

Congratulations Letters

Like the letter of condolence, the letter of congratulations may be put away and saved for years. The tone, however, should be quite informal and even breezy.

After first mentioning the reason for the congratulations, every congratulatory letter should say how richly the recipient deserved whatever happy thing happened.

Dear Bill:

My heartiest and most sincere congratulations on your Carnegie grant. What great news! It is a very high honor and one that you so richly deserve. Your work in that field has broken new ground for all of us. Everyone here will miss you during your period of travel and study, and we look forward to your return.

Sincerely,

Peter Grable

Apology Letters

If you have offended someone and are sorry about it, apologize in person and follow it up—promptly—with a letter saying clearly and humbly that you are sorry. If there is some way to make amends, promise to do so.

Writing a Note

Why a handwritten note? Why not e-mail it? Why not just call?

The note is not as cold as e-mail. It is more personal; it takes more effort and is therefore more appreciated. It won't be seen, as e-mail can be, by strangers or anyone other than the intended recipient.

And you know what happens with telephone calls. You pick up the phone knowing generally what you want to say, but not the exact words. You hesitate. The other person says something. You respond to that. The mood turns. The moment is lost. Besides, you can't hold a telephone call in your hand, put it away, and look at it again later. As if all that weren't reason enough, whenever we call someone, we are interrupting that person's schedule; we call them at our convenience, not theirs.

By nature, notes are brief and personal. They need not be poetic. (Also, note that brief notes don't need a complimentary close.)

Dear Mary:

Isn't it about time we had lunch to catch up on all the news? I'll call you next week.

Omar

And don't worry about clichés.

Dear Fred:

It was great seeing you on Wednesday.
You haven't changed a bit.

Tanya

Before you write, think about two things:

1. What is your "root" message? Get to it right away.
2. Who is the recipient? The tone differs depending on whether you're writing to an old friend, to a recent acquaintance, or to your boss.

If you have trouble thinking of an opening, you can fall back on one of these perennials:

"What a grand occasion/terrific surprise/welcome gift."

"I was just thinking (or) remembering .... "

Sometimes a famous quote can convey your message perfectly.

"No wise man ever wished to be younger."

—Jonathan Swift

I cannot foresee a time when the impact of electronic communications will replace personal correspondence. Letters and notes, handwritten on good paper, bring with them the gift of your time and effort. They come from your human hand, not an arrangement of electronic spasms.

It is a good idea to accept the fact that you should—and will—write as well as type in the course of your work day, so keep what you need in your desk. Resist the temptation to hammer out something on your keyboard when you know that a handwritten letter is the better, more gracious thing to do.

Choosing Your Stationery

The medium is part of the message, a vital part. Sometimes, how your correspondence looks is as important as what it says.

Happily, the rather rigid rules concerning stationery in past generations have been relaxed, stretched, and in some cases obliterated. One reason is changing attitudes and customs. Another is the easy access to computer programs for word processing and graphics.

Certain basic rules remain in place, however, and it is important to know them.

Paper Traits

You may want to consider certain factors if you are choosing personal stationery or paper for your company's correspondence.

You know when you are handling fine paper, even if you don't know why. The reason is texture and weight. A good guideline is rag content: The best paper is made from unlaundered, undyed, new cotton rag. Cheaper paper is made from vegetable fibers, sometimes combined with wood pulp.

Rag content is often noted on stationery boxes. The higher the rag content, the better the paper.

Watermarks

Another good indication of good stationery is watermarks, which are revealed when you hold the paper up to the light. Genuine watermarks of legitimate manufacturers look slightly blurred. Artificial watermarks usually are betrayed by their sharpness.

Printing

Most printing these days is done by a process called lithography, which is used for most printed material. This is the least expensive method and, with good design, can present a good quality appearance. The highest quality printing, however, is engraving, in which symbols are etched into a metal plate and then are stamped into the paper. You can tell real engraving by the raised, embossed quality. If you turn the paper over, you will note that the paper is slightly indented.

Don't try to get by with a cheaper process called thermography, which is similar to lithography but which attempts to imitate engraving. Stationery, like people, should not pretend that it is something it is not.

Your Personal Stationery

Of course, you will use company stationery for routine business matters. But, in addition, you need personal stationery. For many of us, that means having three kinds of stationery in the desk.

1. **Formal writing paper.** This is used for things such as condolence letters and when replying to formal invitations. It should be plain white or ecru letter sheets or cards.

2. **Personal business stationery.** This is used for correspondence relating to your career and for telling Sears that the refrigerator the store delivered is the wrong color. This correspondence should be on a single sheet and in a neutral color.

3. **Social notepaper.** This is used for things such as thank-you notes, informal invitations (and responses), and most other social correspondence. This stationery can reflect your personality and style with colored paper, borders, and lined envelopes. It may be in the form of a single sheet, a folded note, or a single card.

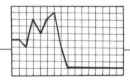

The Bottom Line

If your name can be either male or female, it's best to help the recipient by including a title (Mr., Mrs., Ms., Miss) on your printed or engraved stationery.

You also may want to consider "house stationery" as a single solution to many of these requirements. This is usually a single sheet with your address at the top, and it can be used by all members of the household.

Folding Stationery

There's a classic way of folding a piece of paper and putting it into an envelope. Fold the bottom up to approximately one-third of the way down from the top. Fold the top down so that the edge meets the bottom edge. Slide it into the envelope without turning it. Thus, when the letter is opened, it may be read at once without turning it. The read-at-once theory applies also to cards and fold-over notes.

Identity: Women

Gone are the days when only fold-over notes—not flat stationery—were used by all well-bred women. Nowadays, women select personal stationery that reflects their personal style, taste, and handwriting. For example, women with a large, generous script style will use large, letter-size sheets. However, it is still a good idea to avoid extreme ink colors in favor of multiuse, conservative colors such as blue, black, or gray.

How you identify yourself on stationery is important. A married woman may use "Mrs. Robert Smythe" or the more contemporary "Ms. Mary Smythe." It is unnecessary and, perhaps, pretentious, for a single woman to use "Miss" before her name. "Ms." is fine, or the name alone will do.

Insert a fold-over note into the envelope in this way.

Men

A man's name should appear on his stationery without a title, unless he happens to be a medical doctor (in which case "Dr." may be used; "M.D." is used only professionally). A man will also use a title if he is a clergyman or a member of the military.

Both

Men and women will find that the correspondence card is a very useful piece of stationery—it may be the most used item of stationery for some business people. These notes can be used for any kind of short note, including thank-you notes.

These cards come in different forms. Mine are single cards, about 4 by 6 inches. They can be colored or have a colored border, and they can be plain or engraved with your name or monogram. They can also be used for sending or responding to informal invitations.

Doctors

When a person has a Ph.D., these initials should be used only in a professional context:

Janet Duncan, Ph.D., Department of Anthropology, University of Pennsylvania (When writing to such a person, use the salutation "Dear Dr. Duncan.")

A medical doctor may use "Dr." before her name. Women in the military and the clergy also use titles.

It may be more practical for you to have your personal stationery printed with your address only if you use different names for different circumstances (for example, using your maiden name for business and your married name socially).

Memo to Myself

You may not need custom-printed or engraved stationery. You can find plain stationery in all the appropriate forms at stationery stores, department stores, and some jewelers. Personalizing is a nice and useful luxury, however.

Monograms

You may want to monogram your stationery. If so, it is generally best to use three initials—unless, of course, your name is something like Arnold Steven Sanders. In such cases, two initials are best. One initial leaves too many unanswered questions and strikes me as rather useless and silly.

Generally, monograms are three initials in consecutive order or with the surname initial set larger and placed between the two others.

Monograms should be centered at the top of the page or, on a folded note, centered on the front or in the upper-left corner.

A married woman who uses her husband's name uses the initials of her first, maiden, and married names. A single woman or one who retains her maiden name uses the initials of her first, middle, and last names.

See the following page for some examples of monograms.

Sending Invitations

During the course of your career, you almost certainly will have occasion to invite colleagues and bosses (or be invited by them) to weddings, formal dinner parties, or other occasions that call for a proper invitation and a correct reply.

In past generations, it was considered somewhat shabby to include a reply card with a formal invitation. Nowadays, however, the RSVP card is commonplace and generally is accepted. It evolved into general use because so many people stopped replying formally and in writing.

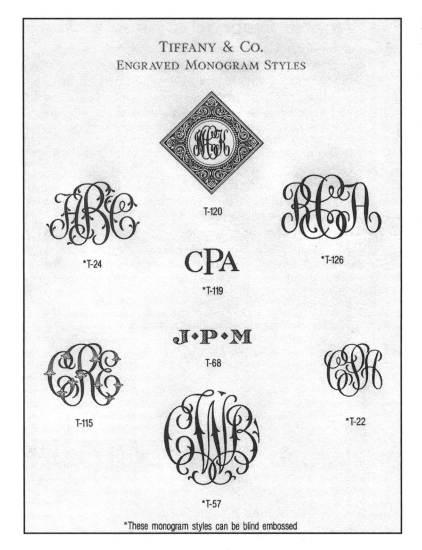

Engraved monogram styles.

The reply card is acceptable in all situations and is a lot less stressful than a telephone blitz before the event to find out how many people are coming. The card should be in the same style as the invitation and should be made of the same paper stock. If you don't use a reply card and you need to know who is coming, be sure to have an RSVP on the invitation along with an address or a telephone number.

Memo to Myself

Replies should be in the same form as the invitation, as an acknowledgement that you accept the sender's standards in reference to the occasion. A casual or flip response to a formal invitation means you think less of the event than the person who is inviting you.

How to Respond to an Invitation

If you receive an invitation without a reply card enclosed, respond in the same general form as the invitation. Write by hand and in the third person: "Mr. and Mrs. Thomas Tolson are pleased to accept ...." Use conservative stationery or engraved personal stationery. You can also use a personal letter sheet or a half sheet.

If you are sending regrets, remember the two standard reasons for refusing an invitation: "due to a previous engagement" and "because of absence from town." Don't use illness as an excuse; this requires the host to make some response concerning the illness. If you don't know the host very well, an excuse is not needed. Simply write: "... regrets that she will be unable to attend." If you know the host well, you might want to make a call explaining why you can't attend, but mail your regrets as well.

Sending regrets in response to a formal invitation.

> *Mr. Paul Gallagher*
>
> *sincerely regrets*
>
> *that because of a previous engagement*
>
> *he will be unable to accept*
>
> *Mr. and Mrs. Smith's*
>
> *kind invitation for the tenth of June.*

Sending and Responding to Informal Invitations

Though informal, these invitations are still written in the third person. However, they are less structured and are written on personal note paper or on an informal or correspondence card. You also can use a "fill-in" invitation, or you can write on informal note papers or on a folded note with a monogram. (With a monogram, start writing on the front if the monogram is placed to one side, or start inside under the fold if the monogram is in the middle.)

Lisa and Steven Price

invite you

to cocktails

on Wednesday, May 3rd

6-8 (or six to eight) o'clock

430 Prince Street

R.S.V.P.

555-4203

An informal fill-in invitation from more than one person.

requests the pleasure of the company of

at

on

at   o'clock

An informal fill-in invitation from one person.

When replying, call if there is a telephone number given. If there is no number but an address is included, reply on your own stationery. Even if the invitation says "regrets only," it is still a good idea to call to let the hosts know you will be attending.

Forms of Address

For women, "Ms." is the correct form of address in the business arena, and it is widely accepted in the social world as well. Also, a divorced woman will often use "Ms." because "Miss" is reserved for women who have never married.

➤ A married women who keeps her maiden name may be known professionally as Mary Mitchell and socially as Mrs. Daniel Fleischmann, for example. When a married woman hyphenates her name, the maiden name comes before the hyphen, and the married name comes after.

➤ A woman using her husband's name does not change her name if she becomes a widow.

➤ A divorced woman may choose to drop her married name entirely. If she is known professionally by her former husband's name, she can continue to use it, even if she remarries. When she resumes her maiden name, she drops the "Mrs." and uses "Ms.," not "Miss."

➤ A woman who is legally separated continues to use her husband's given and family name until she is divorced.

➤ For single mothers, "Ms." makes more sense than "Miss."

For men, a man uses "Jr." if his name is identical to his father's. (If you spell out *junior*, use a small j.) If the father dies, the son drops the "Jr." The surviving son's mother may add "Sr." to her name to avoid confusion with the daughter-in-law. If a woman marries a "Jr.", her married names includes the "Jr." If the junior gives his son the same name, the son adds "III" or "3rd" to his name.

If a man is named for a family member other than his father (perhaps an uncle or grandfather), he adds "II" or "2nd" to his name; that is dropped when the family member dies.

Memo to Myself

Only one person can write a letter, so only one person can sign one. However, you can end the text by saying, "Grady joins me in wishing you good luck in your new job." It is perfectly fine for one half of a couple to sign both names to a postcard or a greeting card.

Signing Off

A married woman should sign checks and legal documents with her given name and married name: Helen Cartwright. If it is a common name such as Mary Smith, she might want to use her maiden name as well: Mary Simpson Smith. A single Mary Smith might wish to use her middle initial.

Never give yourself a title when signing your name. If you are on a first-name basis with the recipient, write "Mrs. Grady Smith" under the Mary Smith signature. If "Mrs. Grady Smith" is printed on your stationery, simply sign as Mary Smith.

➤ When writing to someone you know very well, sign using your first name only.

➤ A single woman may write "Ms." or "Miss" in parentheses to the left of her name.

Addressing Envelopes

These other important tips will help you make sure your correspondence is properly addressed.

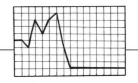

➤ It is no longer necessary to write out the names of states in full when addressing formal correspondence. Thankfully, the ancient affection of writing numbers out in full is passe.

➤ Type or write all social envelopes; it is okay to address an envelope by hand if the letter is typed.

The Bottom Line

No matter how cute odd–sized envelopes may be, the U.S. Postal Service won't deliver envelopes that are not at least 3.5 inches by 5 inches.

➤ Keep lines aligned, or indent each slightly more than the previous one. City, state, and zip code go on a single line.

➤ Middle names are not always written out. If Thomas Joseph Clancy uses Thomas J. Clancy, follow his lead.

➤ It's acceptable to write the return address on the envelope flap, but it is more convenient all around to put it on the front, in the upper-left corner.

When addressing an envelope to a married couple, the woman's name goes first if the wife uses her maiden name:

Ms. Betty Miller
and Mr. Adam Blake

The exception is when the husband uses a professional title:

The Reverend Adam Blake
and Ms. June Friday

If it's social correspondence, and Betty uses her maiden name only professionally, the address is Mr. and Mrs., or The Reverend and Mrs. If the husband is deceased, remember that widows continue to use the husband's first and last names. If divorced, it's Ms. (not Miss) Betty Miller. A separated woman uses her husband's name until the divorce. Use Ms. for single mothers.

If both halves of a couple are doctors, you can use The Doctors Blake, or Doctors Betty and Adam Blake, or Dr. Betty Miller and Dr. Adam Blake.

If he is the only doctor, it's Dr. and Mrs. Adam Blake, or Dr. Adam Blake and Ms. Betty Miller. If she is the only doctor, it's Dr. Betty Miller and Mr. Adam Blake.

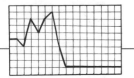

The Bottom Line

The Post Office will still deliver mail with the return address on the back, a long-standing formal custom. However, it's best to put the return on the front, in the upper-left corner for all but the most formal invitations.

Memo to Myself

A good way of "bribing" children into writing is to get them their own stationery. For younger children, the paper should be lined.

Unmarried Couples

When addressing an envelope to a couple living together but not married, place each name on a separate line, flush left, alphabetically with no *and* in between. (The *and* on an envelope signifies marriage.) This is also the way to address envelopes to gay couples living together.

Kids

Girls are "Miss" from birth to 21, but in practice, envelopes are generally addressed without the "Miss" until they become teenagers. At 21, girls may wish to change to "Ms."

Boys are correctly, but not necessarily, addressed as "Master" until age 8, when the title is dropped. He becomes "Mr." at age 18. There is a comma between the name and "Jr.", but not between the name and the letters II or III.

If you must mess with "Messrs.", remember that it applies only to brothers and not other male family members, such as uncles and fathers. If the envelope is going to all the brothers, it is addressed to The Messrs. Jones. If it's going to two of the three brothers, it's addressed to The Messrs. Steven and Robert Jones.

Honorifics

When it comes to honorifics, certain persons should be addressed in very specific ways.

➤ *Esquire* is used now only for lawyers, and is almost always abbreviated as "Esq." When using this title, you drop the prefix "Mr.", "Ms.", and so forth. When writing to a lawyer and a spouse, drop the "Esq." and use Mr. and Mrs. Steven Jones.

➤ *Honorable* goes before the names of a former President of the United States, cabinet members, Senators, Congressmen, American ambassadors, governors, and mayors.

➤ Judges are addressed as "The Honorable."

➤ Roman Catholic clergy: The Pope is His Holiness the Pope, or His Holiness Pope John Paul II. Cardinals are addressed as "His Eminence." Bishops are "The Most Reverend." Monsignors are "The Right Reverend."

➤ Protestant clergy are addressed as "The Reverend." Episcopal bishops are "The Right Reverend," and archdeacons are "The Venerable."

➤ A Jewish rabbi is addressed as Rabbi Thomas Jones, and cantors as Cantor Thomas Jones.

It matters a great deal how your correspondence looks—in some cases as much as what it actually says. Select your stationery and printing with the same care and attention you give to selecting a wardrobe.

The forms and conventions that have grown up around such things as sending and responding to an invitation have evolved in certain ways for very good reasons, and they should be acknowledged. The same is even more true when it comes to how people should be addressed. All of us are sensitive about how we are addressed, and we're appreciative of those who have the good manners to address us properly.

The Least You Need to Know

➤ The pen is still mightier than the computer; no printout, however eloquent, can replace a letter or a note.

➤ The appearance of a letter sends a strong message about you and your company.

➤ The two most important qualities of any letter are clarity and sincerity.

➤ The thank-you note must mention the gift and say how it will be used and how much it is appreciated.

➤ Most people need three kinds of stationery: formal stationery, personal note paper, and personal business stationery.

➤ Most invitations now include reply cards. If you don't include one, mark the invitation RSVP and give an address or telephone number.

Part 3

Making Contact

This part of the book explores something most people think they know lots about: communication. The trouble is, most of us know a lot less than we think.

Good communication is essential to good manners: What might seem an insignificant or meaningless gesture could turn out to be a sensible and deliberate move when we know the reason behind it. What we initially perceive as an annoying memo or note might become a friendly reminder. An impossible task, when outlined and explained clearly, might become a rewarding and successful endeavor.

For openers, we look at the dynamics of communications: what happens and what doesn't. We'll examine how we erect barriers to communication—and explore how we can tear them down. We'll also look at the craft and art of conversation and uncover some tricks and techniques that will help you in the board room as well as at the cocktail party. In addition, we reveal some secrets of the successful public speaker. After all, no matter what kind of business you are in, there's an excellent chance that you will find yourself speaking in public.

And then there is the old and new electronic etiquette. We'll look into how to make the new wizardry of the workplace work for you, from teleconference to e-mail to the most misused instrument of instant contact: the good old telephone.

Chapter 9

How We Communicate

In This Chapter

➤ How you come across—and how you fail to

➤ The way you look, how you sound, and why it counts

➤ Recognizing learning styles and getting people to listen

➤ He said, she said—gender differences

➤ When it's the boss talking

Steve walked out of his supervisor's office, got himself a mug of coffee, sat down at his desk, and moaned—softly.

> "I just spent 20 minutes talking with Hilary," he said to no one in particular, "and I still don't know what she wants me to do."

Steve has just passed through a communications dead zone, probably because of a flawed understanding of how people communicate. And, until he and Hilary realize this, they will spend a lot of time sending and receiving empty, incomplete, or contradictory messages.

Communication Basics

Remember two basic rules when it comes to effective communication:

1. What we say is not necessarily what people hear.

2. What they hear is more important than what we say.

We have to accept the fact that there is more to getting a message across than speaking the right words.

Three aspects are involved in the way we communicate:

1. What we say

2. How we say it

3. What people see

In certain circumstances, particularly upon first meeting someone, the last of these aspects is the most important. Studies have shown that 55 percent of how people first perceive us is based on what they see, 7 percent is based on what we say, and 38 percent is based on how we say it. No matter how well developed our verbal skills are, we are still visual creatures.

Another crucial factor is understanding that different people receive information differently, and it is important to be aware of and be able to recognize communication styles.

So, skillful and effective communication depends not only on what we say, but also how we say it, how we look, and how the other person receives information.

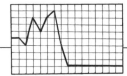

The Bottom Line

Gestures do not always accentuate your message—in fact, they may obscure it. This is particularly true of such gesture as finger-pointing (accusatory) and table-pounding (threatening).

Body Language

The messages your body is sending can obscure or enhance any verbal message. Try these tips to make sure your message is getting across:

➤ **Open up.** Communication is enhanced by an open appearance. Crossing your arms "closes" the body and creates a barrier between you and the person you are trying to reach. Unfortunately, this is a habit that will take time and effort to break. Women also tend to cross their arms more than men and will have to try harder to break this habit.

➤ **Watch your posture and gestures.** Slouching or, at the other extreme, sitting or walking rigidly, can send negative messages. Studying your shoes also can come across as a negative action. Gestures that interfere with clear communication include jabbing with the fingers, clenching the fists, twirling the hair, and fidgeting.

➤ **Space wars.** Keeping the right distance is critical. If you are too far away—or, even worse, if you are crowding the other person—you create a discomfort level that will interfere with communication.

Generally, Americans are more comfortable speaking about an arm's length from one another. The comfort zone differs in other cultures. (See Chapter 19, "The Global Stew," for more on global diversity.)

In any case, watch for clues. If you are speaking and the other person moves a little closer, don't back off unless you find the proximity disturbing. On the other hand, if the listener backs off, resist the urge to close the gap again. He is probably moving away because he feels that you are too close.

Business Blunders

If the person you are speaking to backs off, don't pursue him. Let the listener establish a distance that is comfortable for him.

Sound Advice

The sound of your voice may be something less than music to the ear, and people have a tendency to arbitrarily assign certain personality traits to you based on how you sound. If your first contact with someone is by telephone, that person may even develop a mental picture of what you look like without seeing you.

When is the last time you listened to your voice? It might surprise you. There's a good chance that you are still using your "child voice," continuing the vocal patterns you learned while growing up.

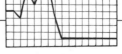

The Bottom Line

Studies show that raising the voice in tense or confrontational situations causes people to "hear" you less. Conversely, lowering the voice in these circumstances causes people to focus on what you are saying.

Tape yourself, preferably during a conversation. You may be startled by what you hear. Listen for and try to eliminate nasal tones, raspy sounds, and thinness. Try to develop resonance without booming like some camp meeting book-walloper.

You may consider investing in voice classes or in an acting class that stresses vocal development.

Speaking of actors, you may recall being in a theater and, when the plot takes a tragic turn, thinking, "I should be feeling something." If you're not, it's probably because the actors are not. The point is, no amount of vocal acuity will replace sincerity. You may have asked yourself how you can successfully sell a product or an idea you don't really believe in. The answer is, you can't, no matter how good an actor you think you are. If you want to be a convincing advocate, you must first find something you can support. Once you have done that, you can go about convincing others with confidence and authority.

113

Memo to Myself

Your voice may sound fine to you, but not to others. Listen to yourself on tape. If you don't like the way you sound, it certainly is possible to change.

What's Your Personality Type?

People receive information in different ways. Three major factors affect the way people accept and process information:

1. Personality type
2. Learning style
3. Gender

You don't have to be a shrink to understand and deal with the dynamics involved with these three factors. The first thing you want to recognize is personality type. A good way to begin is to divide personality types into four categories:

1. Activist
2. Controller
3. Consensus seeker
4. Logician

If you can learn to look for signals that will help you to decide the categories into which people best fit, you will find communication greatly facilitated.

Before describing the qualities of folks in these four categories, it is important to point out that as we become more sophisticated, we tend to develop qualities from all the four groups. But one or two of these will always be our most dominant characteristics. None of these four groups is good or bad, better or worse—they're all just different.

One of the first things we must do is to look for the unwritten rule or prime motivator shared by those in each group. Let's examine each category in more detail.

The Activist

The prime motivator for the activist is to be appreciated. If you (or a colleague or client) are an activist, you thrive on appreciation and, of course, action.

The activist absorbs information quickly and tends to make decisions spontaneously, based on enthusiasm and intuitive or "gut" reactions. He wants his information in terms of the big picture and is impatient with details. He is a people person and, because of this, works well with a team.

Clues: Because the activist is not detail-oriented, a clue is a messy work environment. In addition to being appreciated, the activist wants to have a good time. If he remembers to bring a notebook to a seminar, he will write down all the jokes so he can repeat them the next day at the office.

The Controller

The unwritten prime motivator for the controller is "Let's get it done!"

Being results-driven, the controller wants information promptly and completely. Time is important, and wasting time is not only annoying, but also downright sinful. The controller is energized by phrases such as, "Let's get to the bottom of this," and "Let's cut to the chase."

The controller likes challenge and risk, and responds to remarks such as, "This could be a risky proposition," or "This is a challenging project." The controller likes action, control, and results.

Clue: The controller tends to stick with a task until it is completed, preferring to work on while others take a break.

Memo to Myself

It may take a little while for you to pick up enough clues to assign someone to one of the four categories described previously. But thinking in terms of these traits can help you better understand the people you are dealing with and can be valuable in helping you to communicate effectively with them.

The Consensus Seeker

The prime motivator for the consensus seeker is "Let's get along."

The consensus seeker wants a lot of information and a number of points of view. Don't expect a quick decision from this person, but when the decision is made, it will reflect the feelings and position of his coworkers and often will accurately reflect the will of the majority. The consensus seeker is an excellent and valuable team player.

This type of person is conscientious, introspective, loyal, appreciative, and caring. He wants to be certain that everyone understands what is going on and is as comfortable as possible with it.

Clue: The consensus seeker wants his working environment to be orderly and, as far as possible, peaceful. He functions poorly, if at all, amid chaos.

The Logician

The prime motivator for the logician is "Get it right!"

The logician wants his information in great detail and, preferably, in writing. If given a choice between two pages of data and 50, he will opt for the 50. He wants hard data—numbers, graphs, and confirmation from more than one source.

If you want a decision quickly, don't go to the logician. He makes decisions slowly and with great caution.

Clue: The logician works best and is happiest when working alone.

Learning Styles

Another important way to determine the best means of communicating with someone is to look for indications of that person's learning style, or how he or she receives information. You do this by observing the person's reaction to how new information is presented.

Three basic learning styles exist:

1. Visual
2. Auditory
3. Tactile

A good way to think of this is to imagine three persons assembling a bicycle on Christmas Eve. One reads the instructions twice and studies a diagram intently before taking the parts out of the box. This is the visual learner.

The second gets the parts out of the box, throws away the manual, spreads out the parts, and calls his brother Ted for advice. This is the auditory learner.

The third just starts putting parts together in a trial-and-error fashion. This is the tactile learner.

Imagine that your boss has assigned you to come up with a new, more efficient telecommunications system for your offices. You know from experience how the boss best receives information, so you plan your presentation based on that knowledge.

If the boss is a visual learner, you write everything out and include graphics.

> "Here's a description of the system I have in mind, along with a couple rough graphs. Look it over, and let me know what you think."

If the boss is more auditory, the best tactic is to set up a meeting and talk things over.

> "I'd like to get together with you and go over my idea for that new telecommunications setup."

If the boss learns best in a tactile environment, look for a way to have her experience things.

> "I can show you how a console at key locations can thoroughly upgrade our telecommunications."

Differences Between Men and Women

When it comes to equal treatment and equal respect, it doesn't matter whether the person you are dealing with is male or female. But, when it comes to the most effective and efficient means of communication, gender can make a difference.

116

For one thing, studies have shown that when men nod their heads, they are most often saying, "I agree." However, with women, a nod does not necessarily mean approval. When women nod their heads, they are most often saying, "Yes, I understand. Keep going."

Where Do You Stand?

Another significant difference is that men tend to be more comfortable talking side to side, while women are most comfortable talking face to face. It is very important to be aware of—and accepting of—this difference. A woman should not be put off by the fact that a man has a tendency to move out of a face-to-face situation during a conversation. Conversely, a man should be aware that a woman feels more comfortable conversing face-to-face. Couples may find that husbands tend to bring up important topics while in the car on the way to the restaurant, whereas wives would much prefer to wait until the two are facing each other across the table. (Business aside, learning this was a major breakthrough in my marriage.)

Speaking Styles

Women tend to enhance their narratives with color and detail, whereas men tend to hurry to a conclusion.

A woman might say

> "The meeting was held in that drab, dark conference room on the second floor, the one with those hard, uncomfortable plastic chairs. This might account for the fact that so little was accomplished. All we really agreed on was the agenda for tomorrow."

A man might say

> "Nothing was accomplished but setting tomorrow's agenda. I think the venue might have been all wrong."

Because of this difference, men tend to become impatient and may interrupt a woman's narrative by saying, "So what finally happened?"

And women may become annoyed with the tendency of men to "tell" rather than "discuss." Women may consider men's voice and body language intrusive when they are trying to make a point. They might not like the fact that a man is more apt to say, "Hand me that McCarthy report," rather than, "Would you please pass me that McCarthy report?"

Bonding

Men and women have different ways of solidifying relationships. Men like to advise one another. They enjoy talking about the best ways to find, accomplish, or get rid of

117

something. In fact, if you bring up a topic, a man's first reaction is to think of some way to advise or help you in that area, whether or not you need or want any help or advice. In conversation, men use humor, sarcasm, and even mild insults. They talk about external, nonpersonal things, such as sports.

Women form bonds by sharing personal information and by complimenting one another. They are disappointed when men refuse to talk about their feelings. On the other hand, men tend to run for cover when women try to get them to open up.

So, effective communicating with the opposite sex takes some tolerance and some extra effort.

Fighting Fair

Resentment, hostility, and defensiveness are the mortal enemies of good communications. That's why I offer the following "fair fighting tips." Keep these in mind when communicating, and see if they can improve and clarify your message.

➤ **Use "I" Language.** Substituting "I" for "you" can avoid a defensive response. For example, imagine someone saying to you, "Do you understand? Are you sure?" Now, imagine the same person saying, "I've been over this so often that I might not be coming across clearly. Please let me know if I've skipped over any questions you might have had."

➤ **Avoid zingers.** "Your hair looks nice today. Did you wash it?" When we zing somebody, that person's reaction is to zing back. Soon, we're more interested in zinging than listening and communicating.

➤ **Avoid sarcasm.** The word *sarcasm* is derived from the Greek word *sarcous,* meaning to rip and tear flesh. If that's not your intention, avoid using sarcasm.

➤ **Avoid chasing rabbits.** This phrase means going off on another topic or not following the meeting agenda. Studies tell us that our first reaction to this is confusion, followed by impatience and resentment. Not sticking to the point creates a negative emotional reaction in others.

➤ **Don't interrupt.** It's not only rude, but it also creates the opposite of what we want when we interrupt.

➤ **Restate what you heard.** "If I've understood you correctly, you feel that the problem can be solved by negotiating, rather than by going to court. Is that correct?"

➤ **Ask questions that clarify.** It's a good idea to avoid beginning questions with "why." That tends to create a defensive reaction. Preferable are *who, what, when, where,* and *how.*

➤ **Stay in today.** References to the past too often connote blame and generate defensive responses.

➤ **Don't disparage feelings.** Don't tell someone how to think or feel—that's a judgment. Saying, "That's a silly way to feel about this," or "I can't believe you feel that way," causes defensiveness. Rather, talk about behaviors you would like to see or have seen.

➤ **Listen.** When someone believes we are not listening, his reaction is to feel demeaned, disrespected, and unimportant.

Talking to Your Staff

Good managers are good communicators, and they know that communicating with their staff requires some care and skill. Here are some of the most important consideration to keep in mind:

➤ Praise in public; criticize in private.

➤ Show respect for ideas and contributions. Thank the staff, in public, if possible. Write a personal note of appreciation.

➤ Foster the team concept. Your staff represents you to the company, your customers, and clients.

➤ When giving instructions, have staff members restate what they heard. Asking "Do you understand?" will get you a nod, whether they understand or not. Better is, "I want to make sure I was clear about that. Would you mind reading back to me what I've asked you to do?"

➤ Deal in observable fact and observable behavior. The statement "We're losing customers because you're not interested in serving them" will get you an "Am too" type of response. Better is: "I noticed that the last customer stood at the counter five minutes before he was served. We need to serve all customers in one minute." Also deliver such comments in the same tone of voice you would use to say, "It's raining outside."

Memo to Myself

If you are explaining something and the other person is "just not getting it," it doesn't help to simply repeat what you said more slowly. Try a whole new approach.

At the heart of the above items, and at the heart of all discussions about effective communications, is the concept of respect, which implies a willingness to listen and learn and to accept individual differences.

The Least You Need to Know

➤ Communicating involves more than just saying the right words.

➤ Recognizing the personality types of activist, controller, consensus seeker, and logician can facilitate communication.

➤ People learn in three learning styles: visual, auditory, and tactile.

➤ Important gender differences affect efficient communications.

➤ You can reduce resentment and defensive reactions by observing the "fair fighting" rules.

➤ When talking to your staff, praise in public and criticize in private.

Chapter 10

Making Conversation

In This Chapter

➤ Small talk certainly isn't small

➤ Tricks of the great conversationalists

➤ The vanishing art of listening

➤ The uses and misuses of clichés

➤ What you don't say and do

➤ When it's time to break it off

What people often refer to as small talk is anything but. No matter how well you know software applications or diesel engines, you will not rise above a certain level without people skills. That means being able to hold up your end of a conversation not only in the board room, but also at the dinner table and at the office picnic.

You may have encountered people who say almost proudly that they are "just not good at chitchat." They say it's because they are serious people. What they really are is seriously mistaken. In reality, they have not had the will or the energy to learn the skills and techniques that make casual conversation easy, pleasant, and rewarding.

And, yes, being a good conversationalist is a learned behavior. Despite appearances, learning the art of conversation is easy, and anyone can become quite good by applying some thought and preparation.

Let's look first at how a conversation begins and how you can make the kind of start that gets things going comfortably and smoothly.

Memo to Myself

Look at the person who is speaking. Then look at the person you are introducing when you speak that person's name.

Approaches

The conversation begins when you approach the other person, or vice versa, or when somebody introduces you.

If you make the approach, do it from the front rather than from the rear or the side. You want the person to see you coming and to avoid the tap on the shoulder or the theatrical throat-clearing to get attention. Say the other person's name, if you know it. If not, smile, put out your hand, and say, "Hello, I'm Jane Carter." Add some information that will identify you and/or outline the reason for presenting yourself: "I understand we'll be working together on the Jackson watershed case."

If someone approaches you, immediately give the person your full attention. Fix the name in your mind by repeating it silently to yourself. If you are not sure of the name, ask the person right away to repeat it. Listen for any nugget of information to hang a response on; if none is forthcoming, try to elicit something.

"Are you here with the Jackson group?"

If someone is introducing you, look first at the introducer and then at the person you are meeting. Again, listen carefully to the name. Repeat it in conversation as soon as possible. (See Chapter 3, "Greetings and Introductions," for more on this.)

If you are already engaged in conversation and another person joins you, say

"We were just talking about the problems we'll be facing with the Jackson watershed situation."

Listening

When people describe someone as a good conversationalist, they often really mean that the person is a good listener. We listen not only for nuggets of information upon which to build conversational exchanges, but also for the tone of voice that might tell us the person's attitude toward or position on a certain subject.

It is necessary not only to listen carefully, but also to give the appearance of listening carefully. You do this with body language. Look at the speaker. Lean forward slightly. Nod, or say, "I see," or "Yes." If you are uncomfortable looking into the eyes of another person, try the "Cyclops" technique, focusing on a spot between the other person's eyebrows. Actually, you can probably select any spot between the chin and hairline. But don't stare fixedly. Shift your gaze occasionally.

From the File Drawer

The most common irritant in conversation is the interruption. If you have something to contribute, no matter how witty or cogent, wait for a pause. There will be pauses—everybody has to breathe.

Don't allow yourself to be distracted by what is happening elsewhere in the room or which people are coming and going. Being disinterested in what the other person is saying is no excuse. Good manners often require extra effort.

Prompting

It's more important to get the other person talking than to deliver what conversational ammunition you have in the arsenal. Ask people about themselves. Ask open-ended questions that are not answered with a simple "yes" or "no." Rather than saying, "Do you like Seattle?" say, "What do you think of Seattle?"

If the person says that she is from Brooklyn, for example, don't say, "I was in Brooklyn last month and toured that marvelous art museum there." That will force the question, "What did you think of it?" And then you find yourself talking about yourself instead of the other person. A better response would be, "Oh, do you get back there much?" Or, you can talk about how Seattle and Brooklyn differ, how East Coast living differs from West Coast living, and so forth.

The Conversationalist

You know when you have enjoyed speaking with another person, but you may not have been aware of the characteristics that led you to that conclusion. Here are some of the characteristics that make a good conversationalist:

Business Blunders

Avoid topics that arouse strong or angry feelings, particularly religious or political philosophies.

➤ Curiosity. It is always pleasant to meet someone who is interested in who you are and what you have to say. These people ask intelligent questions and really listen to the answers.

123

➤ A sense of humor. Nothing breaks the ice like people laughing together. It's a good idea to have an arsenal of jokes, but real-life stories—particularly about familiar and famous persons—are sometimes better than the best jokes. Sarcasm and irony are fine, as long as the object of the remarks is remote enough from the lives of those listening. Politicians, business moguls, and celebrities are fair targets.

➤ A sincere desire to please others. This can't be faked.

➤ A willingness to play down your own achievements and expertise and to direct the conversation to others.

➤ A good vocabulary that allows you to speak vigorously without profanity, vulgarisms, and blasphemy.

All these features add up to one thing: a good conversationalist.

Clichés

Of course, you can rely on conversational clichés to get things going. After all, these became clichés because they are so useful. So go ahead and talk about the weather and politics and jet lag:

Memo to Myself

When invited to a party, find out as much as you can about others on the guest list. It will make the experience of meeting more comfortable, and will be an aid to starting and continuing a conversation.

"I imagine you find the weather here quite a bit more challenging than back in San Diego."

"That sure is true, but I don't mind a little snow. I grew up in Maine."

Now you can talk about Maine and about "down east" life as compared to "laid back" life.

Another useful and even welcome cliche is asking about possible mutual acquaintances. A good place to start is with the person who introduced you:

"How do you know Tom Fitzsimmons?"

"We met at that Chicago seminar on diversity training."

"I'm sorry I missed that. Was it interesting? Did you see much of Chicago? Had you been to Chicago before?"

And so on.

Another useful conversational cliché is the news. Everybody has an opinion on current events, and they like being asked for it.

You Don't Say

Avoid these conversational mine fields:

➤ Bad news, such as airplane crashes or a mutual acquaintance who has cancer

➤ Religion

➤ Political philosophies

➤ Your health, or lack of it

➤ Your promotion, or lack of it

➤ The cost of things these days

➤ The faults or misfortunes of others

Business Blunders

Yes, bad news—a plane crash, news of someone's death—will get you attention, but this is negative attention, not the kind you want at a social occasion or during a casual conversation.

You can explore plenty of fertile fields of conversational fodder without straying into these danger areas.

Don't Ask

If the other person is over 30, don't ask his or her age.

Don't ask the weight of an over- or underweight person. If you think someone has lost weight, has had cosmetic surgery, or is pregnant, just say, "You look terrific." If the other person volunteers the reason for the new look, you can then ask a few polite questions.

Don't ask a person why his or her spouse in not at the party. A question such as "How's Harry?" may bring forth an explanation. If not, don't press.

Avoid all questions concerning firings or layoffs, sex lives, miscarriages, serious or terminal illnesses, or divorces. Money questions to be avoided involve salaries and bonuses; the cost of a person's fur coat, house, or car; the size of his mortgage; or the cost of the latest vacation.

You Don't Do

Also avoid these no-nos in conversation:

➤ Don't slouch, but don't stand at attention either.

➤ Don't fold your arms, and keep your hands away from your hair and your face.

➤ Don't tell long, shaggy-dog jokes. Never tell vulgar or sexually explicit jokes. Jokes should relate to the topic under discussion.

➤ Don't perform. This happens when you concentrate too much on yourself and the impression you are trying too hard to make.

Business Blunders

Don't tell dirty or vulgar jokes, no matter how funny you think they are.

➤ Don't speed-talk, trying to cram in as much information as possible into every pause. This also happens when you have prepared "set pieces" that you like to trot out whenever the opportunity presents itself.

➤ Don't slow-talk. It doesn't make you appear thoughtful, just boring. You know you're doing it when people start finishing your sentences for you or nodding to indicate that they understand even before you have reached your point.

➤ Don't watch other people moving around the room while somebody is talking to you.

➤ Don't fight. Avoid phrases such as, "That's way off base," or "You're wrong about that." It's okay to disagree, but try, "Another way of looking at it is …" or, "I disagree because …."

➤ Don't pepper your conversation with obscure or arcane words, foreign phrases, or technical jargon. Don't introduce slang expressions that are obscure or offensive.

➤ Never begin a conversation with, "I'll bet you don't remember me" or, "I'll bet you don't remember my name." The other person might respond, "I don't remember you, and now I know the reason why."

You Do Say

So, you find yourself in the position of having to introduce a topic of conversation because the other person is shy, the present topic has been exhausted, or one of those awful, self-conscious silences has fallen over the group you are conversing with. Try one of these topics that never fail:

➤ A funny movie you just saw

➤ A major local company's bankruptcy, merger, expansion, or relocation

➤ The latest miserable or heroic showing of the hometown sports team

➤ A terrific restaurant you have discovered

➤ The latest technological miracle coming out of Silicon Valley

➤ A mutual friend's promotion, marriage, pregnancy, or transfer

➤ Developments in a provocative court case or criminal investigation

➤ What's opening on Broadway or in your own theater district

➤ What hot singer is coming to town and whether it will be possible to get tickets

When opening a line of conversation, stay away from the negative and choose something that will bring forth comments and opinions and lead to other areas of conversation.

Your Job—or Lack of It

When you meet someone for the first time, it is almost certain that the question will come: "What do you do?"

Responding with a joke or a flip answer is insulting. The question may be unwelcome, but it must be answered with sincerity. If you are unemployed, say that you are looking for a new position, and talk about your field or the kind of job you are looking for.

If you are retired, say: "I just retired after 30 years in the chemical industry, and I've seen that field transformed completely several times over."

Whatever you do, speak about it with pride; never be apologetic about it. Self-deprecation has a dampening effect on conversation. How can the other person speak with enthusiasm and pride about his work if you have just denigrated your own job?

People ask this question not only because they are curious, but also because they want to advance the conversation. Cooperate. Don't just say: "I'm a lawyer." Say: "I'm a criminal defense lawyer." Or, say: "I'm a tax lawyer with Microsoft."

Speak in general terms about what is happening in your field. If the other person doesn't continue with questions about your work, it's your turn to ask the "What do you do?" question.

Don't Be a Bore

I once was at a party during which a man said, "I know this is boring, but I really want to finish saying this."

He had enough brains to know that he was boring people, but not enough sense to stop doing it. Unfortunately, most people don't know when they are being boring, even though there are lots of clues. Here are some boredom signals to look out for.

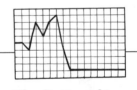

The Bottom Line

Keep current. Newstalk is a rich field for conversational exploration.

➤ The listeners' eyes glaze, they look away or at their watches or shoes.

➤ Listeners say things like, "What's the point of this story?" or, "Yes, we know."

➤ It occurs to you that you have been the only one speaking in the last few minutes.

Business Blunders

Avoid telling jokes that take longer than 30 seconds. Brevity, somebody said, is the soul of wit.

➤ You hear yourself using technical or obscure terms.

➤ You notice that you are the only one laughing (or even smiling) at what you thought were the amusing or witty parts of your story.

➤ You hear yourself repeating or rambling.

➤ You are using worn-out, hackneyed folk wisdom, such as these phrases: "Better late than never;" "Can't beat 'em, join 'em;" "Let the chips fall where they may;" or "Here today, gone tomorrow."

Talking About Your Children—Ho-Hum

If you want to create a conversational coma, talk to strangers or casual acquaintances about your children—or, even worse, your grandchildren.

Yes, they are fascinating and adorable creatures. But the other person does not care and has zero interest in their virtues and accomplishments. If someone asks if you have children, give the sex and ages, and move on: "I have two sons, 8 and 11." If the other people press for more information, they are just being polite or are looking for an opening so that they can tell you how fascinating and adorable their own children (or worse, grandchildren) are.

You may talk endlessly with family and close friends about the children, but not with people you have just met or that you know only slightly. And, if you happen to have that really cute picture of Timmy and the puppies in your pocket, leave it there.

Memo to Myself

A good time to break away from a conversation is when someone else joins you. In fact, you can snare a passing acquaintance and introduce him or her before excusing yourself.

Breaking Away

When it's time get out of a conversation, it won't do for you to just bolt or say, "I gotta go," and walk away.

One point that I stress while teaching is that people need acknowledgement and closure in their dealings with others. You recognize the need for acknowledgement when you are standing in front of someone's desk or a teller's window and the person on the other side refuses to look at you. You are less annoyed waiting in line when a clerk at least says, "I'll be right with you." You also probably get annoyed when someone blurts out, "Please hold," and cuts us off before we have a chance to identify ourselves.

The same feelings of annoyance occur when someone departs abruptly without a word, or just drifts away without any acknowledgement that a conversation has occurred.

At parties, I like to have a half-empty or nearly empty glass so that I can say, "I think I'll go to the bar for a refill. It was nice speaking with you."

Try these other tactics as well:

"I've got to say hello to our host (or my mother, or good old George)."

"That food looks delicious. I think I'll try some."

If others have joined your conversation and it is not possible to say goodbye without interrupting things, it is still important to make some kind of parting gesture: eye contact, a smile, a wave.

The Least You Need to Know

➤ The most important thing to remember about becoming a good conversationalist is to focus on the other person and concentrate on keeping the conversation going. Then your fears about your ability to engage in casual conversation will disappear.

➤ You don't need to be brilliantly witty, exhaustively well-read, or incredibly sophisticated to be a good conversationalist. You need only to be interested, considerate, and a good listener.

➤ Being a good conversationalist is a learned behavior. Anyone can learn to use skills and techniques for conversation.

➤ Listen. Pick up on nuggets of information dropped by others, and use them to get the conversation going and to keep it going.

➤ Don't be afraid of conversational clichés. The weather can warm up a conversation, particularly at the beginning, when you know little about the person's background or interests.

Speaking in Public

Like it or not, these are some immutable facts of business life: Sooner or later, every-body has to become a public speaker, whether it's during a dinner party with a dozen colleagues, at a meeting of the board of directors, or before a few hundred people in an auditorium. Saying that you suffer from stage fright is no excuse—everybody does, to one degree or another.

That's the bad news. Here's the good news: Stage fright can be conquered, and anyone can do it. As with becoming a good conversationalist (see Chapter 10, "Making Conversation"), becoming a good public speaker is a learned behavior. We learned. You can. Just about anyone can.

Panic City

The elevated blood pressure, the trembling fingers, and the quickened heartbeat are the normal reactions of humans in certain situations. It happened to old Uncle Orf, your cave-dwelling ancestor when he heard the husky huff of some jungle beast. It happens to some people when they are called upon to speak in public.

Memo to Myself

Two common mistakes made by inexperienced speakers are speaking too loudly and speaking too quickly.

Experts call it the flight-or-fight reaction. When hit with this adrenaline surge, Uncle Orf grabbed his club or scampered up a tree. The public speaker employs other tactics. He reminds himself that the flight-or-fight reaction is a right-brain function that is both instinctive and emotional. Therefore, he counters with activity involving the more logical left brain. He thinks about how his talk is organized and about the principle points he wants to make. Or he does a mental math problem, or counts forward or backward, or both.

His left brain tells the remnant of old Uncle Orf that dwells in each of us that the audience is not a 500-pound tiger looking for lunch. The speaker then reminds himself that the audience wants to relax and have a pleasant experience, almost as much as he does. The audience wants to like him, wants to be on his side, and wants him to do well.

The Four Big Questions

I do a lot of speaking before groups. My audiences vary from a handful of children to a board of directors, to hundreds in an auditorium or thousands in a television audience. And, before each and every event, I take some time to ask myself the same four questions:

1. "Who does the audience think I am?" What relationship do you have, if any, with the audience? How would you like them to perceive you?

2. "What do I want to accomplish?" Focus on your objective. Are you going to ask for a raise, praise another person or project or institution, explain a situation, or present a problem and possible solution? Is your mission to welcome, instruct, persuade, or motivate?

Business Blunders

Speakers should try to avoid situations in which audiovisual aids are absolutely imperative. You must be prepared if the aids don't appear or break down.

3. "To whom am I speaking?" Ask yourself why the members of the audience are there. What are their expectations? What are their shared characteristics? What is their point of view concerning your topic?

4. "Where am I?" Find out ahead of time all you can about the physical space you will be speaking in. This will influence how you use your voice and gestures. Will there be a microphone? Will you be standing or sitting? (Stand whenever you have a choice.) Check out the audiovisual equipment, and think about what you will do when it breaks down (assume that it will).

How to Begin

You are ready to begin when you have asked yourself the four big questions, when you are sure that
you are well-groomed and dressed appropriately
(see Chapter 4, "The Job Interview," and Chapter 6,
"Business Attire and Accessories"), when you are
confident about your grasp of the material, and
when you are convinced that the audience wants
to like you and wants to hear what you have to say.

Before speaking, I often ask myself, "What do I
want them to know?" rather than, "What do I
want to say?" This helps to take the focus off me
and puts it on the audience.

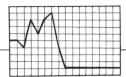

Memo to Myself

The average attention span of an
audience is 8 seconds. Variation in
visual and vocal delivery is imperative
in holding an audience's attention.

Your First Words

Make sure that you have your first few words and
your first few ideas firmly in mind before you open
your mouth. You may want to begin by introducing yourself, even if somebody has already introduced you. (If somebody has, you may want to
begin by thanking that person.) If possible, mention something that connects you to the audience
as part of your self-introduction: "Like many of
you, I have been working in biotechnology for
some time."

The Bottom Line

To help you relax before the
speech, inhale deeply through your
nose and exhale through your
mouth. It works. And smile—this
helps to relax not only you, but also
the audience.

Your Opening Options

Here are some examples of ways to open your presentation.

➤ Some speakers open by complimenting the audience or the institution they are
  associated with.

➤ Some like to begin with a startling or provocative statement.

➤ Some lead with a quote from a prominent or historical person.

➤ Some open with a joke or an anecdote.

Be careful here. The two absolutely unbreakable rules for using jokes or anecdotes is
that they must not be vulgar or offensive and that they must have a direct connection with the audience or the subject of your talk. (Books with good and useful opening jokes and anecdotes can be found in libraries and the larger bookstores.)

Memo to Myself

Try delivering your speech in advance to a friend, and remember the experience while making the speech in public. I usually record my entire speech and listen to it while I'm driving.

Your Delivery

Before you begin to speak, remind yourself of the fact that *you* are more important than the material. The audience wants to hear what *you* have to say and how *you* present the material. Otherwise, they could have stayed home and read a report. Remind yourself that you believe in what you are going to say and that you will present your idea with sincerity and feeling.

Talk Tactics

Some basic points will help you with your delivery:

> ➤ When possible, stand.

➤ Adjust your language to the audience. You don't use the same language speaking to scientists as to artists.

➤ Some people just can't tell a joke. If your humorous sallies are often met with quizzical looks and strained smiles, leave jokes out of your speeches.

➤ Don't talk down. Just because the audience is unfamiliar with the topic doesn't mean that you need to employ a slow or repetitious delivery. (With children, you will need to employ lots of gestures, jokes, and vivid images because their attention span is shorter than that of most—but not all—adults.)

➤ Keep your head up and your voice clear.

➤ Don't let your voice volume get out of control. Inexperienced speakers tend to get louder the longer they speak. Think in terms of projecting rather than loudness.

➤ Take your time. Inexperienced speakers sometime speak too quickly, as if points must be made before someone interrupts, or as if every moment must be filled with as much information as possible.

➤ A good rule of thumb is that you should not try to make more than two major points during any 20-minute talk. Studies indicate that, 72 hours after your presentation, the average audience member will remember 20 percent of what you said. What is the 20 percent you most want them to remember?

It's a good idea to mentally run though the above list repeatedly while preparing to make your speech.

What to Do When You Are Through

The closing is every bit as important to the success of a speech as the beginning. Good openings and closings will make up for lapses or tedious material in the middle of a speech.

Significantly exceeding your allotted time will not be forgiven, however. When your time is up, stop, whether or not you have covered all the material you had planned to cover. The audience does not know that you intended to say more. You may offer to stay after the talk for those who wish to speak with you.

Saving the Best for Last

The ending should be as strong and satisfying as possible.

If your talk has been light, save your best joke for last, or put a humorous spin on the material covered.

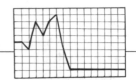

The Bottom Line

Every conversational topic has a natural life span—it blooms, flourishes, and dies. When it begins to wither, dump it. The easiest method is switching to a related topic.

If your talk has been the "call to action" or "lest we forget" kind, don't hesitate to bring forth some dramatic or emotional language at the end. If such language does not spring immediately to mind, quote a portion of some great speech or a few lines of stirring (and preferably familiar) poetry.
Whether you are writing a speech or not, it's a good idea to commit some of these stirring quotations to memory so that you have them at your disposal at all times. Good sources are *Bartlett's Familiar Quotations* and *The Oxford Book of Quotations*.

The End

When the speech is finished, just say thank you and sit down. Do not wave or otherwise acknowledge applause or any other expression of approval (or disapproval) from the audience.

Q&A

If there is to be a question-and-answer period, say so and raise your hand to indicate the protocol to be followed by questioners. When posed a question, do not say, "Good question." This implies that you are judging or comparing the quality of questions. Do not address the questioner by name, unless you are prepared to address everyone in the room by name.

When you think enough time has been devoted to Q&A, one tactic is to say, "I'll take one more question."

If you mingle after the talk and someone compliments you on your performance, just say, "Thank you," or "Glad you liked it." Don't attempt to expand on your remarks, and never apologize for anything you said during the speech.

From the File Drawer

"The human brain starts the moment you are born ... and never stops until you stand up to speak in public."

—George Jessel

"We'd rather be in the box than give the eulogy."

—Jerry Seinfeld

Introducing a Speaker

If your job is to introduce the speaker, keep it simple. Your mission is to get the speaker to the podium with the least possible fuss or delay. Leave yourself out of it— don't go into a story about what good pals you are.

Get a biography, and pare it to the highlights, emphasizing the things that are of particular interest to this particular group.

Keep the tone warm and welcoming.

If it's a family affair, a retirement party, or a similar event, you can be somewhat more sentimental. Still, brevity is the best policy, and the introduction should not last longer than a few minutes.

The Good Audience

You will be on one of the folding chairs more often than you will be at the podium. It is important to know how to be a good audience member, which means having a good grasp on audience etiquette.

First of all, if you are behaving beautifully and some lout behind you is not, don't make a big deal out of it. Say something like, "It's difficult to hear the speaker." This is a non-confrontational way of getting your point across.

Now let's look at some other pointers.

Audience Etiquette

Following are some pointers for audience members:

1. Be on time. Speakers may not show it, but they are bothered by late arrivals. It throws them off their pace, interferes with their concentration, and disrupts whatever mood they were trying to build.

2. Be quiet, turn off your cellular phone, and switch your beeper to vibrate mode.

3. Don't slouch, slump, stretch, and grunt.

4. Ask questions, and thank the speaker if the circumstances permit.

You may be in a crowded and/or confined space, so go easy on the perfume, take off your hat, and try not to arrive at your seat encumbered with garments and packages.

You don't have to be an actor or a professional emcee to become a good public speaker. But you do have to be prepared and as relaxed as possible. Some anxiety about getting up in front of people to speak is to be expected. Accept it and handle it, and get on with presenting the information.

The Least You Need to Know

➤ Everybody gets stage fright, and everybody can get over it.

➤ You are more important than the material.

➤ Be prepared.

➤ Remember that the audience wants to like you.

➤ Have a strong beginning and a stronger ending.

➤ Limit your message to the time allotted.

Communicating by Telephone

It's hard to believe, but you may be misusing that comfortably familiar instrument of communication: the telephone. Because it's so familiar, you can lose sight of the fact that your old friend can be a potentially deadly enemy.

A lot of otherwise smart people repeatedly make basic and serious mistakes when using the telephone, even though it is estimated that upwards of 75 percent of business gets done by telephone. That means that an awful lot of business can get "undone" by telephone.

In the largest study of its kind, the International Customer Research Institute asked 20,000 nonrepeat customers why they became nonrepeat customers. Here are the answers:

➤ 1 percent died

➤ 3 percent moved

➤ 5 percent cited friendships

➤ 9 percent cited competition

➤ 14 percent cited product dissatisfaction

➤ 68 percent said the reason was an attitude of indifference by employees

And you can believe that, in many, many instances, this attitude was communicated over the telephone.

Who's There?

The mistakes can begin as soon as the other person answers your ring. In the business world, the caller must begin by completely identifying himself, giving first name, last name, and company. (This holds true even for inter-office calls, particularly in large companies.) Unless the other person is a friend or relative, say "hello" instead of "hi."

Memo to Myself

When you dial a wrong number, apologize and say, "Is this 123-1234?" to find out whether you made a dialing mistake or have an incorrect number.

"Hello, this is Gail Baker from Colgate Steel. May I speak with Mr. Bainbridge?"

Repeat that when Bainbridge gets on the line, and add something like this: "I'm glad I reached you," or, "We met at Thompson's seminar." The tired, "How are you today?" always sounds insincere and is often ignored.

Then say, "I'm calling about the Miller printing project."

This way, you sound confident, in control, and ready to do business. And being ready to do business means knowing in advance what you want your call to accomplish. It's a good idea to jot down notes before you dial because the call can be interrupted, or the other person may change the subject, and you will forget some of what you had intended to say. This means a second call that begins, "I forgot to ask you …."

Whenever possible, place your own calls. Some people—and I am among them—find it annoying to pick up the telephone and be told to "hold for Mr. Smith." A journalist friend of mine routinely hangs up as soon as he hears that phrase. He feels that the underlying message here is that Mr. Smith thinks his time is more valuable than yours. He can't take time to dial your number, yet he expects you to wait until he gets on the line. Getting in touch this way can mean that your conversation will begin in an atmosphere of hostility.

Speak Up

About 70 percent of the impression you make during a telephone conversation depends on vocal quality, so speak clearly and think about the tone of your voice.

(It's true—a smile can be "heard" over the tele-phone.) Maintain a constant distance from the mouthpiece. Don't engage in nonverbal communi-cations with someone in the room—smiling, gri-macing, and so on. Don't chew gum or food. If you sneeze or cough, apologize.

Business Blunders

Don't think that putting your hand over the mouthpiece means the person on the telephone can't hear what you are saying.

Hold It!

The person you are speaking with always has precedence over a ringing telephone. If possible, it is much better to have someone or some machine pick up the second line. If this is not possible, don't just reach for the hold button—ask. It's not good enough to just say, "Please hold." Ask if that person minds being put on hold, wait for the response, and thank them for agreeing to wait. Many people find the very word *hold* annoying. Think about possible alternatives:

> "Would you mind waiting for one moment?"

> "One moment, please."

> "Please stand by."

> "I'll check that out for you."

Be brief. Never keep someone on hold for more than one minute. Think of "hold" as holding a hot potato. Answer the second call, but say that you are busy and will call back. If you absolutely can't do that, say, "I'll have to finish up the call on my other line."

Apologize to the first caller, promise to call back promptly, and do so. A good rule of thumb is that people should not be dangling on hold for more than a minute.

Warning—if the call comes a few minutes before a meeting begins or just as you are preparing to leave the office for an appointment, explain and ask if you can return the call at a more convenient time. If you are expecting a call you can't afford to miss, explain that, too:

> "I may have to break this off and call back because I'm expecting a call from a client I've been trying to reach all week."

Then hang up. If you are the one on hold, it is perfectly acceptable to hang up after a minute or so. In fact, it may not be good strategy to let the other person think you have nothing better to do than sit there with a silent telephone to your ear.

It's Not My Phone

Answering another person's telephone can be a tricky business. A lot depends on the culture of your workplace. In some offices, it is routine for colleagues to pick up calls when you are not at your desk. In some places, only the receptionist does this, or voice mail picks up the call.

Memo to Myself

When you get a call from someone you really don't want to speak with or whom you haven't time to speak with, make sure that you sound very glad to hear from him, and quickly say, "I really can't talk right now. I'll get back to you."

In office situations in which employees are expected to answer the telephone of an absent coworker, the answering employee may be resentful about having to interrupt work to take a message for someone else. This resentment often is conveyed to the caller.

If you answer another's telephone, say something like, "CalTech Industries, Peter Thompson's phone." Or, simply say, "Peter Thompson's office." Then explain that Thompson is not there, and offer to take a message.

It's a good idea to train yourself to answer the telephone politely and correctly, no matter what the circumstances. You never know who is calling. Wise supervisors call their own offices to check on the telephone manners of their workers.

It's a completely different story if you happen to be in someone else's home and your host leaves temporarily just before the telephone rings. Do you answer it? That depends.

If the host has asked you to pick up any calls, fine. If not, and if there is no answering machine, it's a judgment call. If you don't know the host very well, you may feel safer just ignoring the ring. If you decide to answer, pick up the phone and say, "McGinley residence," before the caller has time to say something unguarded, such as, "Hello, love muffin."

Voice Mail: A Useful Annoyance

Sure it's annoying. But voice mail is a useful tool that is a permanent and ubiquitous part of the business universe. You can make it less annoying in several ways.

Your answering machine message should be brief and should provide some choices—the fewer, the better. After you identify yourself, give the choices:

1. Leave a message.
2. Call another extension.
3. Hold for the receptionist.

Longer messages may be required by circumstances:

> "Hello, this is Nancy Goodman. I will be traveling today, Friday, and will not be able to return calls until after 7 P.M. Eastern time. Please leave your name, telephone number, and a brief message."

If you are going to be out of town, you may want to leave a message saying that you will be at the Orlando Imperial Hotel all week, and then give the telephone number and fax number. If you are traveling with a laptop, add that you can be reached by e-mail.

From the File Drawer

Always check your voice mail before heading out to an appointment. The person you are expecting to meet may have called to cancel. If so, return the call to let him or her know that you received the message. I learned to do this every time after making an unnecessary trip.

Recording Your Message

Before you record your message, follow these tips:

➤ Adjust your machine so that it will pick up after four rings, which seems to have become the unofficial standard in most places.

➤ Write out what you are going to say on the tape, and practice once or twice.

➤ Briefer is better. Start by giving your name or your telephone number so that people will know whether they have reached the right person. End with, "Please leave a message." You don't need to flog the obvious by saying, "I am either out of the office or unable to come to answer the telephone right now."

➤ Unless you are a musician or a professional comic, stay away from sound effects, gimmicks, and jokes.

Leaving a Message

If you are the caller, follow these tips:

➤ Be prepared to speak promptly, whether the telephone is answered by a person or a machine.

➤ Once you hear the beep, leave a message even if you dialed a wrong number. You don't have to identify yourself: "Sorry. I dialed the wrong number."

➤ Give your full name and affiliation and your telephone number up front so that the receiver doesn't have to replay the whole message to get the number.

➤ Briefly say why you are calling. This is especially important if the call concerns a time-constrained matter: "I need to speak with you prior to tomorrow's auction."

➤ Leave your complete telephone (and/or beeper) number slowly, pausing between the area code and the local number. Leave your number even if the other person already has the number.

➤ Say when you can be reached.

➤ Just hang up. You don't say goodbye to a person you haven't talked with. Don't say you are sorry you missed the person, or that it's the second time you've called.

➤ Don't leave multiple messages. It is unnecessary and annoying to leave a message at 10 A.M. and call back with the same message at noon.

Don't use voice mail as a way of avoiding speaking with someone. If you make your callbacks during lunch hour or after office hours, the other person would have to be terminally dense not to figure out what you are doing. In fact, a lot of voice mail systems let you know the time that the call was made.

On the other hand, in some situations the call must be made during off-hours. In that case, you can say, "I know you're not in the office right now, but I'm headed out to the construction site and thought you should know that ...."

Business Blunders

Never, ever say "I'll let you go now." The implication is that you are in charge of the conversation and are being generous in allowing the other person to hang up. It's rude and simple-minded.

Gatekeepers

Part of a good secretary's job may be to screen calls and to make sure that Mr. Biggs is not interrupted unnecessarily. Learning some tactics will help to make even the most diligent gatekeeper an ally.

First, learn the secretary's name. On your first call, you can get the name from a receptionist or simply by asking the secretary. Then use the name every time you call, but don't use the first name unless he or she suggests that you do. Very often, being overly familiar or casual with the secretary can have an effect opposite from the one intended. Be cordial and friendly, but don't push it. The secretary can be a good source of information, such as when Mr. Biggs usually is available and when he is never available. When you get a "best time" response from a secretary, make it clear that you will be calling back at that time:

"Fine, I'll call back at 4:00 with the figures on the Barclay transfer. I know he's been expecting them."

If Mr. Biggs is not available at 4:00, don't complain—it's not the secretary's fault.

Playing Phone Tag

The best way to avoid getting on this irritating merry-go-round is to leave specific messages. Even specific messages can be brief messages, though. If you are calling to find out what time the meeting begins, say so and add, "If I'm not at my desk, please leave the time on my tape."

Also, if you are calling simply to convey information, be prepared to leave it on the answering machine tape with, "If you have any questions, call me back. Otherwise, I'll see you there."

Another way to avoid phone tag, and thereby make the world a better place, is to say, "I'll be at this number until 5:00. After 6:00, I'll be at 123-1234."

It's good manners to return calls as promptly as possible. If there is a delay in returning the call, explain the reason for the delay when you finally do return the call.

Call Waiting

If you really need this service, accept the fact that you will have to annoy people who are already on the phone when the call-waiting signal kicks in. If possible, wait until you are speaking and interrupt yourself, not the other person, to say, "Can you hold on a second?" Then listen to the response before you click over to the other call. The first caller then has the option to say, "No. Call me back."

After you switch over, get the second caller's number, promise to call, and return as promptly as possible to the first caller. Remember that the person already on the line has priority, except in the case of an emergency:

> "Paul, I'm speaking with someone on the other line. Give me your number, I'll get back to you right away."

Memo to Myself

Don't be rude to telephone solicitors—they're just trying to earn a living. But don't waste time on them, either. As soon as it becomes apparent that it's a sales pitch, interrupt with, "I'm sorry. I don't respond to phone solicitations," or simply, "I'm not interested, but thanks for your call." Then hang up.

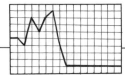

The Bottom Line

When calling someone at home, avoid calling around mealtime or after 10 P.M., unless the call can't wait. If it's a "just chat" call, start by asking if the other person is busy. The response will give you a clue as to how long that person can comfortably chat.

Chatty Cathy

If you are friendly with the person you are calling about a business matter, it's fine to open the conversation with, "How was the ski trip? Glad you're still in one piece," or, "Wasn't that a great game on Thursday?" But then get right down to the reason for the call. Rambling or just chatting during business hours gives the impression that you have little to do—or little interest in doing it—and that you think the other person has time to waste. If you're lonesome, take up ballroom dancing.

On the other hand, if you have an overly chatty caller on the line, don't hesitate to cut off the call:

"We'll have to make this short because …."

"I've got to hang up now because my lunch date has arrived (or the meeting is about to start, or that's the other call I've been waiting for)."

You should always sound delighted to hear Chatty Cathy's voice before apologizing for having to dash off.

Speaking on Speaker Phones

This is a "convenience" that should be avoided whenever possible. People have a tendency to yell into speaker phones, and no matter what they do, they always sound as if they are speaking at the other end of a dark tunnel.

If you *must* use a speaker phone, follow these pointers:

➤ Never begin a conversation on the speaker. Ask if you can switch over to the speaker, and explain why: "George Miller will be working with us on this project, and I would like him to hear this."

➤ Identify every person in the room.

➤ Only one person should speak at a time, and that person should move closer to the phone. Speakers should identify themselves each time because the instrument distorts voices.

➤ Avoid sidebar conversations.

➤ If you have to leave during the call, say so.

Once again, the speaker phone should be used only when needed.

Cellular Phone Rules

Remember telephone "booths"? They were created with the idea that only the person you were calling should hear what you were saying. That's still a useful concept to keep in mind when you are using your cellular phone. Let's look at some basics:

➤ Use your cellular phone in public only when absolutely necessary.

➤ If you are not expecting an urgent call, turn off the phone during business meetings, at social gatherings, in restaurants, and at the theater. In these situations, rely on your beeper, and have the beeper set to vibrate mode.

➤ If you absolutely must keep your phone on during a meeting, explain in advance.

➤ If you must make a call at a social gathering or at a restaurant, excuse yourself and find a reasonably private nook in which to make the call.

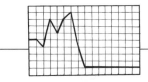

The Bottom Line

If it's not an emergency, don't ask to borrow another person's cellular phone when you can get to a pay phone.

➤ If you must speak while others are near, speak softly. Your conversation may be fascinating to you, but it's intrusive for others.

➤ Don't ask to borrow a phone unless it is a matter of urgency. Then, use it sparingly. Remember that the lender pays for the call, and the person receiving the call is also charged for air time.

If you use your cellular phone while driving, you deserve whatever happens. Others, however, do not. Even if you are lucky enough to do this repeatedly without crashing, you will develop a reputation for reckless and dangerous behavior.

Pull over, and take the few minutes you need to make your call.

The Teleconference

Teleconferencing—instant, personal, global, and intimidating—is putting the formality back into meetings and creating a whole new field of business etiquette. In other words, you can put on an intercompany, intercity, international display of bad manners unless you are clued-in on the new rules. It's not only about how you look, but where you look. It also involves gestures, expressions, and voice and camera know-how.

In the Wings

If teleconferencing hasn't reached you yet, it probably will eventually, and you have to be ready. The cost of travel and the increasing sophistication of the equipment have combined to make teleconferencing the wave of the future. The amount of money spent on teleconferencing equipment doubled to $10.8 billion from the mid- to late-1990s.

You may have to prepare even more carefully for a teleconference than for your usual meetings. You don't want to walk out of the room and leave colleagues, clients, or anyone else at the other end staring at a blank screen until you return.

If there is the remotest chance that you might need something, make sure it is with you. If there is a *good* chance that you will need something, keep it within reach.

Take One

The camera may magnify or distort clothing and makeup. Bright tones and patterns will come across more intensely on the screen, and the camera may distort bright colors. Reds may become glaring oranges, for example. Your best bet is to wear conservative grays and blues. A pale blue shirt also is generally better than a white shirt. Remember that bright colors and large white areas cause glare; when the camera compensates for the glare, it will make the faces darker.

Go very easy on the makeup. That subtle blush in the mirror might look as if was applied at Clown College. If possible, men should minimize five-o'clock shadow as well. Jewelry should be low–key—no dangling earrings or big, bright pins or brooches. Don't flash your Rolex.

Dress should be more conservative than casual, particularly if meeting with people in or from Europe and Asia. Suits are more suitable than sweaters and shirtsleeves.

The rapidity with which teleconferencing is spreading suggests that a rehearsal or two before a camera would be a good investment in time and resources. Get together with colleagues or friends, and stage a meeting. Viewing the tape will provide you with some interesting and even surprising insights.

Memo to Myself

Make a tape of yourself in a business meeting situation, and watch it a few times. This will help you eliminate some things that might be annoying to others and will give you more confidence at your next teleconference meeting.

The Meeting

The usual rules for meeting manners (see Chapter 5, "A Fact of Office Life: Meetings") apply here, yet with some important additions. You will find that teleconferencing requires even more formal behavior and consideration of others than the more common human-to-human meetings, the ones without the cameras. Posture, which is always important, counts for even more in these circumstances.

On Camera

Resist the temptation to look at the monitor. Look at and into the lens of the camera when you are speaking.

This is the electronic equivalent of looking the other person in the eye. You can look at the monitor when the other person is speaking, but remember that the other person sees you looking away from him when you shift your gaze to the monitor.

Also remember that peripheral vision doesn't work here. Stay within range of the camera.

Speaking

You may encounter a slight sound delay, particularly with overseas transmissions. If so, expect pauses, and wait for them.

Speak slowly and clearly in your normal tone of voice. If the people at the other end have trouble hearing you, they will let you know, and you can raise the level of your voice a bit.

Only one person should speak at a time. If there is a team on hand at your end, elect a captain and have him do most of the talking. Remember that faces will appear on the screen one by one, and you can't hand out business cards. Thus, under some conditions, name cards with dark, easy-to-read writing are appropriate.

The team captain must try to keep people speaking one at a time. So, he would avoid saying "Any questions?" and instead address each member: "Ted? Any questions?" And so forth.

Don't Goof Off

You may be on camera at any time. Perhaps you can see only one person at a time on your monitor, but that doesn't mean that the same situation applies at the other end—that end may have the capacity to see a wider picture. So don't make faces at one another, give thumbs up or thumbs down gestures, yawn, scratch, or otherwise behave as if you are attending a poker game and not a business meeting.

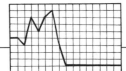

The Bottom Line

Remember that your behavior during a teleconferencing meeting may become part of a permanent record that can be saved and viewed over and over.

Don't drum your fingers, tap your foot, bend paper clips, click your pen, tilt your chair, or wiggle. The camera and microphones pick it all up—and sometimes they give more power to facial expressions. The meeting may be long and tedious, and you may be bored out of your socks—but don't let that show on your face.

Nobody in the meeting room should be holding sidebar conversations within range of the microphone. Those can be picked up and amplified.

Also remember that interrupting, speaking too loudly, and using broad gestures are exaggerated on camera. Be cool.

The Least You Need to Know

➤ Don't assume that you have good telephone manners just because you use the telephone a lot.

➤ How you present yourself over the phone is as important as how you present yourself in person—about 70 percent of business is done over the phone.

➤ Keep voice mail messages as brief as possible, and forget about gimmicks and jokes.

➤ So-called conveniences such as call waiting and speaker phones should be used sparingly.

➤ Teleconferencing involves a whole different set of meeting etiquette rules, involving not only how you look but also where you look.

➤ You can't get away with little asides, nods, scratching, and other small diversions that may be overlooked at no-camera meetings.

Chapter 13

Nethics and E-Mail

In This Chapter

➤ Getting in line with online etiquette

➤ Different uses for different e-media

➤ The use and abuse of e-mail

➤ Responding, forwarding, and editing

➤ Some caveats about newsgroups and mailing lists

The electronic "Wild West" is a thing of the past. In frontier days, cyberbandits roamed the range, causing trouble, spreading viruses, committing cybercrimes, and then hiding out in the badlands.

There are still a few of these varmints out there. But, as time goes on, it becomes more evident that those who commit cybercrimes will be traced. The probability of getting caught has a chilling effect on electronic vandals.

Netiquette

But that doesn't mean that rudeness, inconsiderate blundering, and downright bad manners have been eliminated—far from it. This has resulted in the creation of a new word, *netiquette*, and a new set of rules for electronic manners. In the business world, ignorance of or flouting of the rules of netiquette will damage your reputation as much as bad table manners or rude behavior during meetings.

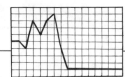

The Bottom Line

Don't think that electronic messaging is so ethereal that you can be anonymous. E-mail messages do not "go away" when you hit the Delete button. Computer users who break the law can be traced.

Some of the rules are obvious. Just because you may never meet or even see those you deal with on the Internet, that is no license to be rude. If you ask for information, say "please." If someone does a favor or responds to a question, say "thank you."

Some users, mostly kids, are deliberately rude. That's because they are young and dumb and want attention. Don't play into their hands by responding with an angry tirade—it's a waste of time.

Use the Shift Key

Don't write entirely in upper- or lowercase when writing an e-mail, a posted message, or a chat room contribution. Using all capital letters is considered to be the equivalent of shouting. All lowercase is not exactly whispering, but it's annoying. You will become a better and stronger writer if you resist the temptation to use capitals to emphasize a word. Look for ways to make the sentence or the context give stress to the word or phrase.

Lurk Before You Leap

Lurking means observing what is happening with any online discussion before jumping in with your contribution. You may happen upon a mailing list for your favorite bluegrass band and feel eager to write something about its last album. If you lurk awhile, you may find that the album has been talked to death over the span of three weeks, and everything you wanted to say has been said at least 30 times.

Lurking also gives you time to pick up the general tone and direction of a discussion. Many newsgroups and mailing lists will provide access to past discussions so that you won't be repeating the oft-said. Also, look for FAQs, or Frequently Asked Questions, before making yourself known to the group. Somebody went to a great deal of trouble to compile the FAQ list or lists; it's not polite or sensible to ignore the resource. Checking it out will save everybody a lot of time and annoyance.

Lurking will also allow you to avoid things such as asking a group interested in wood carving about hiking in the woodlands of Maine.

Flaming

Flaming is sending insulting and vulgar messages, usually because some user has made a mistake, has expressed a controversial opinion, or has revealed ignorance of a subject that another user holds dear. Flaming is a little like calling someone a name or starting an argument in a bar, except that you don't risk getting punched out for it.

You can save yourself a lot of trouble and emotional involvement by simply deciding that you will leave flaming to more inflammatory personalities. It is more sensible and good training in real-world interpersonal relations to respond gently to errors, flawed arguments, and wrong-headed opinions. Just correct the error. You can say, "The trouble with your argument is …" or, "That may be your opinion, yet I believe …." People are more apt to read and remember such responses.

Memo to Myself

If you absolutely must flame, start with "FLAME ON" and end with "FLAME OFF" so that people can skip your outburst if they wish.

Of course, you may elect to spare people your angry retort by sending it directly to the e-mail box of the person who has offended your sensibilities. Taking the dispute to e-mail makes a lot more sense than engaging in a flame war that others in your newsgroup may find tedious.

Spamming

Spamming is sending junk mail or inappropriate messages, everything from advertisements to pyramid schemes. The best way to deal with it is to ignore it. Delete it and never forward it. If your company has set up a means of tracking e-mail spammers and cutting them off, notify your systems manager or other appropriate person when you receive spam. Certain software will filter out stuff from known spammers.

Never pass along a chain letter, even if the letter says that failure to forward it will cause your leg to fall off. You're too old to fall for any of that superstitious kid stuff.

Security

Your computer is not a safe deposit box. Unless you are using encryption software, your secrets may not remain secret.

Secret Passwords

The use of passwords is your one best protection against snooping. Here are some things to remember:

➤ Never tell anyone your password.

➤ Don't look over the shoulder of someone logging on. That person may think you are out to steal a password.

➤ Don't use an obvious password, such as your name spelled backward, your birthday, or the name of your dog.

➤ The most secure password contains numbers, punctuation, and upper- and lowercase letters.

If you think you might forget your password, write it down and put it in safe place. (Not your address book, please.)

Copyright Protection

It is a violation of the law to use, copy, or forward copyrighted material, whether you are using a computer or a printing press. Don't assume that material is in the public domain because it does not have the little circled C on it.

When to Use E-Mail

It's wonderful to have so many ways of communicating—telephone, cellular phone, beeper, e-mail. However, all those choices bring up the question of which method of communicating is preferable under which circumstances. A basic rule is, a handwritten letter or note is still king when it comes to gracious personal communication.

In certain situations, no amount of electronic wizardry can replace a letter. The thank-you note is a good example. People have defended substituting a telephone call or an e-mail for a handwritten note on the grounds that, "I knew I'd never get around to writing, so this was better than nothing." This is another way of saying that e-mail is a license to be lazy. How many people are so desperately busy that they can't find five minutes to write a note?

It's a mortal sin to even think of e-mailing a letter of condolence.

It's fine to use the telephone or e-mail to invite people to an informal party, particularly when you're giving short notice. For more formal occasions, send invitations through the mail.

Making Contact

Where there are options, there are preferences. Find out how people wish to be contacted in different circumstances. If it's e-mail, should it be to the office or to the home PC? Is the cellular phone number for business only? Let people know how you wish to be reached under various circumstances:

➤ Leave a message on voice mail.

➤ Fax a copy.

➤ Call my beeper number on Tuesdays when I'm in the field.

➤ Don't contact me at home after 7 P.M.

Cellular phones and answering machines have made people so mobile these days that, when you leave a message, you should always include your telephone number. The message might be received when the person is nowhere near his or her list of telephone numbers.

Whenever possible, call the intended recipient to say that you are sending a fax, particularly if the whole office or department is sharing one or two fax machines. The fax you send could end up in the wrong person's mail slot, on the floor, or in a wastebasket.

Travel and Communication

Good electronic manners should not be suspended just because you are on the road. Here are some pointers:

➤ If you must make a cellular phone call in the airport boarding area or any other crowded space, walk to a less congested spot.

➤ Don't advertise the fact that you are traveling with a laptop—it's too tempting for thieves. Some of the fancy carriers scream LAPTOP, so get an inconspicuous one. Keep your computer in a bag or other camouflaging conveyance while at the airport, train station, and so on.

➤ Send your laptop through the security gate on the conveyor belt rather than carrying it through the metal detector, which emits a magnetic pulse.

Business Blunder

Don't send things by overnight mail unless you have a good reason. Aside from the expense, it will give the recipient the impression that he should reply in kind, even it is not necessary.

Memo to Myself

Always carry spare batteries for your laptop and cellular phone.

➤ Using the laptop in flight can annoy the person sitting next to you, particularly if he or she is trying to sleep. If you have your computer on the seatback tray, don't move it around or pound on it in a way that sends vibrations to the person sitting in front of you.

➤ Everybody around you is listening to your in-flight telephone call. Don't say, "Hey, I'm calling from the airplane!" If you can, use a phone in an unoccupied row of seats, or take the phone to the back of the plane. Be brief, too—such a call can easily cost you more than dinner for two at the House of Chateau Chez Maison Restaurant.

➤ In the car, don't talk and drive, no matter how good you think you are. And don't leave evidence of expensive technology where it can be seen. An adapter cord can inspire a thief to break in to see what else is available.

E-mail Etiquette

Those in the business world must look at e-mail as a business tool and approach it with as much care as any form of business communication.

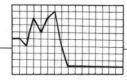

The Bottom Line

Don't send anything by e-mail that you wouldn't want to see posted on the office bulletin board.

The Write Way

To some kids, hackers, and casual computer users, e-mail is a toy. People in business know better—or at least they should.

If you are serious about your career and your reputation, you will take e-mail very seriously. Just because it is a relatively new form of communication does not mean that you can make up your own rules when using it. People will judge you by your e-mail just as critically as they would judge you by the quality and correctness of a formal business letter.

And, because some companies monitor employee e-mail—and because e-mail messages can be saved, forwarded, and passed around—there is no such thing as a "casual" use of e-mail in business.

Legally, your company owns and has the right to read all employee e-mail on the company computer system—and don't think they won't. It's so easy for a supervisor to say, "Let's see what Gibson is up to these days," scan your e-mail, and find messages such as, "Thank you, darling, for last night."

Also remember that when you delete e-mail, it does not "go away" forever. It *can* be recovered and traced.

E-Mail Supplements Communication

It's easy to get carried away with the ease and novelty of e-mail, but always remember that it should supplement your other methods of professional communications. In many situations a telephone call, a formal business letter, or even a handwritten note are required. Of course, e-mail should never be used to avoid a face-to-face discussion or confrontation when that is clearly called for. In other words, don't hide behind your computer terminal.

Use and Abuse

The fact that you can "talk" to people through e-mail in your pajamas doesn't mean that your messages can look as disheveled as you. The generally accepted rules for written communication apply. Don't fall into the trap of being quick and careless while using e-mail, even though the medium is quick and easy. Here are some basics:

➤ Observe the rules of English grammar and usage when using e-mail. The same goes for punctuation: Don't use dashes and dots as substitutes for periods and commas.

➤ Avoid the temptation to write in lowercase only, which makes the message look trivial and also harder to read. Capitalize where appropriate, but don't write in capitals for emphasis. This is equivalent to shouting at the person you are writing to.

Memo to Myself

Use upper- and lowercase (or just lowercase) letters on the e-mail subject line. All caps is an advertising gimmick, and your message could go unread.

Before Your Fingers Hit the Keyboard

Before you start to type, take a few minutes to think about what you are going to say and what the tone of the communication should be. If the recipient is a friend or a longtime colleague, the tone will be less formal than if you are writing to a client, a stranger, or your company's president. But, no matter how friendly the relationship is, the message should not be flip, full of slang, or in bad taste. Your friend might not be the only one to see it.

As with all good writing, your message should be concise and tight. Keep your sentences short. Don't repeat. Avoid rambling, and avoid interrupting yourself with asides or irrelevant remarks. If it's a long message, break it up into paragraphs.

Editing Your Message

Edit yourself. Reread your message at least once with a cold and critical eye. Look for typos and grammatical slips. Break up overly long sentences. No matter how sure you are, recheck the address and header information.

If your system has a spell-checker, use it—no matter how good a speller you think you are. If you don't have access to this tool, use a dictionary. The time it takes to look up a word is time well spent. Misspellings and typos can change the meaning of your message.

Business Blunders

E-mail is unkind to witticisms. Jokes seem to lose their punch. Flip asides morph into insults. Language you consider to be merely emphatic may be perceived as downright vulgar. It's best to stick to forthright language and straightforward sentences.

Then check the tone. Something about e-mail doesn't love a joke. A line that sounds hilarious over lunch looks dumb on the screen. "Hey, big guy" sounds fine over the telephone, but it looks juvenile in an e-mail message. The screen is an utterly two-dimensional medium.

Symbols

Don't pepper your prose with emphatic symbols such as exclamation points or dollar signs—that's kid stuff. And stay away from "smileys," those tricky little icons that are supposed to express emotion, for example :-). This is no better than writing "ha ha" to let people know that you are joking.

Many e-mail users employ acronyms to keep their messages shorter, and perhaps because they think it's clever. Generally, you should avoid using acronyms in business correspondence. I think they look unprofessional, and you can't be sure that the person receiving your message will be familiar with Internet lingo.

However, you should be familiar with the most commonly used acronyms. Here's a list to keep handy.

Common E-Mail Acronyms and Their Meanings

Acronym	Meaning
AAMOF	as a matter of fact
AFAIK	as far as I know
BTW	by the way
BRB	be right back
FWIW	for what it's worth
FYI	for your information
HTH	hope this helps
IDK	I don't know
IMO	in my opinion
IOW	in other words
NRN	no response necessary
PLS	please
RTFM	read the fabulous manual
Sp?	check the spelling
TIA	thanks in advance
WRT	with respect to

You can find other acronyms in Internet manuals at a book store.

Looking Good

Picture your message being printed and displayed on a bulletin board. Your message will look a lot better and will reflect more favorably on you if it is neat:

➤ If your system isn't formatted so that the lines are from 60 to 80 characters long, you should arrange for your copy to follow this generally accepted standard.

➤ Tabs and centered or justified text can be lost in transmission.

➤ For dates, use numbers instead of words. The form is MM/DD/YY. Thus, for New Year's Day, it's 01/01/99.

➤ Type your message single-spaced, and leave a blank line between paragraphs.

In short, neatness and care are emblems of self-respect and respect for those viewing your message.

From the File Drawer

"Deleting" does not make e-mail disappear—neither the mail you send nor the mail you receive. This can be a plus or a minus. It's a plus when you want to retrieve something and a minus when you make a mistake. I know an executive in a Fortune 100 company who wrote a critical and sarcastic e-mail about the assistant to the company president and then, accidentally, sent it to that very person.

Heading and Signature

If you are sending a formal business letter by e-mail, it is not necessary to include the usual heading that contains the recipient's name, company name, and so forth. However, you must still use a salutation ("Dear Ms. Galway") and end with an appropriate closing ("Sincerely"). Leave a space and add your signature block, which should include your company name and e-mail address.

For certain business purposes, you may want to create an e-mail letterhead. Use it sparingly, however, when you want to make sure that the recipient knows that the message is from your company and not from you as an individual. Your signature block should not duplicate the information in the letterhead.

Responding to E-Mail

Whenever possible, respond immediately. It is all too easy to let your electronic correspondence back up—and when there is a great deal to be answered, we tend to approach the task less cheerfully and carefully. If you can't respond fully right away, send a brief message explaining the delay and predicting when a more complete answer will be forthcoming.

If you need an answer promptly, make that part of your message. This doesn't have to sound like a command: Try something like, "I expect to speak to the board about this at tomorrow's meeting, and the information I'm requesting would be a great help." If a response doesn't come, a polite reminder is not out of line.

Forwarding E-Mail

If you want to forward an e-mail message, check with the original author of the message first. It is not only impolite to circulate another's work without permission, but it may also be an infringement of copyright law. This applies even if the message is trivial or contains good news, such as, "Mary had her baby yesterday." Always get permission before forwarding.

Never pass around another person's e-mail address without permission. When you are messaging someone for the first time, it is a good idea to say where you got the e-mail address. If it is from a business card or a Web site, for example, say so.

Business Blunders

If you get a message that was not intended for you, don't forward it. Let the author know that he or she has made a mistake.

Don't "spam," either. That's sending unsolicited material advertising a product or service by e-mail. The negative reaction to this behavior far outweighs any benefits. However, if someone asks for such material, you may send it and add something like, "If you find this material interesting, please feel free to pass it on."

Don't participate in chain letters. In fact, if you receive such a letter, it is best to delete it from your system and inform a supervisor or system manager that one is circulating. Chain letters are unprofessional and annoying, and they waste time and resources.

Going Global

In sending e-mail internationally, it's a good idea to keep the language as formal as possible. For one thing, citizens in many other countries are generally more formal in their business dealings, and it is customary for them to write even more formally than they speak.

Casual language can present difficulties in cross-cultural communications. Certain slang words or phrases have quite different meanings elsewhere, so watch what you write; also avoid clichés and jargon.

Remember also that, in many countries, age and rank are treated with a great deal more deference than in the United States.

What's the Subject?

Use the subject line: It is helpful to those receiving the message and may even be helpful to you, the writer. Selecting the correct subject can help you focus on the meat of your message.

Keep the subject message as brief as possible. Think of it more as a title than a headline. Brevity is also a virtue when it comes to the message. If the message is unavoidably long, use the word "long" on the subject line to tip off the recipient.

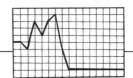

The Bottom Line

People who receive a great deal of e-mail daily use the subject line to sort and prioritize the mail. Thus, the subject can become a headline saying, "Read me first," particularly if it says something like, "Meeting with CEO."

Your E-Mail Signature

Many—in fact, too many—people use their computer signature as a sort of vanity license plate, employing jokes, diagrams, and bumper-sticker witticisms. This is absolutely unacceptable in a business context and is questionable in any other context. What strikes you as hilarious might strike others as simple-minded. Your signature should contain only your name and contact information. Anything more can be seen as inconsiderate, annoying, and a waste of bandwidth.

Mailing Lists

Some companies have established mailing lists to pass along general information by e-mail. Any participant can send a message to the mailing list address, and the message is automatically routed to each subscriber. In many cases, the messages are screened by a moderator, who determines which ones should be posted. If this is the case, don't complain to the moderator if one of your messages doesn't get posted, and don't criticize the decisions about what does get posted.

Contributing

If you are a new member of a company or departmental mailing list, it's a good idea to monitor the messages for a time to get a feel for the sort of behavior that is considered acceptable. (This sensible practice goes by the sinister name of *lurking*.) Each list has its own style, ranging from quite formal to breezy. Don't lurk indefinitely—all members of a list are expected to contribute from time to time.

When writing, avoid slang or references that may not be understood by all people, and be very careful about any language that could be insulting to other people, places, or cultures. You don't know how varied an audience you will be reaching.

Some Pointers

Consider these ideas before getting involved with mailing lists:

➤ If you are invited to join a mailing list, check with your supervisor about whether your membership would be appropriate.

➤ Don't join unless invited, and don't add someone to the list who has not asked to be added.

➤ If there is a mailing-list manager, be sure to send all messages through that person.

➤ Most new subscribers to a list get a set of rules at the beginning. Read and heed.

➤ Don't use the list to advertise things.

➤ Using the subject line is particularly important in this context.

➤ Don't ramble. Use facts and cite sources when you can.

➤ When responding to a long message, don't include the entire text. Summarize, using the original author's words.

➤ Check all responses under a subject heading before sending your response. For example, the question you were going to answer might already have been dealt with thoroughly.

➤ If you are discussing or debating a subject with a particular person, continue the conversation through e-mail and give the group a summary, if relevant.

➤ If you don't have anything useful to add, do nothing. "I agree" or "Good point" is a waste of space and is annoying.

If you are invited to join a mailing list, think it over before accepting, and don't accept unless you are prepared to participate actively.

Memo to Myself

Certain software allows you to ignore newsgroup postings from particular individuals or those that concern topics that don't interest you.

Participating in Newsgroups

Newsgroups are similar to mailing lists, but messages are posted in a common place instead of to individual mailboxes. Subscriptions are not necessary, and anyone can participate, although some newsgroups are moderated.

It's a good idea to lurk for a time to be sure you are interested in participating and to learn the group's culture and netiquette. It is also useful to remember the rules of mailing lists when joining newsgroups.

Some additional considerations apply here. Read the news.announce.newusers and news.newusers.questions before getting started. Also take a look at the FAQ (frequently asked questions) list. If you are testing how to post a message, use one of the testing sites.

When responding to an article, you may want to e-mail the author directly instead of posting to the group if you simply want to clarify a point. Post to the group if you have new or relevant information. And read all the other postings before responding to an article to be sure that someone else hasn't already made the same points.

If you are sending a personal message to a group member and it doesn't go through, don't just send the message to the whole group. Wait until that person messages the group again, and check the e-mail address.

Limit cross-posting. It is quite possible that the audience in one newsgroup may also participate in other groups to which you are cross-posting. When you cross-post, indicate to which group the responses should go.

The Least You Need to Know

➤ These days, there is no such thing as the anonymous voyager on the seas of computer technology. You cannot get away with flaming or spamming, but lurking is a good idea.

➤ The usual traditions and rules of good manners are not superseded by the availability of electronic wizardry.

➤ As important as knowing how to use cellular phones, e-mail, and so forth is knowing which to use (and when) according to the circumstances.

➤ E-mail is easy, but it's not a toy. How you use it will reflect upon your good sense and good taste.

➤ E-mail should neither supplement, nor replace other forms of communications, and it should not be used to duck one-on-one contact.

➤ Never forward the e-mail of another person without permission.

Part 4

Dining and Entertaining

Your first meeting with important clients or a prospective employer may be over lunch. The company president might invite you to dinner at his home. You might find yourself sitting at the same table with Lord and Lady Fitzhugh at the black-tie awards banquet, or maybe you must give a dinner party at your house and find the prospect daunting.

Each of these situations is a test, and you will be judged—perhaps harshly—on your behavior and your manners. And, if you fail the test, nobody will tell you why. But don't worry—you'll be fine. You just need to get clued in about the rules, about how to avoid the most common mistakes. That's what this part of the book is all about.

The following chapters will outline the basics of good table manners, walk you through a formal dinner, and dissect a typical business lunch. Along the way, they'll point out the potential pitfalls and tell you all you need to know about afternoon tea, banquet halls, and buffet tables.

This part also deals with the ins and outs of home entertaining and covers such as topics as what to serve, who gets invited (and how), and how to cope with caterers (and without them). In short, the following chapters will provide you with all you need to know to feel relaxed and confident in any situation that involves entertaining and dining with others, including Lord and Lady Fitzhugh.

Chapter 14

Table Manners

In This Chapter

➤ The 10 most common mistakes

➤ Handling napkins and cutlery

➤ Accidents will happen

➤ Dealing with foods from hell

➤ Culinary cultural diversity

Some years ago, the president of a hotel management firm asked me to help the newly appointed manager of an old, much respected hotel in Charleston, South Carolina, with his table manners. We met for an instructional dinner in a private dinner room at the Ritz Carlton in Philadelphia, and I was immediately impressed by the charm and intelligence of the manager. His only problem was that he hadn't learned some of the rules of dining etiquette. The problem was effectively dealt with and the man returned to Charleston for a lengthy and successful tenure at the hotel.

The point of this story is that, while common sense and respect for others will take you a long way, you must also learn the rules. I had to. Everyone does.

How to Behave at the Dinner Table

These are some of the most common mistakes people make at the table—along with the best ways to avoid them.

Cutlery

Hold cutlery with the fingers, not the fists. The knife is not a dagger; the fork is not a broom handle.

Do not put silverware partly on the table and partly on the plate.

Once you have picked up a piece of cutlery, it should never touch the table again. Knives go on the plate, blade facing in.

Never lift a piece of cutlery substantially above the plate. Don't wave or thrust with your cutlery to emphasize a point.

The coffee/teaspoon, which may be found above the dinner plate together with a dessert fork and spoon in some banquet table settings, goes on the saucer beside the cup once you have picked it up.

Chewing

Never chew with your mouth open.

Do not speak with food in your mouth, no matter how much you want to inject a brilliant observation at a critical moment. And don't gulp and blurt. Just finish chewing, and swallow the food and the timely remark together.

Be consoled by the fact that you could have said just the right thing at the right moment, but you had too much class to speak with food in your mouth.

Napkins

Don't flap your napkin to unfold it, and don't wave it around.

Dab delicately. Don't rub or blot the lower part of your face.

Don't tuck. The napkin belongs unfolded on your lap.

If you leave the table, put the napkin on your chair and push the chair close to the table. If your napkin is soiled, be mindful of the upholstery.

At the end of the meal, the host places his napkin on the table and others follow suit. Pick up the napkin from its center and place it loosely on the table to the left of your plate. Don't refold it—the server might mistakenly pass it along to the next diner.

Posture

Your mother was right: You should sit up straight. Avoid slouching or leaning on the table.

Keep your elbows off the table.

If you don't know where to put your hands, put them in your lap.

Pacing

Gulping down your food is unhealthy and unattractive, whether you are at the Ritz Carlton or the Dingy Dish Diner.

People dining together should have the same number of courses, and they should start and finish them at the same time.

If you find that you are falling behind the others, stop talking long enough to catch up. If you have almost finished your entree while others are just starting, stall.

Bread

Your bread dish is the one on your left. (Your water glass is on the right.)

Put butter first on your bread plate or dinner plate, not directly on the bread or roll.

Don't butter an entire piece of bread or a roll to have it ready for nibbles during the course of the meal. Instead, tear off a piece, butter it, and eat it—one piece at a time.

Clutter

If it isn't part of the meal, it should not be on the table.

Put purses and briefcases on the floor.

If you absolutely must handle a document or other paper, keep it on your lap, not the table.

Other things that do not belong on the table include keys, eyeglass cases, cigarette packs, hats, gloves, pens, cellular phones, and beepers.

Smoking

Even if you are in the smoking section of the restaurant, it is best to refrain.

If you *must* smoke at the table, wait until the meal is over.

Never, ever use your plate as an ashtray. If no ashtray is available, ask for one or don't smoke.

Panic

Accidents happen—and they can happen to you, even though you are being really, really careful. The most important thing to remember is not to panic. React calmly and, if possible, cheerfully.

If you spill something, don't dramatize the incident by jumping up or yelling, "Watch out." If you are in danger of getting wet, back away a little from the table and blot with your napkin and ask the server for another one.

If you spill something on someone else, apologize—calmly. Then offer to pay for whatever cleaning may be needed. Do not touch the other person. Let the victim handle the blotting and/or wiping. Offer your napkin and ask the server for replacements.

Don't make the incident the next subject of conversation, explaining how the accident happened, who was at fault, and how it all could have been avoided.

You Don't Say

If someone leaves the table, don't ask where he is going.

Don't complain to your fellow diners about the quality of the food or service. If you are the host, talk to the restaurant manager later.

If someone takes a pill at the table, don't ask what it's for. If you must take medication at the table, do so without comment. No explanation is necessary.

Don't talk about your health, good or bad.

From the File Drawer

Small forks for eating were first used in the eleventh century in Tuscany. Prior to that time, even at the most elaborate court banquets, people ate with their fingers and drank their soup and other liquids by raising a bowl to their lips.

Once you pick up a piece of cutlery, no part of it should ever touch the table again.

Quick Tips

This handy list of dos and don'ts can help during all dining situations.

➤ Don't dunk your food.

➤ Pass food to the right.

➤ Cut only enough food for the next mouthful.

➤ When you have finished eating, do not push your plate away, and do not push your chair back from the table.

➤ Never crumble crackers in your soup.

➤ Never blow on a liquid to cool it.

➤ If you belch, cover your mouth with your napkin, and say "Excuse me" to no one in particular.

➤ Don't pick at something stuck in your teeth or go through facial contortions trying to dislodge it with your tongue. If it is driving you crazy, excuse yourself and go to the restroom.

➤ Don't leave a lipstick trail. If you don't have a blotting tissue, detour to the restroom before sitting down, or pick up a cocktail napkin as you pass the bar.

➤ Never tilt your chair.

➤ If you are dining at someone's home, even your own, the cook may be offended if you salt or season your food before tasting it. Even in a restaurant, it's sensible to taste your food before seasoning it.

Memo to Myself

If you use the wrong piece of flatware, don't worry. Continue to use it, and ask the server for a replacement when you need it.

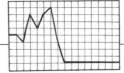

The Bottom Line

What do you say if the person next to you has commandeered your bread plate? Nothing. Use the rim of your dinner plate.

If you see others doing the things we warn against in the above list, say nothing.

How to Eat Anything with Aplomb

Some foods are difficult to deal with gracefully. Following is an alphabetical list of such problem foods and tips on how to approach them. Remember, it is perfectly correct to eat some foods with your fingers. The general rule is, when in doubt, use cutlery correctly. If you have already touched the item, go ahead and eat it with your fingers. And, please, don't say, "They invented fingers before forks, right?"

Artichokes. Bravely pick up an artichoke and remove one leaf at a time. Dip the soft end into the sauce, and pull, don't yank, it through your teeth to remove the edible part. Discard the rest. At the center, use a knife to scrape away the fuzzy part, and proceed with knife and fork.

Avocados. These fruits can be eaten with a spoon or with a fork when cut into pieces.

Bacon. When crisp, bacon strips can be eaten with the fingers; use cutlery when they're not.

Memo to Myself

Pass food to the right. If you don't care for the food being passed, accept the dish anyway and pass it along. When asked to pass the salt or pepper, pass both.

Berries. All berries should be eaten with a spoon except when served with stems. In that case, hold the berry by the stem and bite.

Cake. If it's bite-sized, cake can be eaten with the fingers. If not, or if it comes with a sauce or ice cream or is sticky, use a spoon in your right hand to eat it and a fork in your left to push the piece onto the spoon.

Caviar. Spread this on toast with a knife, and eat the toast with your fingers.

Celery, radishes, and pickles. Take relishes off the service plate with your fingers, place them on your dinner plate, and eat them with your fingers.

Chicken or fowl. Poultry requires a knife and fork unless you are at a picnic.

Corn on the cob. Even if you're not at a picnic, use both hands. Butter just a few rows at a time. This food is never served on formal occasions and is never served at all in Europe, where it is considered food for livestock.

Grapefruit halves. Section these fruits to avoid a lot of digging with the spoon. Never squeeze the juice.

Hard-shell crabs and lobsters. Crack the shell with a nutcracker and extract the meat with a seafood fork, a small implement with three tines. If it's a large piece of meat, cut it with a fork. Pull off the small claws and treat them as if you were drawing liquid through a straw. Stuffed lobster is eaten with a knife and fork.

Lemon wedges. Handle these with care. Secure them with a fork and squeeze with the other hand or pick them up, using one hand to squeeze and the other to shield so that your neighbor doesn't get an eyeful of lemon juice.

Olives. If pitted, these can be eaten whole. If not, pick up a large one and eat it in small bites instead of popping the whole thing into your mouth and chewing. To discard pits, kiss the palm of your hand, discreetly putting the pit in it, and deposit the pit on the edge of your plate.

Oranges and tangerines. Peel these fruits with a knife or your fingers, and eat them by sections. If they're served sectioned on a plate, use your fork.

Pasta. Don't cut the strands with your knife, and avoid that business of using the bowl of a spoon to twirl. If it's small-sized pasta—ziti, penne, and the like—use only a fork. For strands, twirl two or three strands on your fork at a time.

Peaches. These fruits should be halved, quartered with a knife, and eaten with a fork. You can eat the skin or peel it off with a knife or your fingers.

Pineapple. Eat these with a spoon when served in small pieces and with a fork when sliced.

Potatoes. Eat the inside of a baked potato with a fork. Don't try to convert the inside into a mashed concoction. If you want to eat the skin, cut it into manageable pieces with a knife and fork. Cut fries in half, and eat them with your fork.

Shrimp. Eat shrimp with your fingers if the tails are left on. Shrimp cocktail should be eaten with a seafood fork, in two bites if large. Better still, put the shrimp on a serving plate and cut them with a knife and fork.

Sushi and sashimi. If you must take sushi or sashimi from a platter with chopsticks, use the ends that have not been in your mouth (see the next section, "How to Hold Chopsticks," for help). Eat sushi pieces whole if they are small, or cut them with a knife and fork or with the ends of chopsticks. There's nothing wrong with using your fingers.

Tortillas. Eat from the end when held, or cut starting from the end when using a knife and fork.

Watermelon. Eat this fruit with a spoon when in small pieces. Otherwise, use a fork. Put the seeds in the palm of your hand and transfer them to your plate.

From the File Drawer

The custom of breaking bread and taking only as much as you intend to eat began when what was left of the communal loaf was given to the poor. Similar consideration for the poor is embodied in the ancient custom of "gleaning," leaving part of the crop in the field to be collected by the impoverished and hungry. This practice of "gleaning" is even mentioned in the Bible.

How to Hold Chopsticks

These pointers will help you handle chopsticks comfortably:

1. Put the bottom chopstick in the web of your right hand, between the thumb and index finger.

2. Use your two middle fingers to keep it steady. This chopstick will remain fairly stationary.

3. Hold the top chopstick like a pencil between your thumb and index finger. This one does most of the moving.

Hold the rice bowl under your chin and scoop with the chopsticks.

In a restaurant, it's fine to ask for a fork.

The bottom chopstick is placed in the web of your right hand, between the thumb and index finger.

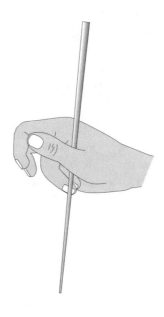

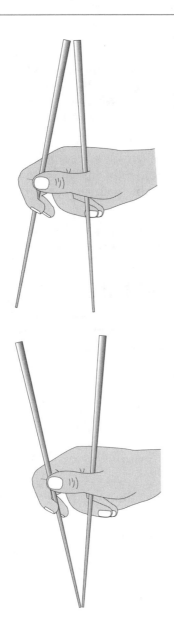

The top chopstick is held like a pencil between your thumb and index finger.

The top chopstick does most of the moving. The bottom chopstick remains stationary.

175

It's a Pleasure

The tips and guidelines in this chapter will keep you out of trouble in most dining situations. But it is also important to remember that dining with others is—or should be—one of the great pleasures of life. This is a pleasure that can be enjoyed only if you approach the experience with confidence—and confidence comes with experience.

When dining out, alone and with others, watch what is going on around you. Note the behavior of those who appear to be confidently enjoying themselves and those who seem ill at ease. Don't save your good table manners for special occasions. Practice, especially when dining alone.

With some knowledge and experience and a willingness to please, anyone can become the poised, informed, and confident dining companion he wishes to be.

Foreign Words to Help You Order

This list of foreign words will help you function more smoothly and avoid surprises in restaurants where Spanish, French, or Italian is spoken.

English	Spanish	French	Italian
Please	Por favor	S'il vous plait	Prego
Thank you	Gracias	Merci	Grazie
Salad	Ensalada	Salade	Insalata
Vegetables	Legumbres	Legumes	Legumi
Fish	Pescado	Poisson	Pesce
Chicken	Pollo	Poulet	Pollo
Broiled	Ala parilla	Grille	Alla griglia
Steamed	Al vapor	Ala vapeur	Cotto a vapore
Baked	Asado	Au four	Al forno
Beef	Carne	Boeuf	Manzo
Without	Sin	Sans	Sanza
Sauce	Salsa	Sauce	Saisa
Butter	Mantequilla	Beurre	Burro
Oil	Aceite	Huile	Olio
Cheese	Queso	Fromage	Formaggio
Salt	Sal	Sel	Sale
Sugar	Azucar	Sucre	Zucchero

Keep this list and add to it as you come across other useful terms.

From the File Drawer

"Don't, when offered a dish at a friend's table, look at it critically, turn it about with the spoon and fork, and then refuse it."

—G. R. M. Devereux, Etiquette for Women, 1901

The Least You Need to Know

➤ Once you pick up a piece of cutlery, it must never touch the table again—and don't gesture with it, either.

➤ Practice good posture, and keep elbows off the table.

➤ If it isn't part of the meal, it should not be on the table.

➤ Don't chew with your mouth open or speak with food in your mouth.

➤ Don't flap or wave your napkin; don't put it on the table until the end of the meal.

➤ Cut only enough food for your next mouthful.

➤ The food itself is the least important part of the business meal.

Dining for Dollars

First, be assured that the business lunch or dinner is not just a meeting with food. In fact, it might be wise to think of it as a test that spotlights your social skills and your level of sophistication. If you can't function smoothly and with confidence on these occasions, it will cast doubt on your ability to do so in other circumstances.

To examine the dynamics of a business meal, we will start with the premise that you are the host, putting on trial your ability to plan and organize, as well as to practice good table manners and demonstrate your grasp of the basics of business etiquette. Learning about what makes these occasions successful from the point of view of the host also will make you a more considerate and savvy guest.

The Mission of the Meal

First, you must have a clear idea of what should be accomplished during this meeting. If more than one objective is to be met, prioritize and write them down. It is your job to create the best circumstances for achieving these ends, and that means controlling the process from beginning to end.

Make sure your agenda is short. One reason for the meal is to foster a relationship by getting to know the other persons—you can't do that if you are trying to get through a 50-item agenda.

Guidelines for Dining Out

Keep these two basic guidelines in mind from the beginning:

1. Don't experiment. You want to select a restaurant that you know—really know. Frequent a couple of good, convenient places. Become a "regular," which means being familiar with the menu and the dining room and being friendly with the maitre d' or manager. Even if you have heard that a restaurant is very good and well-suited to your purposes, save it until you have time to check it out yourself.

2. Watch costs. Don't skimp, but remember that extravagance—except perhaps for important celebrations—shows bad manners and bad judgment. You don't need a gorgeous French restaurant with classic service; choose a quality restaurant known for reliable service. For one thing, your guests might feel that they must reciprocate in kind and may not choose or be able to. Worse, they may conclude that you are reckless with money and may therefore be reckless in other areas.

Issuing Invitations

When you have chosen the restaurant, organize your party. Start with the most important person or the hardest to pin down. The conversation might go something like this:

"Hello, Jeff. This is Hilda Lucas. I'm calling to invite you to lunch to talk about our new marketing proposal. Does that sound like a good idea?

"Sounds good."

"I'd like Tom Finch and Marge Cutter to join us."

"Good idea."

"How about Monday or Tuesday?"

"Let's do it Tuesday."

"Fine. How about Anthony's or The Palm?"

"The Palm sounds good."

"Is 12:30 all right, or would you prefer another time?"

"Twelve-thirty is fine."

"I'll make the reservations. Smoking or non?"

"Non-smoking."

"Great. See you at 12:30 on Tuesday at The Palm."

If it's a breakfast meeting, confirm the afternoon before, and give your guests your home telephone number in case an emergency arises. For a lunch or dinner appointment, confirm the day before. If the meeting must be canceled, call the restaurant promptly. You should make these calls yourself, not have a secretary do it.

Dress Rehearsal

Do yourself a favor, and invest the time it takes for a dress rehearsal. This does not mean that you are a bumbling clod; it means that you care enough to do this right. Visit the restaurant well in advance of the meeting, preferably at mealtime. Is the place too noisy? Is the room too large or too congested? Look for a table in a good position, perhaps in a corner and a little distance from other tables. Reserve it, if possible.

Speak with the owner, maitre d', or manager. Make the reservation both in your name and in the name of your company, which helps to send the message that this is a business meeting. Make it as clear as possible that the meal is important and that you and possibly your associates will be returning if all goes well.

Set up a corporate account, or allow them to take a credit card imprint. Let them know that you may be ordering wine. Talk about the price range that you expect to operate in, and ask for suggestions. It may be a good idea to tip the maitre d' before you leave the restaurant if he has been the one you have been talking with. Such a tip is usually $10 or $20, depending on the level of the restaurant.

Arrive Early

Get to the restaurant about 10 minutes before the appointed time. Being early means that you will be there to greet your guests as they arrive. If you did not tip the maitre d' during your "dress rehearsal" visit, do so now, and remind him of how many guests will be arriving. "We'll be four for table 12."

If possible, wait near the door for your guests to arrive. In some places, this is inconvenient or impossible. If you must wait at the table, do not eat or drink anything, and leave the napkin on the table. The table setting should be undisturbed when the others arrive.

Memo to Myself

Try this technique for tipping the maitre d' without flashing cash. Fold the bill in half, then half again, and then half again so that the amount shows on both sides. Put it into the palm of your hand, and shake. The bill will magically and smoothly disappear.

Stand up and greet your guests when they arrive (see Chapter 3, "Greetings and Introductions"). If it is not convenient to shake everyone's hand, a small wave or other gesture will suffice. Remain standing until everyone is seated.

If someone at your table excuses himself during the meal, it is not necessary for you or anyone else to rise.

Where Does Everyone Sit?

Try to control the seating order as subtly as possible. This may be done simply by pointing to or touching a chair or by saying to the first person to reach the table, "Tom, why don't you sit here." If someone has obviously laid claim to a position at the table, don't fight it.

If possible, try to work it so that your principal guest—in this case, Jeff—is at right angles with you, preferably on your left if you are right-handed. If there are two principal guests, or two guests who will be doing most of the talking, try to avoid sitting between them, or you will be doing the tennis-match head swivel throughout the meal. A better arrangement is for them to sit opposite you or both on one side of you.

Don't set up shop. Keep papers in your briefcase, and keep your briefcase on the floor. If it is likely that a certain document will be passed around, make sure that you can put your hands on it immediately. Pass only that document, and put it away as soon as you can. The basic rule of table manners that says, "if it isn't part of the meal, it shouldn't be on the table," may have to be modified at a business meal, but keep it to a minimum. For example, if you must use your pen, put it back in your pocket, purse, or briefcase, not on the table in front of you.

If you have a cellular phone, it should be turned off unless you are expecting an urgent call that you absolutely *must* take. If so, explain in advance. If you have a beeper, set it to vibrate mode. (See Chapter 12, "Communicating by Telephone.")

Ordering Drinks

The server will ask if you want anything from the bar. Let your guests reply first. If they do not order drinks, neither do you. If they order drinks, follow suit. You may order something non-alcoholic, even if you are the only one to make that choice; you don't have to explain why. However, as a host, I have sometimes said, "I'm not having any wine today, but please do have some if you like." The "today" makes it clear that there is no general disapproval of wine or drinks with meals.

If no drinks are ordered, spend a few minutes in minor conversation before ordering. If there are drinks, the server will return to ask about refills. If the answer is no, ask for menus. If the answer is yes, ask for menus when the second round arrives.

Ordering Dinner

Your previous perusals of the menu, and perhaps your experience as a diner at this particular restaurant, will pay off here. You can make some recommendations and encourage those at the table to order appetizers. (If you are a guest, feel free to ask the host at this point if he or she has any suggestions.) Have the server take your guests' orders first, and order the same number of courses yourself—whether you want them or not.

Now, stop talking and look at the menu. This is no time for dawdling or changing your mind. Make a decision and put the menu down. One thing to consider while deciding is the wisdom of avoiding user-unfriendly foods during a business meal. Stay away from things such as large sandwiches and spaghetti, things that could be messy or difficult to handle.

Memo to Myself

The napkin should remain unfolded on the lap. If it's one of those over-sized formal dinner napkins, don't unfold it completely.

Selecting the Wine

Sooner or later, you will be in the position of ordering wine. Again, extravagance is bad manners and bad strategy.

If you are in a fine restaurant, remember that these establishments generally won't have inferior wines on their lists. So, look for mid-priced wines, and figure one bottle for three persons.

In a modest restaurant, it's fine to order the house wine, and it is never wrong to order a bottle and add glassfuls.

Wait until your guests have ordered their meals before you order the wine. Generally, white wines go with chicken and fish, and red with meats. Try a sauvignon blanc for white and pinot noir for reds; these are not as overpowering as the standard Chardonnay and cabernet sauvignon, and they go well with both fish and meat.

From the File Drawer

The custom of clinking glasses began as a means of driving away evil spirits. Avoid clinking today, though—it ruins glasses and china.

The phrase *powder room* was originally used at formal balls in England to designate the room in which servants attended to the wigs of the guests. The term for the most part has passed out of usage.

Check the wine label to be sure you got what you ordered.

The server will open the bottle and present you with the cork. Pinch it to be sure it is not dried out, and then lay it on the table or give it back to the server. This is the signal to pour. You will get a small amount in your glass. Taste it. If it has not "turned" and doesn't taste vinegary and rancid, nod your approval to pour. Your guests will be served first.

Checking the Service

Part of your responsibility as host is to see to it that your guests are served properly. If you discern or even suspect that something is missing or that something is wrong, ask your guest if there is a problem. If there is, summon the maitre d' and ask him to fix it.

Business Blunders

Never get into a dispute with restaurant staff in front of your guests. You can say something like, "I'm sorry. They seem to be having a bad day." Then excuse yourself and talk to the manager or maitre d', or wait until after the meal.

Don't Skip Dessert

Encourage everyone to have dessert: "The chocolate mousse is terrific here." Again, follow their lead, whether you want dessert or not. Ask if they would like coffee or tea; when it is served, ask for the check.

This is a very important time. Decisions and agreements are often made over dessert and coffee. As host, you should review what has been discussed during the meeting meal and perhaps summarize what still must be decided. Make sure that everyone understands what arrangements have been made and what future meetings have been agreed to. The end of the meal is a good time for writing things down and passing things around.

Paying

Do not pull out your pocket calculator. It is perfectly fine to review the bill—briefly—for accuracy, but don't study it like a prenuptial agreement. If you think there is a mistake, deal with it after your guests have left.

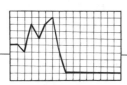

The Bottom Line

The best way to avoid anyone haggling over who pays the restaurant bill is to leave a credit card imprint in advance so that no check comes to the table.

Haggling over who should pay the bill is stupid, annoying, and unnecessary. The person who did the inviting pays the bill—period. Contributions from the guests should be limited to "thank you." Unfortunately, however, these haggling situations do arise. It happens more often when a woman is the host, in spite of what we like to think of as progress in this "enlightened" time.

Just say, "I invited you—and besides, (name your company or corporation) would like to buy you lunch."

If you have left a credit card imprint so that no check comes to the table, be sure to arrange beforehand that a tip of 18 or 20 percent may be added to the bill.

Before you leave the table, collect the checkroom tickets from your guests; on the way out, tip the attendant $1 per garment.

Leaving

Escort your guests to the door. You can remind them about the next meeting, or tell them you will be contacting them to set up a meeting if one is needed.

Shake hands and thank them for joining you. If there has been a problem with the food or service, apologize.

If you are one of the guests, thank the host and, if warranted, praise the restaurant. Even if you didn't like the food, you might say that you were impressed by the service or the ambiance. You should send a handwritten thank-you note to the host within two days. And, no, a telephone call will not do—neither will a fax or an e-mail.

Afterward, you, as host, might want to take a few minutes to make some notes on what went well and what could be improved, and to congratulate yourself on staging such a successful business meal.

Anatomy of a Restaurant

You will feel more confident in dealing with restaurants if you know how a restaurant functions and understand the role of the various staff members who make it function. When you enter a restaurant, staff members essentially become your employees for the duration of your visit. Smooth dining is basically a team effort, and it is important to know the functions of the team members.

Maitre d' or Host

This is usually the person who seats you. He may also be the general manager or, in a smaller place, the owner. The maitre d' is in charge of staffing and coordinating reservations with seating. This is the person you speak with if you want a special table or if you have a special request, such as orchestrating a birthday surprise or having an engagement ring appear in a champagne glass.

Memo to Myself

Getting to know—and be known at—a couple good restaurants is a wise investment in time and money.

Captain, or Head Waiter

These terms are pretty much interchangeable. If one person takes your order and another actually serves the food, the first person is the captain, or head waiter. If the restaurant has such a person (and many do not), he is the one to consult if there is a problem with the food or service.

Sommelier

This is the wine steward. In restaurants that have no sommelier—and that's most of them—his duties are assumed by the maitre d' or captain. The sommelier is the one to ask about which wine will best complement both the rack of lamb and the lobster. The sommelier may also present the wine and pour it.

Servers and Bussers

These are the people you will have the most contact with while at the restaurant. Refer to them by these gender-neutral titles rather than *waiter* or *busboy*. (We have actually heard people use the obnoxious, politically correct word *waitron*.) If you have a problem with either servers or bussers, speak to the maitre d' or host. The busser is the one to inform if there is something missing, such as a water glass or a piece of flatware.

Tipping

Here are some specific pointers when it comes to the always difficult subject of tipping:

➤ The captain or head waiter gets 5 percent of the bill in cash, or specified on the bill if you use a credit card.

➤ The server gets 15 percent to 20 percent if service has been especially efficient, friendly, or both. Remember that this tip is generally divided among the entire service team, including bartenders and bussers.

➤ The sommelier gets 15 percent of the wine bill if he performs a special service, such as helping you choose the right wines.

➤ The check room attendant gets $1 per garment and another dollar for a brief-case, boots, or umbrella.

➤ If you are a regular at a restaurant, it pays to tip the maitre d'—and to do so in cash. The maitre d' who provides you with the perfect table, oversees a complicated seating arrangement or business meal, or provides another special service deserves a cash tip of $10 or $20, depending on the extent of the service.

Trust your own judgment when you think it is appropriate to deviate from these suggestions and when unusual or special tipping situations arise.

Dining at Work

If you are planning to order food for a meeting, remember the two basic rules: Keep it simple, and keep it tidy. Drinks should include diet and regular, decaf and regular.

As for eating, use a knife and fork if they are provided, and use your fingers for foods such as pizza and sandwiches. You may find it easier to use your fingers for other food as well if the only alternative is using those flimsy plastic knives and forks.

Don't spread out. Keep your area as clean and tidy as possible. Use plenty of napkins or, better, those packaged towelettes. Your place should not resemble a compost heap. Bones and scraps go on the side of your plate, not on the table. Keep things such as keys or other items not related to the meal or the work off the table. Put them in your pocket or in your purse or briefcase on the floor.

While it is very important to treat a business meal seriously and to prepare for it as carefully and professionally as possible, it is also important to remember that there is a social component to any meal, whether or not business is being done. Something about sharing food brings people together. Sharing a meal provides the opportunity to get to know others better as people, not just as bosses, clients, or colleagues.

The Least You Need to Know

➤ Don't lose sight of the fact that the reason for the business meal is to foster a relationship and then get business done.

➤ Use a restaurant you have checked out and that you have confidence in.

➤ Learn who gets tipped and how much.

➤ Never haggle over a bill.

➤ Use dessert or coffee time to summarize what happened at the meeting and to arrange for future activities.

The Formal Dinner

You open the invitation to a formal dinner, and the cold fist of dread clutches your heart. You have a vision of stern, important people in formal dress watching you drink from your finger bowl and wash your fingers in the consommé.

If that's your reaction, it is because you don't know what to expect. Formal dinners were not part of your upbringing, and your pals think that a formal dinner is one in which a knife and fork are required. The truth is, you are probably less likely to encounter the unknown at a formal dinner than at any other social gathering. The more formal the dinner, the more predictable it is. And, if you know what to expect, what's coming next, and what to do about it, you can relax and enjoy yourself.

So, let's go through an imaginary formal dinner, step by step. When we finish, you will be able to open a formal dinner invitation with pleasure and attend the event with grace and confidence.

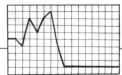

The Bottom Line

At a large dinner party or a banquet table, greet the others before sitting down. If no one introduces you, do it yourself.

Preliminaries

Before approaching the table, make a stop at the restroom. Check your general appearance. Make final hair repairs. Make certain your lipstick will leave no traces anywhere. Then proceed to the table.

➤ Greet everyone before sitting down. Smile, whether you feel like it or not.

➤ A server will draw the chair for you. Enter from your left.

➤ Gentlemen must rise to greet newcomers. They may also rise when ladies leave and return to the table, but that may seem extravagantly courtly these days.

You may remark on how grand the table looks—and it will look grand and, at the same time, daunting. You'll see lots of silver and glass and candles. Don't worry—we'll sort out of that presently.

Napkin Niceties

When you're safely seated, wait for your host to make the first napkin move. When the host places the napkin on his or her lap, the others at the table follow suit. Similarly, at the end of the meal, the host will be the first to place the napkin on the table (to the left of his or her plate) to signal that the meal is over, having first made sure that everyone at the table has finished.

Memo to Myself

It's a good idea to take your cue from the host, beginning with sitting down and putting the napkin on your lap and ending by not putting your napkin back onto the table until the host does so.

Don't flap your napkin to unfold it. In fact, don't unfold the napkin at all if it is one of those large dinner napkins. Leave it unfolded on your lap, with the fold facing inward.

If you leave the table during the meal, place the napkin on your chair. If the server does not push your chair back under the table, you should do so. Be advised that the server may refold your napkin and place it on the arm of your chair. (The uninformed might interpret this small courtesy as a rebuke, incorrectly assuming that napkins always should be left on the chair arm.)

At the end of the meal, do not refold your napkin. Pick it up from its center, and place it loosely on the table to the left of your plate.

All About Wine

Wine will be served during the meal, beginning with the first course, the soup course. If you don't want wine, place your fingertips on the rim of the glass when it is being poured and say, "I'm not having any today (or tonight)." The use of the word "today" indicates that you do not disapprove of wine or those who drink it.

Wine is poured from the right.

White wine and champagne glasses are always held by the stem, so as not to diminish the chill. Red wine glasses also may be held by the stem but generally are held by the bowl because the warmth of the hand releases the bouquet of the wine. The same is true of brandy glasses.

Don't be dazzled by the glasses at your place. The largest is the water goblet. If there is a tall, thin glass, it is the champagne flute. The red wine glass is larger than the white wine glass; if there is a sherry glass, it is the smallest.

If you are not accustomed to drinking alcohol, be careful. Remember that different wines may be served with different courses, and drink sparingly or not at all. Simply decline, as described earlier.

Counting Courses

Take a look at the place setting. The number of courses to be served will generally be indicated by the number of pieces of silverware, although the server may replace silverware between courses at some formal dinners. The general rule is to start from the outside.

You may expect the formal dinner to include seven courses, in this order:

➤ Soup

➤ Fish

➤ Sorbet, or palate cleanser

➤ A meat or fowl dish

➤ Salad, often served with cheese

➤ Dessert

➤ Coffee

Subtle and Not-So-Subtle Signals

It helps to know which directions things are coming from. Courses are served from the left and removed from the right. Liquids are poured from the right. (Soup, no matter how thin, counts as a food, not a liquid.)

Memo to Myself

The fish fork *is* smaller than the others, and the soup spoon *is* larger. The coffee/teaspoon is sometimes found above the dinner plate and belongs on the saucer when not in use.

Keep a subtle watch on your fellow diners, and try to finish each course at about the same time as the others. When you have finished with a course, signal the server with your flatware. You do this by visualizing a clock face on your plate: Place the knife and fork in the 10:20 position on the plate, with the points at approximately 10:00 and the handles at approximately 4:00. The prongs of the fork may face up or down, and the blade of the knife should face you. If you have been eating the course with a fork only, place it prongs-up in the same position.

Finished position.

You send a different signal when you wish to stop eating temporarily during a course and don't want the server to remove your plate. In this case, the knife and fork are crossed on the plate with the fork over the knife and the prongs pointing down. The knife should be at the 10:20 position, and the fork prongs should be at 2 o'clock with the handle at 8 o'clock.

Resting position.

Sipping Soup

When eating soup, it looks better and reduces the dribble danger if you tilt the spoon away from you, dipping the outer edge into the soup first, rather than the edge nearest you. Sip from the side of the spoon, rather than the tip, making no more noise than a snoring spider. And, yes, you may tilt the soup plate (often inaccurately called the soup bowl) away from you to access the last of the soup.

When you have finished, leave the soup spoon in the soup plate. However, if the soup is served in a soup cup, leave the spoon on the saucer under the cup. If soup is served in a two-handled cup, it's okay to drink the soup, holding it by both handles.

When eating soup, tilt the spoon away from you.

Tilt the soup plate away from you to access the last of the soup.

A two-handled soup cup.

Fish Dishes

In fine restaurants, and perhaps at some elegant private dinner parties, the fish course is served with special fish knives and forks.

In this case, hold the fish fork in the left hand, as in the continental style of dining. (The continental and American styles are compared elsewhere in this chapter.) The knife is used to break the fish and put it onto the fork. You will hold the knife differently because it is used to break or separate the fish, not to cut it. Hold the fish knife between your thumb and your index and middle fingers, like a pencil.

If the fish is soft and boneless, you need not use the knife and can leave it on the table. Hold the fork in your right hand, prongs up. Leave the fork on your plate when finished, with prongs either up or down.

Fish bones are removed with the thumb and index finger and are placed on the side of the plate.

How to hold a fish knife.

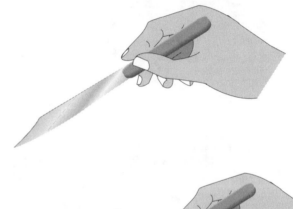

How to place the fish on the fork.

Sorbet: A Refreshing Pause

"Ices" have been served at meals at least as far back as the Roman Empire, when packed snow was brought down from the mountains to chill the palates of the rich and powerful. The emergence of "sorbetto" was not seen until the middle of the sixteenth century in Italy.

At one time, the sorbet was served between every course to clear the palate and prepare it for the next part of the meal. These days, however, it is served only between the fish and the meat or fowl courses.

Yes, you may eat the garnish, if you wish. Sorbet is sometimes served with mint leaves, fresh herbs, or flower petals.

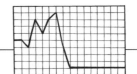

The Bottom Line

At the table, never give a fellow diner advice about table manners or criticize anything another person does or fails to do.

From the File Drawer

Pearl Mesta, "the hostess with the mostest," once demonstrated that good manners are more important than etiquette rules when a foreign visitor drank the water in his finger bowl. She immediately followed suit, so as not to embarrass the visitor, and others at the table then did likewise. This is a good example to remember when someone, particularly the host, does something unexpected at the table.

Cutting Meat and Fowl

You will use your knife during this course more than any other. However, you will use it more like a surgeon than a lumberjack. Place your index finger on the back of the blade about an inch down from the handle to help you press down firmly. With the fork in your left hand, prongs down, hold the meat firmly in place while you cut. Cut only enough food for the next mouthful. It is okay to put a small amount of potatoes and/or vegetables on the fork along with the meat.

Knives and forks are held this way.

When using the meat knife, place your index finger about an inch down the handle to help you press down firmly.

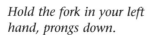

Hold the fork in your left hand, prongs down.

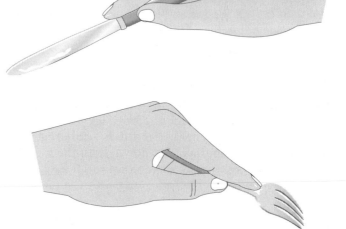

Salad Greens

As with the fish course, the salad course has its own knife and fork. If you don't need the knife, leave it on the table. If cheese is served with the salad, place a small portion of cheese on your salad plate, together with crackers or bread. Use the salad knife to put cheese on crackers or bread.

In some places, the salad is served before the entrée. The story goes that this change originated in California, where restaurateurs made the change to accommodate hungry, impatient diners who wanted some food when they sat down.

Dessert Cutlery

When dessert is served with both fork and spoon, the spoon is used for eating and the fork is used for pushing. Hold the fork in your left hand, prongs down, and push the dessert onto the spoon in your right hand. Pie and cake require only a fork. Ice cream and pudding require only a spoon. Leave the other utensils on the table.

Coffee Time

Coffee signals the end of the formal dinner, but that's no time to get careless. Following are some don'ts:

➤ Don't turn your coffee into a milkshake by adding excessive amounts of cream and sugar.

➤ Don't swirl too vigorously, banging the spoon against the cup and leaving a puddle in your saucer.

➤ Don't slurp. Sip silently.

➤ Don't blow on your coffee (or any beverage, ever) if it is too hot. Let it sit for a while.

➤ Don't leave your spoon in the cup; put it on the saucer. Don't put the spoon in your mouth.

Take your time. Coffee time is often the best time for conversation.

Continental vs. American Style

Both of these styles of handling cutlery are correct, whether you happen to be in the United States or abroad. What is important is to use one or the other consistently.

Some experts believe that what we now call the American style was used in Europe when the use of knives and forks first became popular during the early seventeenth century. Later, the upper classes in Europe began using what is now called the continental style, which gradually spread, but apparently not as far as the United States.

American Style

In the American style, the knife is used only for cutting. The fork is held in the left hand while holding down the object that is being cut. Then, the knife is put down on the edge of the plate (blade facing in), and the fork is transferred to the right hand to convey the food to the mouth. The prongs of the fork face upward while eating. Hands not in use are in the lap.

Memo to Myself

In either style, if you are left-handed, simply switch knife and fork, if that is more comfortable. However, when you finish, the knife should still be on the plate with the blade facing in.

Continental Style

In the continental style, there is no switching. The knife stays in the right hand and the fork in the left. After the food is cut, the knife is used to push it onto the fork. The prongs of the fork remain facing down, unless the food (peas, for example) requires a different tactic. The hands remain above the table from the wrist up through the entire process. Once again, both styles are correct. Choose one, and stick with it.

Be aware that in backwaters in this country, using the continental style could engender some unpleasant commentary.

The Ceremony of Tea

Say you want to have an informal, relaxed meeting later in the day, but without alcohol. Or, you want to fire someone gently, and you dread the prospect of a long lunch or dinner session. The answer could be tea.

Afternoon tea is served in England, without fail, at 4 P.M. My collaborator on this book, John Corr, recalls that, while covering the fighting in Northern Ireland, he and a British reporter learned of an IRA bombing in a town north of Belfast. John headed out for the scene, but the British journalist said he would be along later: It was 4:00, and he had to stop for tea.

The tradition of afternoon tea began with Anna, Duchess of Bedford, who lived in the late 1700s and early 1800s. At the time, the aristocracy ate two heavy meals. Breakfast was just after sunrise, and dinner was after sundown. The duchess got a bit peckish in the afternoon and began taking tidbits in her chambers. The idea spread and became formalized.

In the United States, hotels sometimes begin serving tea at 3:30 P.M. Tea consists of finger sandwiches, which are eaten first, followed by scones, miniature fruit tarts, and pastries. Cut the scones in half, and apply butter, jam, or Devonshire (or clotted) cream. The tarts and pastries are eaten with a fork because, though small, they are sticky.

Tea generally is served one pot per person with sugar, milk, and lemon. The usual tea choices are these:

➤ Darjeeling, the "champagne of teas," comes from the foothills of the Himalayas. It has a strong color and delicate flavor.

➤ Lapsang comes from south China and has a smoky, tarry taste.

➤ Earl Grey tea is a blend of Darjeeling and Chinese teas created for the Earl by the Chinese. It's usually taken with lemon.

➤ China Oolong has a delicate flavor, like ripe peaches, and is taken black or with lemon.

➤ Keemun has a delicate, light flavor.

➤ English Breakfast is a robust blend of Ceylon and Indian teas.

A drink growing in popularity here, particularly in cafes and coffee shops, is *chai,* which is the Hindi word for *tea.* This hot, milky tea is spiced with cloves, ginger, anise, vanilla, or other flavors and has long been popular in India and Nepal.

High Tea

No, high tea is not a more elegant version of afternoon tea. In fact, it is quite the opposite.

The tradition of high tea began in the late 1800s to provide a hearty meal for miners returning from a day of hard labor. It was called "high tea" because it was generally served on the mantle over the fireplace so that the miner could rid his body of the subterranean chill as he ate.

High tea is generally served between 5:30 and 7:30 P.M. and usually begins with meat or fish and treacle, a sort of molasses syrup food. Other traditional foods are roast chicken, baked ham, pork, poached salmon, hearty whole-grain breads, and Cornish pastries or meat pies.

Toasting

When well timed and well delivered, the toast can bring a festive air to a gathering and create a sense of community around the dining table.

The toast is proposed by the host at the beginning of a meal (particularly when welcoming an honored guest), during the meal, or during coffee and dessert at the end of the meal.

The toast should be brief and can be amusing but not flip. An excellent example is a toast proposed by President Kennedy during a dinner for Nobel Prize winners at the White House: "I think this is the most extraordinary collection of talent, of human knowledge, ever gathered at the White House, with the possible exception of when Thomas Jefferson dined here alone."

If you don't have something clever and brief in your quiver at the moment, you can't go wrong with something similar to these:

Welcoming: "I am so pleased that you all could be here to share each other's good company and this good food. Welcome."

Honoring: "I am so pleased that you could all be here to welcome my dear friend Elizabeth, who has come all the way from Paris to visit." (Often, it is advisable to add some of Elizabeth's sterling qualities as part of the toast.)

One-word toasts, such as the Danish *Skol* or the Spanish *Salud*, are generally accepted everywhere as symbols of welcome. It's a nice gesture to toast people in the native tongue, but be sure to get the pronunciation right.

Irish: Salante (SLANT-tay)

Yiddish: L'chaim (leh-KHY-yim)

German: Prosit (PRO-sit)

Japanese: Kanpai (kahn-PI)

Toasting Blunders

Go ahead and propose that toast, but here are some things to be careful about:

➤ If you are being toasted, don't even put your hand on your glass, much less drink.

➤ You don't need alcohol to toast—water will do. It's the thought that counts.

➤ Don't toast when you're toasted. People are most tempted to propose a toast after they've already had a few, and that's the worst possible time.

➤ Don't clink; it's bad news for the glassware.

➤ Don't read the toast. If it's too long to memorize easily, forget it.

➤ Be sincere, be upstanding, and be brief.

➤ Toast the host in return if you are the honored guest. You can do it immediately after the host's toast or wait until the end of the meal. Keep it short.

➤ Don't tap your glass to get attention.

➤ The host is the first one to toast. Don't pre-empt.

Memo to Myself

At a crowded banquet table, remember that your place setting is bounded by your water glass on the right and your bread dish on the left.

Toasting is a tradition that brings people together, and it is important to have the event go as smoothly as possible.

Entering the Banquet Hall

It's a fund-raising dinner, or a wedding reception, or an awards banquet, and the huge ballroom of the Ritz-Hyatt-Plaza is a sea of linen, glassware, candles, and confusion. The tables are too close together and are not nearly large enough for all the paraphernalia on their surfaces or the dressed-up people at their edges.

No wonder you approach the table, which doubtlessly includes people you don't know, with trepidation. But you can handle it. Just take it one step at a time.

Finding Your Seat

Find the table, and look for the place card with your name on it. Do not move place cards so that you can sit next to the alluring Miss Pinknee. If there are place cards, someone (maybe even someone at your table) went to a lot of trouble deciding about seating arrangements. These plans should not be arbitrarily superseded. It is an even more egregious breach of etiquette to move place cards at a private social occasion, and it will earn you poisonous looks from a host who gave a lot of thought to the seating arrangements.

Business Blunders

You can cause more trouble and resentment than you might think by fiddling with place cards and thereby altering seating arrangements.

Before you sit down, greet and shake hands with the others at your table, introducing yourself to those you don't know. This avoids shouted, across-table introductions later, which most people forget. If you want to distinguish yourself, take a short walk and shake hands with the others.

Enter the chair from the left side.

Men: It is neither sexist nor theatrical to hold the chair for the woman on your right.

Women: Accept the gesture with grace, but don't wait for it if it does not seem to be in the cards.

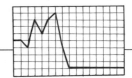

The Bottom Line

At a dinner party, a gentleman may hold the chair for the woman at his right, but a woman should not necessarily expect or wait for this to happen.

The Place Setting

At first glance, utter chaos lies before you. So much "stuff" lies in front of you that your principal problem is determining which belongs to you. Here's how to tell:

➤ Knives and spoons are on your right.

➤ Forks and napkins are on your left. The single exception is the cocktail fork, which will the be farthest right, if there is a seafood course.

➤ Glasses are on your right. (One way to remember is that DR means "drinks right.")

➤ Plates for solid foods, such as bread and salad, are on your left. The bread plate may have a butter spreader lying across it.

➤ There may be a dessert spoon and fork above your dinner plate.

If someone takes over your bread plate, don't retaliate by using someone else's. Put your bread on the rim of your dinner plate.

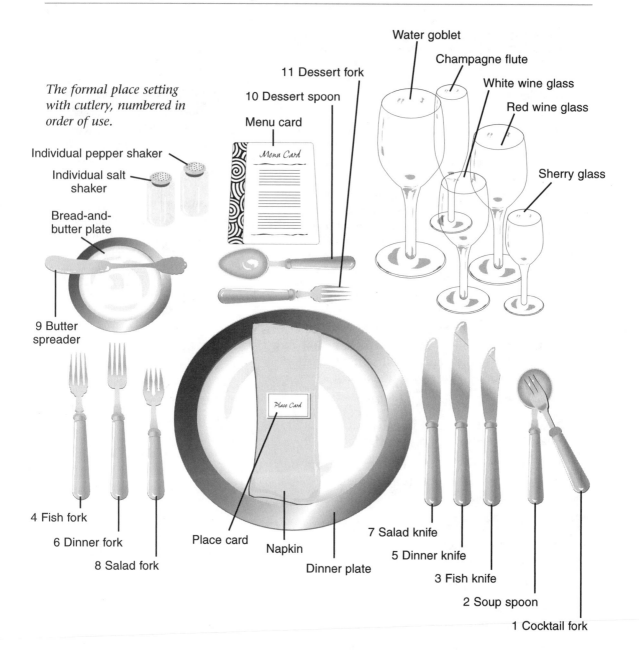

The formal place setting with cutlery, numbered in order of use.

Individual pepper shaker

Individual salt shaker

Bread-and-butter plate

9 Butter spreader

Water goblet

Champagne flute

White wine glass

Red wine glass

11 Dessert fork

10 Dessert spoon

Menu card

Menu Card

Sherry glass

4 Fish fork

6 Dinner fork

8 Salad fork

Place card

Napkin

Place Card

Dinner plate

7 Salad knife

5 Dinner knife

3 Fish knife

2 Soup spoon

1 Cocktail fork

Table Tactics

Because of the crowding, it is even more important to put nothing on the table, including your elbows. If you don't know what to do with your hands, put them in your lap. If you are encumbered with objects, put them under your chair. Remember the no-return rule for silverware: Once you have picked up a utensil, it never touches the tabletop again. Cutlery goes entirely on the plate, not leaned. The coffee or teaspoon goes on the saucer. Food is passed to the right. If you leave the table, it is especially important in these circumstances to push your chair back under the table.

The Buffet Table

Something primal and irrational happens to some ordinarily sensible and polite people when they see food on a buffet table. It's as if they think the food will somehow be taken away or consumed by others before they get any. A kind of panic seizes them, and it can be contagious. The result can be people bumping into each other, racing around and between others, and overloading their plates. You, of course, are above all of that.

Scope It Out

Check out the scene before you even approach the table. Are the plates and utensils on the dining tables or on the buffet table? Are there place cards on the dining table? If so, you may want to leave something you are carrying at the table before getting your food. Check whether there are one or two lines at the buffet table. If two, notice whether there are plates and utensils on both sides. When you get into line, remember that there are no male/female preferences, but it is polite not to break up a couple or a group going through the line together.

Serve Yourself

Here are some things to remember when you approach the buffet dining situation:

➤ Don't overload your dish. You can always go back for more. In fact, you may wish to start with soup and/or salad, return for the entrée, and return again for dessert or fruit.

➤ Don't bring back food "for the table." Let others make their own decisions and mistakes.

➤ If an item seems to be in short supply, it is gracious—particularly at someone's home—to go easy or skip it altogether. If at a restaurant or hotel, it is okay to ask a server or busser to replenish a particular item.

➤ Use only the serving spoon or fork intended for each dish, and leave it beside—not in—the dish. A spoon left in the dish can heat up enough to burn the fingers of another diner.

203

At a serving station, don't ask the attendant for things not easily provided. For example, don't ask for end cuts of beef if you can see there are none left. Don't ask for "over easy" if you can see there are no whole eggs in sight. Don't ask for omelet ingredients if you can see they are not readily available.

Fresh Plates, Please

You should not have to reuse your plate or utensils during a buffet meal at a restaurant or hotel. If you don't see replacements, ask the server or busser to replenish the supply. At a private party, use your head and reuse your plate if it seems advisable.

In either circumstance, do not scrape or stack plates. It's fussy, annoying, and generally unappreciated.

Where to Stand or Sit

If someone invites you to share a table, you should accept unless you have been assigned a seat: "Sorry, but they've got me seated over there."

Also decline if you've been asked previously: "Sorry, but I promised Tom and Jerry I'd sit with them."

People will be coming and going, so don't stand up when someone joins your table or leaves it.

It is even more important not to overload your plate if you will be eating standing up, as at a cocktail party. Move away from the buffet table and take up a position that is out of the obvious traffic lanes and that does not block access to doors or anything else.

Don't let all the dining rules, guidelines, and strategies in this chapter obscure one basic and very important fact: Sharing food with others can be one of life's real and enduring pleasures. However formal the dining occasion, try to approach it with the expectation that it will be pleasant and interesting and even memorable. And, remember, at mealtime, the best sauce is conversation.

The Least You Need to Know

➤ The more formal the dinner, the more (safely) predictable it is apt to be.

➤ Use utensils from the outside in, and remember that your bread plate is on the left and your glasses are on the right.

➤ The formal dinner generally consists of seven courses.

➤ The American and continental styles of dining are equally correct, so choose one and stick with it.

➤ At the banquet, what is yours is what is between the bread plate on the left and the glasses on the right.

Entertaining

Your business instincts tell you it's time to invite some colleagues to a party at your house. But there are problems. The house is a mess. Besides, it's too small. And you don't have enough dishes or even chairs. You don't know what to serve, and even if you did, you probably would burn everything. Besides, you don't have the time. Besides .... These are the symptoms of a typical case of host heebie-jeebies. The best cure is to recall a really great party you have attended and then ask yourself what made it really great.

Chances are, what sticks out was that you were warmly welcomed and felt at home, that the atmosphere was relaxed and cheerful, and the conversation flowed freely. Chances are, you did not leave that great party thinking about whether the china was chipped or the dip was too tangy. So, take heart. You can do it. Here's how.

Start Small

The primary truth is that everything must be neat and clean—all else can be forgiven or easily handled. The best way of dealing with the host heebie-jeebies is actually to give a party. Start small. Try inviting a few friends and neighbors for an after-dinner dessert party. Have plenty of coffee and other drinks, and pick up some things at a good local pastry shop.

Remind yourself of these points:

➤ Giving a successful party does not depend on how much furniture you have or how much money you spend.

➤ People who are worth impressing are not impressed by expensive appointments.

➤ Sophisticated people never boast about what they have and never apologize for what they do not have.

On to Bigger Things

After having had experience hosting smaller gatherings, you can go on to bigger things with more confidence. You don't try running a marathon before trying a few 5K runs.

Memo to Myself

Use candles only at evening meals. Place them in the center of the table or elsewhere, as long as the arrangement is visually appealing and the candles are not in the guests' sightlines.

Improvising Equipment

No party was ever lost for lack of a silver chafing dish. Friends and relatives can supply you with any missing necessities, and you can improvise in ways that will make the party more fun. For example, a man I know puts a big, galvanized-metal washtub in the middle of his large kitchen, fills it with ice, and puts the beer, soft drinks, and wine bottles in it. People tend to gather around it like a campfire.

And do you really believe that friends and colleagues will think less of you if your spoons are not monogrammed or your furniture is not tastefully antique?

Help!

You can probably handle the hosting duties alone. However, if you have strong doubts, why not hook up with a friend or two and jointly host the party? Or, you may want to assign a friend to act as a co-host during the party. One of you can work the back of the house, making sure food and drinks flow efficiently, while the other works the front of the house, greeting people, keeping the conversation flowing, and so forth.

Can't Cook?

Caterers, local restaurants, or the neighborhood deli can supply complete meals or sandwiches with all the trimmings. Or, you can have guests bring dishes. This tactic has the added advantage of making your guests feel that they have a vested interest in the party. (This works well with office friends, but not with clients or the boss.) And there is now a plethora of gourmet take-out shops you can exploit. A good trick is to bring your own serving dishes to the shops to be filled.

Or, you can surprise yourself and prepare the food on your own. You don't need to be Julia Child or Martha Stewart, and you don't need a great culinary repertoire. I have a friend who has only two dishes in her bag of tricks: a fish dish and a chicken dish. These form the centerpiece for her parties, and she fills in with prepared side dishes and desserts.

Your main course can be just a casserole accompanied by a salad: Baked ham is another easy one. Roasts, however, are not a good idea because they depend on precise timing and are just something else to worry about.

If you are planning to serve something exotic or unusually spicy, check with your guests when you invite them. If everyone except Uncle Henry likes the idea, you can have a simple alternative for him.

Memo to Myself

As a guest, it is your responsibility to tip off your host if you require vegetarian or kosher meals, or if you have food allergies or any other special dietary needs.

Balance is important when planning your menu. If the main course is light, a heftier dessert works well, and vice versa. But *do* serve dessert. Even the diet-conscious feel that they can enthusiastically welcome dessert when it is served at someone else's house.

Cocktail Hour

If you will have a cocktail hour before eating, make sure it lasts no longer than that. In fact, shorter is even better. The drinks period should last just long enough for people to settle down and become accustomed to the group. You are not doing anyone a favor—particularly yourself—by letting the booze flow too freely. And, if the pre-dinner drinks period lasts too long, people may have that second or third drink just because they are hungry.

When dinner is ready, announce it clearly and with authority.

Remember that people are using less alcohol and caffeine these days, so have non-alcoholic and decaffeinated drinks available as well.

Conversation Igniters

What will people talk about? This is something that probably will take care of itself. You can help by preparing a mental list of topics to bring up if the assembly begins to resemble C-Span. Even better, supply some conversation-starters when you introduce people.

> "Clara just wrote a book about how computers drive people nuts and what you can do about it."

> "Mark is a writer, so be careful—you might end up in his next book."

> "Gil is a detective and has some wonderful stupid-crook stories."

Infallible Seating Plans

Consider these time-tested tips when making decisions about where people will sit:

➤ Try to pair up a talker and a listener. Consider this when placing people across from one another as well as beside one another.

➤ Don't seat spouses or couples together.

➤ Try to seat each guest near at least one familiar person.

If you want to follow the old rule about not having persons of the same sex sitting next to each other, here is how the table might look at a party for four, eight, or twelve persons:

The host is seated at the head of the table, and the guest of honor of the same sex is seated opposite. The guest of honor of the opposite sex sits to the right of the host. This effectively separates the sexes. I personally consider this old separation rule of little importance when drawing up a sitting plan.

Business Blunders

As a guest, never assume that an invitation means that you can bring along a guest.

Hosting a Buffet

The buffet offers many advantages over the sit-down dinner party. For starters, it is easier to prepare, and much of it can be done in advance. The buffet also can reasonably consist of just a main course and dessert.

The buffet also creates more opportunity for people to move around and mingle, and it accommodates stragglers more easily.

Place your table where people can get to it and away from it easily. For a large crowd, you may want to set up two tables or one long table that can be approached from both sides.

Avoid placing dessert on the table at the same time as the main course. Unfortunately, people tend to combine the two on their plates, which can make things messy. Use two tables, or clear the main course before bringing out the dessert.

Guests should remember that they are guests in a private home, not at an all-you-can-eat cafeteria. If something seems in short supply, go easy. Compliment the host. Don't scrape and stack dishes to "help out"—it's annoying.

Glitches

Accidents happen. There will be last-minute cancellations and additions. Somebody—perhaps you—will drop something or spill something. These things will not ruin your party, though; they may, in fact, enliven it. Minor disasters have a way of becoming amusing anecdotes and topics of conversation.

The only way an accident can have a negative effect on your party is if you let your guests know that it has upset you.

Guest List Do's and Don'ts

Keep a couple lists handy when you are deciding who to invite.

Guest List Do's

Invite people whom you know will appreciate the invitation and will make an effort to help make the party successful.

Invite people who don't know each other but will probably enjoy meeting one another.

Invite old friends who never seem to have enough time to get together.

Guest List Don'ts

Don't invite people you know have an adversarial relationship on the theory that they will make the party livelier. They may make it livelier than you would like. Even if nothing untoward happens, their presence can create an atmosphere of tension.

Don't invite just one type of person. A room full of nothing but doctors or school teachers can be deadly.

Don't invite someone you know won't fit just because you "owe" that person an invitation.

Think about your motives for having the party before you start putting together your guest list. Do the motives include

➤ To score points with your boss or your clients?

➤ To get to know new colleagues or neighbors?

➤ To honor someone?

➤ To pay back for invitations you have received, or to say thanks to people who have helped you?

➤ To rekindle or reaffirm friendships?

Once you have fully recognized the reasons for hosting your party, you will be able to think more clearly about other aspects.

Memo to Myself

Don't be afraid to tell friends that you are giving a party and not inviting them. Tell them the reasons for the party, and explain that they probably would not have a good time or feel comfortable with the crowd you have invited.

An Interesting Mix

When compiling your guest list, think in terms of people who will "sing for their supper." By that, I mean people with personality and people who like to talk, even if it's only about themselves. You want some guests who can be depended upon to be positive and cheerful and who love conversation.

Here is our personal formula for making up a guest list. We always try to include these types:

➤ Somebody involved with politics

➤ A journalist, because they ask great questions

➤ A restaurateur, because everybody is interested in food and how restaurants "really" work

➤ A banker, because they know something about a lot of industries and can talk about what's happening with the economy

➤ Someone in marketing, because they can talk about trends, popular culture, and what people are buying and why

Gone, thank goodness, are the days when hosts had to be sure to invite an equal number of men and women. It's a bother, it can cause you to invite someone you really don't want, and it tends to make people feel they have been "assigned" to someone. You can think about having a reasonable balance, but it's always a bad idea to try to match people up.

Handling Gatecrashers

The unexpected guest. The last minute addition. Generally, the best policy is to accept this as cheerfully and as gracefully as you can. However, in some circumstances it is necessary to refuse to accept the unexpected guest.

You can't produce another place setting if you don't have one or there is no room. You can't fabricate a seventh Cornish game hen. And, it may be that the presence of this extra person will have a decidedly negative effect on the party.

Deliver the refusal with as much grace and good humor as possible. You can say something like, "The way things are arranged, I just don't have room to accommodate another guest. I wish I had known in advance."

You can then say something vague about including the person in future gatherings.

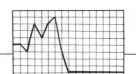

The Bottom Line

Yes, you may refuse to accept last-minute additions to the guest list. Welcome the person, if you possibly can. If you can't, explain pleasantly and graciously, but don't apologize.

Inviting Your Guests

If your party is coming up soon and the guest list is not long, you might want to invite guests by telephone. Be prepared to give all the details concisely if your call is answered by voice mail or an answering machine. Ask for a prompt return call.

The invitation should be cheerful and welcoming and should convey the idea that this is to be a happy occasion. You don't need engraved stationery. If you write a personal note, make it upbeat and friendly.

Be sure to include all the vital information: what, where, when, and why (or for whom). If necessary, supply directions and/or a map. Also give some clue about how to dress. If the guest is someone you don't know well, it is a good idea to give that person an idea of who the other guests will be. If you have no problem with the invitee bringing a friend, say so verbally or on the invitation.

You Don't Have to Do It All

Don't feel guilty or self-conscious about hiring help for your party. Sometimes this is the only way for you to get things done and still have time to be with your guests, to relax and enjoy the party with them.

And, in business, you want to be perceived as a host, not a server and short-order cook.

A convenient rule of thumb is to hire one person to help you if you are entertaining more than six people for dinner. This could be a friend's college-age child or, even

Business Blunders

Never criticize the hired help in front of guests. If you can, wait until the party is over and then direct your remarks to the supervisor or the manager of the catering firm.

better, your own children. They know where things are and will be more relaxed in familiar surroundings. Be sure to pay them fairly.

If these alternatives are not available to you, you may have to engage an agency. You either pay the agency, which pays the workers, or you pay the workers, who give a commission to the agency. In either case, it is not necessary to tip the workers, although I usually do.

Keep these tips in mind:

➤ If you don't pay in advance, make sure before the party starts that terms are clear. You don't want to be bickering with workers at the end of a party.

➤ Accidents happen. Do not attempt to take the cost of broken objects out of anyone's wages. Deal with an agency whose workers are bonded and insured. If something is broken or stolen—and you can prove it—the insurance company will pay to replace it.

➤ It's a good idea to book the help before you invite guests, and make sure the workers show up well in advance of the guests.

➤ Specify how you want the workers to dress. Generally, a woman should wear a black or white dress, or a black skirt with a white shirt and apron. Dark pants are also acceptable. Hair should be pulled back from the face. Men should wear black pants and a white shirt with a necktie.

➤ The people you hire should take coats, make drinks, serve appetizers and dinner, clear the table, and clean up the kitchen.

When you have hired help, remember that you are the boss and that you have a right to insist on the level of service you are paying for.

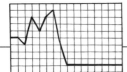

The Bottom Line

You don't have to serve the wine that a guest brings to a dinner party. If someone brings cut flowers, however, you must find a vase for them, although it is annoying.

Wine Protocol

Even if you know your wines, it doesn't hurt to ask the opinion of a knowledgeable liquor store owner or a restaurateur. Tell them your menu and say that you want moderately priced selections. You don't need to be extravagant, but you need to be generous and make sure there is enough. If you are serving wine only, and if your party is to be a longish one, figure on one bottle per person, to be on the safe side. If wine is being served only during the meal, figure a half-bottle per person.

Open red wine about a half-hour before serving to allow the bouquet to develop. Chill white wines about two hours before serving.

As the meal begins, the host can walk around the table to fill the wine glasses for his guests, if there is no waiter/server. At an informal party, the host can fill the glass of the guests next to him and ask them to pass the glasses down. Guests should not help themselves or ask for more wine. Of course, the host may pass the bottle and say, "Please help yourself."

Don't wrap the bottle in a napkin to pour. Glasses should be filled about halfway. At most parties, white and red wines are served in similar-size glasses. Otherwise, the small glass is for white wine and the larger one is for red.

Have some sparkling water or lemon-lime drink on hand as well; nondrinkers find it festive.

If, as a guest, you bring wine, say, "Here's something for you to enjoy later, with your feet up," so that the host knows you do not expect the wine to be served then. Send flowers early in the day of the party or on the day after.

Memo to Myself

If you need to chill white wine quickly, put it in a tub with ice cubes and water up to the neck. This is much more effective and safer than putting the wine in a freezer.

Private Club Decorum

Say the boss invites you to have lunch or a drink at his club. Or, you decide it would be a good career move to join a club. (Make sure you have a strong sponsor; you don't want to chance being rejected.) In either case, you should know a few things about club etiquette.

From the File Drawer

Certain cities, such as Philadelphia, have many old-line private clubs and even what I like to think of as "the club culture." These clubs have their own sets of etiquette rules. They may vary from club to club, but some rules are shared by all. For example, one club may forbid using cash, and another may have rigid dress codes.

In a social club, doing business is forbidden by tradition and/or the fact that the club enjoys tax benefits as a strictly social institution. So, you may invite a client for lunch, but you are not supposed to discuss business, although you probably will. If you do, be discreet. If you take out a notebook or checkbook, you may be asked by a server or a club steward to put it away. The by-laws of some clubs forbid companies from paying dues for members. The members must pay them personally.

As a guest in a private club, make sure you know the rules, including the dress code. Many clubs require jackets and ties for men in the dining room. In general, conservative dress is the norm—that means no skin-baring attire for women. Evening activities usually call for traditional business attire, unless the event is designated as black-tie.

Don't roam around. If your host hasn't arrived to meet you, the doorman will direct you to the lobby or a waiting area. You can ask for a tour later. Members love to talk about the memorabilia and traditions of their club.

Be sure to find out about the club's tipping policy before you go. Some clubs forbid tipping altogether, and an employee can be fired for accepting a tip. However, it is perfectly acceptable to send a check to the club's holiday fund as a gesture of appreciation for excellent service.

If you are a guest, it is inappropriate for you to attempt to pick up the tab. In fact, many clubs accept no cash at all. Everything, including meals and drinks, is charged to the member's account.

In some clubs, paintings, vases, statuary, and other objects may be of museum quality and should be treated accordingly.

The Least You Need to Know

➤ Beginning hosts should start small and keep it simple.

➤ An elaborate menu is not a requirement for a successful party; what is easiest often works out best.

➤ Invite a good mix of people who like to mingle.

➤ Hire help if you need it; hosts should not spend all their time in the kitchen.

➤ Elaborate menus and overly expensive wines are often unnecessary and unappreciated.

➤ The cocktail period should not be longer than an hour—and preferably should be shorter.

Part 5

Beyond the Office

Yes, there is life outside the office. And, yes, you can be gracious and charming even while gasping and perspiring at the gym or humming along at 30,000 feet in the air.

Business people are traveling more than ever these days, and this part of the book deals with the kind of behavior that makes the journey more pleasant and comfortable for you and your fellow travelers.

This next section also deals with proper behavior for when you arrive at a foreign destination (and when folks from far-away places come to your world or your place of business). In addition, Chapter 19, "The Global Stew," addresses how to deal with cultural diversity and the diverse need and expectations of the disabled in the workplace.

And, just as travel should not lead you down the road to disapproval from your colleagues or your boss, so sports and fitness should not strain your relationships. To help in the recreational arena, we will look at the rules of etiquette on the links, the slopes, and the tennis and racquetball courts.

This part of the book concludes with information on appropriate behavior in certain social situations. We'll cover the most familiar social settings, including weddings, baptisms, bar mitzvahs, funerals, graduations, and other ceremonious occasions, both religious and secular.

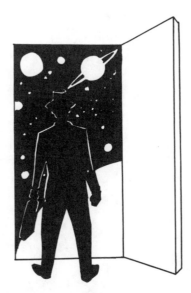

Chapter 18

Travel

In This Chapter

➤ Observing the rules of the road

➤ Learning about language, customs, and money

➤ Hints for the solitary woman traveler

➤ Hotels: luxury, commercial, and other

➤ The etiquette of planes, trains, and ships

A travel editor friend who works for a large daily newspaper has constructed a profile of what he calls "the good traveler." The good traveler, he says, seems to have delightfully serendipitous adventures on his journeys. He or she meets the most intriguing people and somehow gets the most accommodating and cheerful service everywhere, from airports to hotels. The good traveler on business also seems to get more done, makes more friendly contacts, and returns feeling rejuvenated rather than exhausted.

There are two reasons for all this, says my friend, who spends half his life on the road taking notes, interviewing, and writing.

The first reason is that the good traveler begins each journey armed with a positive attitude, a conviction that the trip will be a terrific experience. He adopts a willingness to be open to new situations, new ideas, and new people. The good traveler does not expect to find things as comfortably familiar as they are at home.

The second reason is that the good traveler has a firm grasp of the "rules of the road." We'll explore these rules in this chapter.

Anticipation Is Half the Fun

Some people believe that the most important part of any journey is what happens (and what doesn't happen) before you leave home. After you look at the tour guides, pour over maps, and daydream about possible adventures and stimulating encounters, it's time to sit down and draw up your list of things to do and what to pack. Even the most experienced traveler needs such a list, if only for the peace of mind inherent in the act of checking off items as you deal with them.

Memo to Myself

Check whether your homeowner's policy covers items lost while traveling. Also consider trip cancellation insurance, and find out whether your credit card provides travel insurance.

Travel Agents

A travel agent may or may not come up with the best airline price package. Also check the Internet. It is possible to survey the field and book a flight just by pushing some buttons. If you don't have a personal computer at home, go online at the local library.

Travel agents can save you a lot of time and effort by not only booking flights, but by also arranging things such as car rentals, chauffeur services, tour guides, theater tickets, and even meal reservations. Some agents specialize in handling cruises, hiking trips, or other special interest packages. Find out which travel agents specialize in fields that interest you. (Ask friends who have interests similar to yours.) Be advised that some travel agents charge fees for some of their services—ask first.

Can You Close Your Suitcase?

Rule of thumb: Less is better. Remember that you may not need to bring every file and every document. There's scanning. There's fax. There's e-mail.

An overabundance of luggage looks ostentatious and will probably make your trip unnecessarily complicated or burdensome. Some people pack as if every necessity of life must come out of a suitcase and as if every possible situation must have its own separate wardrobe. Unless you are going someplace remote and primitive, you will be able to buy some small things if you find you need them.

When deciding on what you will wear during your trip, keep a few things in mind:

➤ You must dress as well for a business meeting in another city as in your own town.

➤ Many, if not all of the people you will meet on the road will be strangers, and the only way they have of judging you is by your appearance. The fact that you may have to spend long periods in the same clothes (or in the same cramped airplane seat) does not mean that your clothing has to look sloppy or grungy.

Close quarters demands scrupulous cleanliness. Make allowance for the fact that you may have to clean up and tidy up in unusual circumstances.

➤ Make allowances for the weather conditions and other circumstances you are apt to encounter.

Have identification labels inside as well as outside each piece of luggage. Outside labels can be ripped off in transit.

Itineraries Are Important

If you don't have an itinerary from your travel agent or assistant, it's a good idea to draw one up with dates and telephone numbers. Bring a copy with you, and leave one at the office and another at home in case of emergencies.

Money Sense

Be realistic about how much money you will need to take along. If you are going to another country, try to have a little of the currency of your destination in case you incur small expenses such as taxis and tips before you have a chance to exchange currencies. Airport exchange windows tend to be more expensive than hotels and banks, and hotels are more expensive than banks. Carry a small exchange chart with you for instant reference. Confusion and/or bickering over exchange rates can be annoying not only to you, but also to those around you.

Your financial calculations should include out-of-pocket business expenses as well as things such as tips, admission charges, recreation, and other activities. For example, tips during a stay at a luxury hotel could add 25 percent to your final tab simply because more people are providing more services. Write everything down, even small tips. It will help later with your expense account report.

Limit the amount of cash you carry at any one time. Use traveler's checks.

Before you leave, make sure that you can use your ATM card to get cash in the local currency during your travels.

Documents You Will Need

Find out about passports and visas at least six weeks in advance—it could take that long to get either. To get a passport, you need an old passport, a birth certificate, or a baptismal certificate. You also need two identical passport photos. If you are traveling as a family, every family member needs a passport. If your town does not have a passport office, check at the courthouse or the post office. Check with a travel agent or airline ticket agent about whether you need a visa.

If possible, get an international driver's license. In any case, carry your American driver's license with you.

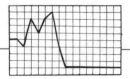

The Bottom Line

The Emergency Center at the State Department (call 202-647-4000) can give you current information about health and security problems for virtually any destination.

Make sure you have your medical and eyeglass prescriptions with you, as well as a record of required inoculations. Some inoculations are mandatory; some are merely recommended. Consider carefully the idea of getting recommended shots. I was not required to get a recommended typhoid shot before going to Egypt, so I didn't—to my later profound regret.

If you are to attend an official function, bring some documentation of it. For example, I was to attend an international banking conference in London and arrived to find that my luggage was lost. I explained the situation and showed my documentation, and the airline gave me a voucher and sent me off to Harrod's to purchase dress suitable for the occasion.

Strictly Business

If you are going overseas on business, your first stop should be the library or book store. Good general guides include *Multicultural Manners*, by Narine Dresser, published by John Wiley & Sons, 1996; and *Do's and Taboos Around the World*, by Robert Axtell, Wiley, 1993.

You can contact the country's consulate in the largest city near to you, or its embassy in Washington, D.C. The Commerce Department Trade Information Center in Washington, D.C., also has a great deal of information on international business matters. The State Department has background notes on each country as well as more detailed "Post Reports."

You might also want to check the Internet for additional sources.

Overcoming Language Barriers

Learn some words and phrases in the language of the country, things like hello, goodbye, I'm sorry, please, happy to meet you, thank you, and no thank you. You may want to have one side of your business card printed in that language.

If you are using an interpreter, make sure he knows the purpose of the meeting and the nature of your business. Look at the person you are addressing, not the interpreter. Stay away from jargon and jokes. Speak clearly and use short sentences.

How to Behave In Other Countries

First of all, find out what the climate will be like and what is considered proper dress. Remember that, in many Scandinavian and Western European countries, black-tie events are more common than in the United States. Also Remember that white is a symbol of mourning in the Far East.

➤ Think before expressing opinions. Stay away from talking about local politics and religious customs as much as possible.

➤ Be punctual, even if you suspect that others will be late.

➤ Avoid scheduling breakfast meetings or night meetings.

➤ Never lecture people in their own country about smoking or complain about smoke.

➤ Be able to talk in terms of that country's currency and measurements, not just in terms of American dollars and American nonmetric measures.

➤ Be prepared to remove your shoes when entering mosques and temples and, in some places, people's homes.

➤ Bring your good stationery, and write lots of thank-you notes.

Always remember that you are a guest in a foreign country.

Women Travelers: On Your Own

Before discussing accommodations and modes of travel, it's important to deal with the topic of women traveling alone, particularly on business trips. In these instances, special considerations must be addressed with regard to safety and companionship.

Although traveling alone in the United States involves some difficulties for a woman, going abroad may be much more complex. Before going to another culture, it is a good idea to get a cultural perspective on the area. For example, while in Cairo, I spent a lot time dining alone in my room while my husband was away. A woman dining by herself there was thought to be less than morally upstanding, and it could lead to some unpleasantness.

Even in the United States, however, there can be problems. A good general rule when talking to strangers—especially men—is to pay your own way, even though you may be invited for drinks or a meal. Make sure that everyone understands that, if you accept an invitation to dinner, it doesn't mean that you will be the dessert.

But don't be afraid to talk with strangers; they might become the most interesting part of your trip. If you begin to feel that the conversation is going in a direction you are not comfortable with, you can communicate the fact that you are not interested in getting to know someone better simply by giving one-word answers, nodding vaguely, or saying that you need to go somewhere or do something.

Memo to Myself

Sometimes your plane or train neighbor will want to chat, and you won't. What do you say? "I wish I had time to talk, but I've got to catch up on my work (or reading, or sleep)."

For men, if a woman wishes to pay for her own meal or drinks, do not insist on treating. It is oafish, stupid, and frustrating. If she doesn't look at you, if she gives you brusque, one-word answers, or if she looks deliberately distracted, disappear.

A woman dining alone doesn't have to be in Egypt to be aware of disadvantages when it comes to service and general hospitality because women are thought to eat less, drink less, and tip less than men.

This is less of a problem when you dine early, say 6:00 or 6:30 PM. Call for a reservation, and tip the maitre d' (see Chapter 15, "Dining for Dollars"). You will get better service if you appear to know what you're doing. Don't hesitate to complain to the manager if you think service is not up to standard, but do so quietly and with no emotion in your voice.

When you are planning activities or responding to invitations, consider the following:

➤ If you are having a drink alone in the bar, sit at a table instead of at the bar, and have a briefcase, a file, or some other diversion so that it doesn't look as if you are waiting for someone to pick you up.

➤ If you agree to have dinner with a man you don't know, eat in the hotel dining room, and arrange in advance to have the meal charged to your room so that there is no ambiguity about the nature of the date.

➤ Women alone should stay at hotels rather than motels.

➤ When traveling on business and staying at a hotel, you may want to let the receptionist know that you are traveling alone. If the reception clerk calls out your room number to the bellman, tell the clerk to give you another room and to be quiet about it.

➤ You might want to have a travel agent find out which hotels are known for safe procedures when it comes to women traveling alone. Double-lock doors and windows are mandatory, not optional.

➤ Make sure the bellman checks all spaces in your room to be sure there is no one there. Check the window locks, and make sure there is no other access to your room.

➤ Never enter your room if you have the slightest suspicion that something has been tampered with. Call security, and have them check it out.

➤ Never admit anyone to your room that you haven't invited or requested through the front desk. If anyone else comes to your door for any reason, check with the front desk before you open the door. For more, see the "Security" section in this chapter.

Yes, it is unfair and annoying that, even in these so-called enlightened times, women must be concerned about travel situations. But all of us must deal with the realities of life. Hopefully the information in this section will make your next trip more comfortable and more secure.

Accommodations

Hotels, motels, and bed and breakfasts all have their advantages, and appropriate behavior in one may be out of place in another. When traveling on business, of course, the first consideration is efficiency and convenience for the working traveler. However, this may not be the only consideration. Another is the company's travel budget and policies.

Memo to Myself

On a business trip, order breakfast from room service. The waiter can set up the meal while you are shaving or otherwise occupied. If a tip is not included on the bill, give the waiter 20 percent.

Most business travelers stay at hotels, and these can be so much more than just places to sleep. In fact, they may be the most interesting nonbusiness aspect of the trip. Hotels can range from elegant establishments with fine service to little more than a bed, a bathroom, and a television set. Generally, they fall into two types: luxury hotels, and commercial hotels of the Hyatt and Marriott type. It is important to know what to expect from each—and what they expect from you.

Luxury Hotels

It's a good idea to book a room at a luxury hotel well in advance. You can count on things such as robes and hair dryers in the bathroom and a mini-bar in the bedroom or sitting room. (Beware of mini-bars, by the way—they can be astonishingly expensive.)

When you arrive, you will be greeted by the doorman, and a porter will take your bags. Tip the porter $1 a bag or more. If the doorman hails a cab for you, tip him $1. If the service involves a lot of time or standing out in the rain, you might want to tip him more. Maids get tipped $2 or $3 a night, left on the pillow or next to the sink. The concierge should get $5 if particularly helpful, and the parking valet gets $2 to $5 for bringing the car around.

At the reception desk, give your name and confirmation number. Couples, married or not, should sign in with both their names. If a married woman uses her maiden name in business, she should include that in registering so that telephone calls can be forwarded accurately.

A porter either will accompany you to your room with the bags or will bring them later. The porter or a bellman will open the door, turn on the lights, adjust the air conditioning, put the luggage on stands, and show you how the mini-bar and television work. If you don't like the room, tell the porter to call the front desk to arrange for another.

The next thing you should do, whatever sort of hotel or motel you are in, is to check out the emergency and fire exits.

Also see if you will need more towels, pillows, blankets, hangers, or an iron. It's best to take care of these things now rather than late at night, when there might be a reduced staff on duty.

From the File Drawer

Luxury hotels and some commercial hotels have a concierge desk, generally near the reception. Here you can obtain theater, concert, and sports tickets; have a look at local restaurant menus; and make dining reservations. You can also find out about car rentals, sightseeing tours, baby-sitters, and traffic and weather conditions. The concierge can do things such as set up a surprise birthday in your room, get you into popular nightspots, or customize a day-trip of local attractions.

Business Blunders

Don't assume that you can steal towels, bathrobes, or other items from hotels. It could lead to embarrassment, and you may find yourself billed for them. If you want a souvenir, visit the hotel gift shop.

Commercial Hotels

Commercial hotels are designed for the business traveler. They are clean, comfortable, efficient, and cheaper than luxury hotels—often considerably cheaper. Available for business travelers are computers, fax machines, copiers, secretarial services, and conference rooms. Most business people I talk with suggest that you avoid doing business in your hotel room. For one thing, you don't want an invitation to your room to be taken as anything other than an invitation to work. Also, such a venue might encourage more familiarity than you might consider appropriate.)

Bring your own travel iron and hair drier. The hotel may be able to supply these items, but you might not be able to borrow them exactly when you need them. You can't afford to be late for a meeting because you were waiting for housekeeping to deliver an iron.

Security

Remember these common sense tips about safety on the road:

➤ Never leave cash or valuables in the room—use the safe at the front desk. An in-room safe is not safe unless it allows you, not the hotel, to set the combination.

➤ Double-lock the door.

➤ Do not open the door when somebody knocks unless the person identifies himself. If it's not someone you know, check with the front desk and/or security before opening the door.

➤ Don't flash a wad of bills in the hotel lobby or bar.

➤ The safest rooms are near the elevator because there is more traffic.

➤ The safest floors are between the fifth and eighth floors. Lower floors have more break-ins, and higher floors may be beyond the reach of the local fire department's ladders.

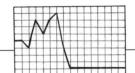

The Bottom Line

Check by telephone with the front desk before you open your hotel door to someone claiming to be hotel staff or security.

Finally, the best security devices are still caution and common sense. Keep your security antenna plugged in while traveling.

Planes, Ships, Cars, and Trains

"The good traveler" has good manners en route, which may not be as easy as it sounds. You may find yourself in crowds of strangers who may be tired, edgy, and frustrated. You may be all or any of the above yourself. Recognize that there will be problems over which you have no control. Stay relaxed—getting there can still be half the fun, in spite of it all.

At the Airport

In some ways, entering the airport is like visiting a different culture, even a different planet. Here are some ideas for making the visit less stressful:

➤ Know where your metal objects are. It is annoying to have security go through an entire suitcase to find a little silver mirror that could have been placed in a pocket or a purse.

➤ If you are carrying anything unusual, let security know up front.

➤ Avoid the "bag lady" look. Don't show up with plastic bags on both arms containing newspapers, souvenirs, and snacks.

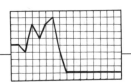

The Bottom Line

It's smart to read the back of your airline ticket. You will learn things such as how much liability the carrier accepts for lost articles and policies regarding to what degree seat reservations will be honored.

Business Blunders

Never leave your luggage alone at the airport; somebody might be looking for a place to stash contraband.

➤ Make sure ID tags are secure—air travel is hard on luggage. A garment/wardrobe bag counts as one of your two carry-on bags. Keep an eye on your bags. Somebody could steal one or add something illegal. Also be careful about agreeing to watch another person's luggage. You don't know what's inside, and you may have to move on before the person returns. Pack medicine, toiletries, pajamas, cash, jewelry, and a change of clothing in your carry-on bags. Luggage does get lost.

➤ Porters are tipped $1 per bag. If no porter is available, look for a cart. To take advantage of curbside check-in, have your ticket and photo ID in hand.

We are often tired or stressed while in the airport. Acknowledge this, and look for ways to avoid further fatigue and stress.

Boarding Passes, Please

If the airport is a strange environment, the inside of an airplane is even more alien.

➤ Remove your coat before boarding so that you can clear the aisle as quickly as possible.

➤ Reserve an aisle seat if you have long legs or expect to be up and down a lot.

➤ Reserve a window seat if you expect to sleep, so that people won't be climbing over you. No matter how experienced you are, wait until after the emergency instructions are given before putting earplugs or blindfold in place.

➤ Bring some cash for onboard purchases such as drinks and earphones.

➤ Don't waste the time of flight attendants with chitchat or trivial errands. But, certainly, push the call button if you need a glass of water and don't want to crawl over sleeping passengers.

➤ You must order a kosher or vegetarian meal when you book the flight. Inform the flight attendant of your arrangement when you board.

➤ The bathroom is no place for a major makeup overhaul, and men should shave before, not during the flight. Leave the bathroom as clean, or cleaner, than you found it.

➤ Look behind you before moving your seat back; there may be coffee or such on the tray.

➤ If working, keep your papers within the framework of your seat. Keep telephoning to an absolute minimum.

➤ When leaving, don't get into the aisle until you are ready to move forward. If a delay means that you have to dash for a connection, tell the flight attendant, who may help you deplane promptly.

When in situations in which people are packed in together, such as in airplanes, consideration and good manners are vitally important.

Dealing with Delays

Temper tantrums don't make you feel any better and are generally counterproductive. If a flight is overbooked or there is some other problem, the person who quietly and politely explains his situation has a better shot at getting that last seat (if one becomes open) than the rampaging bull who is verbally assaulting everyone within hearing.

Traveling with Kids

If you are traveling with children, let the ticket agent know when you book and ask for a bulkhead seat, one where there are no seats in front of you. Bring food, formulas, diapers, wipes, and any other necessities. Attendants will warm bottles or baby food, but they can't be asked to baby-sit.

Children older than five can travel alone, but you must fill out an Unaccompanied Minor form. Brief the children beforehand on how planes work, on seat belts and meals, and on the importance of obeying flight attendants and staying seated. Provide games, books, and snacks.

Cruising

It's a good idea to consult a travel agent who specializes in cruises. Agents will know about dress guidelines, which vary widely from ship to ship. They also will deal with dining preferences and deck chair assignments and will make beauty salon appointments for you in advance.

Accommodations, meals, entertainment, and use of sports facilities are free. You will need cash for wine, liquor, tipping, and personal services such as massage and dry cleaning.

Shipboard Etiquette

Landlubbers beware. Life aboard a ship has its special rules.

➤ Address the captain as "Captain," and the other officers as "Mr.", "Mrs.", or "Ms."

➤ Being invited to dine at the captain's table is a high honor. Dress is usually formal. Introduce yourself to the other diners when you arrive, and wait for the arrival of the captain before ordering.

➤ If there is a reception, don't monopolize the captain in conversation. His duty is to circulate.

➤ There are two dinner seatings: The earlier one is for families, and the later one is considered more fashionable.

➤ You may be seated with strangers. If you are unhappy with your table, you may be able to ask the steward to change your assignment. Don't ask to be seated at an officer's table; this is a bestowed honor.

➤ Bon voyage parties on board are not allowed for security reasons. You can have a party in your cabin for fellow passengers; the ship's porter will arrange it.

➤ Get a diagram of the ship so that you will be able to find your cabin. (The more expensive cabins are larger, higher up, and on the outside.)

➤ Pack light; space is tight.

➤ If you are prone to motion sickness, see your doctor about medication before sailing. If you become sick onboard, the ship's doctor will treat you.

Shipboard is a great situation for meeting people and making new friends. Be open to the opportunity.

Sea Togs

At dinner, jackets and ties for men and cocktail dresses for women are appropriate. Generally, trans-Atlantic cruising is more formal than short-term cruising, and the gala round-the-world cruise is even more formal. Generally, first-class travel is more formal than, say, tourist class.

During the day, dress as if you were at a fine resort hotel. Shorts, slacks, and sweat suits are fine for breakfast and lunch. Never wear a swimsuit without a good-looking cover-up. Men should bring at least one good business suit and a dinner jacket (tuxedo). Women will find a shawl or jacket useful on chilly nights.

Memo to Myself

What do you say if the back seat driver is really getting on your nerves? "You know, your comments are really interfering with my concentration. Could you hold off until the car is stopped?"

Car Travel

On business trips, we often find ourselves riding in cars with others. Remember these tips in those situations:

➤ If you are driving, it's your job to see that there is plenty of fuel and that the car is in good condition. You can remind people to use seat belts.

➤ Never smoke with others in the car, and never smoke in another person's car. The tobacco smell is almost impossible to get rid of.

➤ The seat of honor is front right. Defer to the eldest person or the senior executive in the group. If the passengers include a couple and a single person, put the couple together in back and the single in front.

➤ If you are genuinely frightened by the way someone is driving, tell him to stop and let you out of the car. If the driver says, "Maybe you would like to drive," take him up on the offer.

As with airplanes, the close quarters you can find yourself in while motoring require extra consideration of others.

Taxis

These are the basic rules of taxi etiquette:

➤ If you have invited someone to lunch, you must arrange for a cab or hail one curbside and pay the tab.

➤ If cabs are scarce, both host and guest should do the hailing.

➤ The host should get in first and slide across the seat to make room for the guest.

➤ Say "Good morning" or "Good evening" to the driver on entering, and say "Thank you" on leaving.

➤ If there are three of you, suggest that the tallest or stoutest one sit in front. (Don't be intimidated by the driver's papers and such on the front seat. He is required to move them.)

➤ If the driver is surly, don't reprimand him. The trip is probably hair-raising enough without distracting the driver. If you are angry enough, report the driver to the taxi company. Give a small tip, and say something like, "The tip would have been better if you had treated us better."

➤ If you and your guest are going in different directions, allow the guest to have the first taxi that comes along.

Limousines

The seat of honor here is the curbside back seat. Junior executives take the jump seat or sit in the middle. If you sit up front with the driver, you lose a chance to schmooze with the boss, but the driver is often a good source of local information, which could score points for you later. It is polite to have the seat divider lowered when a member of the party is sitting in the front seat.

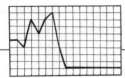

The Bottom Line

The skycap or porter at the airport gets $1 a bag. Tip a private driver or a limo or taxi driver 18 to 20 percent of the bill. Tips in train dining cars are the same as those at a restaurant.

Trains

On AMTRAK, the dining car rules are the same as in any good restaurant. Dress is casual but not careless, and the tip is generally about 20 percent of the tab.

The basic rules of courtesy for airplanes apply on trains.

➤ Don't ask the conductors for favors.

➤ Listen to the radio or tapes with earphones. Keep the volume down.

➤ Keep telephoning to a minimum. (I believe AMTRAK ought to have designated cell phone cars so that callers would only be annoying other cell phone users.)

➤ Smoke only in designated areas, if at all.

➤ Put trash in receptacles, not in the pouch in front of your seat.

One of the good things about traveling by train is the opportunity to get up and move around. This doesn't mean that you should wander aimlessly up and down the narrow aisles, however. That only annoys people and could cause congestion.

Commuter Trains

Rules are different for commuter trains:

➤ Don't hog a seat with your briefcase, coat, or gym bag. It's perfectly fine to ask others to remove such things so that you can sit down, but don't make a big deal out of it.

➤ If you are able-bodied, do the right thing and give up your seat to a disabled person, someone carrying a baby, and so forth.

➤ Lend a hand getting a bag down from the overhead rack if you are able.

You may be riding the same train every day, so make the experience is painless as possible.

The Least You Need to Know

➤ The most important part of the trip may be preparation.

➤ The number one packing rule is: less is better.

➤ Carry a detailed itinerary, and leave a copy at home and at the office.

➤ Tag and watch your luggage; double-lock hotel room doors, and don't open them for strangers.

➤ Don't flash cash in public.

➤ Avoid doing business in your hotel room, when possible.

The Global Stew

American business people are in touch with the world as never before. And it's a world of enormous cultural diversity—it's fascinating, but fraught with dangers.

To move easily in this global cultural mix, there are some important lessons to be learned and some basic lessons about "proper" behavior to be unlearned. For example, the "proper" way that American business people greet each other—stick out the hand, look 'em in the eye, smile, and say hello—would be offensive to some people and even insulting to others.

Cultural Diversity

This chapter will arm you with information that will help you with meeting, greeting, eating, and doing business with persons from other cultures. First, here are some basic guidelines:

Memo to Myself

In other English-speaking countries, "dinner" comes at midday and is the main meal. "Supper" is served at night and is generally a light meal.

➤ No matter what the situation, remember that the basis of good manners everywhere is kindness and respect for others.

➤ In unfamiliar social situations, it is perfectly correct—and a good strategy—to confess ignorance apologetically. This shows a willingness to learn about and, by implication, accept the traditions of others.

➤ Jettison all stereotypes. All Germans are not super-efficient, all Japanese are not overly polite, all Latinos are not emotional, and all Asians are not inscrutable.

These points will help to keep you from making major mistakes, but there is much, much more you need to know.

Americans and Canadians, Take Note

When foreign executives are asked what problems they have in dealing with American and Canadian business people, they most often put forth three complaints:

1. Western "friendliness" is overdone; some relationships call for a more reserved and formal approach. This "friendliness" sometimes amounts to a broken promise. It implies an ongoing friendship and a personal relationship, but it turns out to be shallow and short-lived.

   A German friend of mine was shocked and embarrassed when she visited an American who had said, "Stop by any time." As it turns out, the American gave her the cold shoulder when she opened the door.

2. The eagerness to "get right down to business" is annoying and disconcerting. The hurry-up-and-work-hard approach, reflected in things such as the working breakfast and the stand-up lunch, is grating. Some business dealings should be approached slowly and less directly.

3. Westerners seem to believe that everyone wants to be called by his or her first name. Forcing a relationship into a first-name situation is disconcerting to some and insulting to others.

A Road Trip

Think of a typical business encounter as a road that will take you from point A to point B.

In North America and Western Europe, it is considered virtuous to take the interstate. It's straight, it's quick, and you can't get lost. The best way to work is with unambiguous messages, crystal clear descriptions, and lots of specificity. Time is a linear thing, a measurement, a way of keeping score.

However, in Asia, Spain, Greece, Turkey, Latin America, and the Arab world, the tendency is not to take the interstate. The preferred road has lots of curves, some detours, and plenty of scenery.

The scenic route folks might think of the interstate crowd as pushy, insensitive, gabby, and redundant. The interstate travelers find the scenic route folks devious, slow, mysterious, and inefficient.

Two Scenarios

Imagine that an American goes into a business meeting in New York focused on what needs to get done. He enters, greets others, and find out what everyone's role is. He gets his position "on the table" right away and is prepared to tackle any problems that might arise.

In another part of the world, the savvy American shows up on time but expects to be kept waiting. He may find persons in the room who seem to have no reason for being there. He greets everyone quietly, using last names unless invited to use first names. He does not sit until his host indicates where, and he does not sit until his host is seated. Refreshments are offered and accepted and commented upon. Pleasantries are exchanged, conversations are being held around the room, and there are telephone calls. The visitor does not mention the reason for the meeting until his host does. Even then, talk will digress from the main topic often. But, gradually, opinions and positions become known, and business gets done.

The Middle East, Asia, and Africa

In these regions you may find customs and traditions markedly different from what you are accustomed to, particularly if you have been doing business primarily in North America, South America, and Europe.

The Arab World

This multifaceted world has varying degrees of strictness when it comes to adherence to religious customs and traditional modes of behavior. However, some generalizations are possible.

These are a generous people, but they're easily offended. Polite gestures, such as thank-you notes, are much appreciated. Don't make jokes unless you know the other person well. Even then, there is a danger of misunderstandings. Do not swear or make religious references—particularly, don't mention God. Punctuality is not a celebrated attribute. Be prepared to wait.

Western women should dress modestly, particularly in Iraq, Iran, Pakistan, Jordan, Syria, Libya, Indonesia, Azerbaijan, Tajikistan, Turkmenistan, the Maldives, and the Arabian Peninsula. This means long-sleeved jackets and long skirts. Women should not cross one leg over the other while sitting.

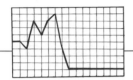

The Bottom Line

Neither men nor women should ever sit in a way that displays the sole of the foot to another person. This is serious social blunder.

➤ Do not schedule business meetings during the holy month of Ramadan.

➤ Alcohol is forbidden in parts of this region. However, you will be served lots of hot, strong coffee. Sip slowly.

➤ Do not point or beckon to an Arab.

➤ Do things (particularly eating and drinking) with your right hand. The left is for handling toilet paper.

Doing business in the Middle East can be complicated enough without adding breaches of the region's rules of etiquette.

Africa

The Arabic language and the Islamic religion are widespread in northern Africa, and customs are somewhat similar to those in the Middle East. In general, Africans tend to not rush into business deals or business discussions. Expect an extended period of small talk. There also is a great deal of handshaking all over Africa—the handshake lasts longer here than in the West, but it is not as strong.

Memo to Myself

You can please an Afrikaner enormously if you memorize a phrase or two in Afrikaans, the South African language that evolved from seventeenth-century Dutch.

In French-speaking countries, manners are more formal, and people dress up more. French social customs have a heavy influence as well: Friends kiss each other on both cheeks when greeting.

The new post-apartheid South Africa is a land of three cultures: African, English, and Afrikaner. In business, the Africans tend to be affable and warm, and the English tend to be rather reserved and initially somewhat distant. The Afrikaner tends to have a robust, straight-ahead attitude toward life and business.

Japan

Business contacts between Japan and the West have been going on so long that a great deal of tolerance for culture differences has developed. Still, there are some points to remember:

➤ This is essentially a polite society. Courtesy and courteous gestures are much valued.

➤ When shaking hands with a Japanese person (or presenting your business card), it is polite to accompany the gesture with a slight bow of the head because the bow is the universal form of greeting in Japan. "Slight" is the key word here, no matter what the other person does. You are not expected to be familiar with the complexities of Japanese bowing protocol.

➤ Don't wear flashy or loud clothing. Conservative dress is best, especially for women traveling on business.

➤ Except for handshakes, there is little touching in public.

Observing the local conventions in very much appreciated in Japan.

Korea

Remember these points when doing business with Koreans:

➤ Dress very conservatively.

➤ Meetings begin with the presentation of business cards, followed by a period of small talk. The host will signal when to begin talking business.

➤ There are no dietary restrictions, and alcohol is drunk by all.

➤ Accept the fact that Koreans smoke a lot—endure it.

➤ Most Koreans are either Buddhist or Christian.

It is important to avoid political discussions whenever possible while dealing with Koreans.

China

As you travel in this country, you will be much stared at and smiled at. Smile back. If someone applauds you, applaud back.

➤ Punctuality is essential.

➤ Dress modestly in dark colors.

➤ Refrain from noisy, conspicuous behavior.

➤ Beyond a handshake, touching is frowned upon.

A smile goes a long way to breaking the ice with casual Chinese acquaintances.

India

English is spoken everywhere in India and is the language of business and business contracts. Remember these tips when traveling here:

➤ Don't expect strict punctuality.

➤ This is a very family-oriented society. Don't hesitate to talk about your family back home; showing pictures is not only acceptable, but also appreciated.

➤ Dress in light clothing in this hot climate. Western women should dress modestly, with skirts well below the knee. In very hot weather, a jacket is not worn.

➤ Indians shake hands on greeting, but some will perform the "namaste," which involves putting fingertips together chest high and bowing slightly. You may respond similarly.

It is generally a good idea to preface business dealings with a period of casual conversation.

Extending Greetings

One of the first things anybody in business learns is that, when greeting someone, you put out your hand, make eye contact, and smile. But, in some places you could be making three mistakes at once.

Hand Signals

While it is true that the handshake is the only acceptable form of physical contact in a business context—and is generally acceptable in most places—some caution is necessary. When meeting an Asian for the first time, it is a good idea not to be the one to initiate the handshake; you may be forcing the other person into contact that he is not comfortable with. Wait until the other person offers his hand. (See Chapter 3, "Greetings and Introductions," for more handshaking strategies.)

To Touch or Not to Touch?

People in some parts of the world—particularly Asia—are touchy about touching. Don't use the two-hand "sincerity" handshake with the Japanese. Don't grasp the elbow, and especially don't put an arm around the shoulders. Some Americans are annoyed or even insulted when Asian shopkeepers place change on the counter instead of in the hand, as if they were reluctant to touch the customers. Actually, they are just being polite.

On the other side of the coin are Latinos, who are much more open to touching. People who know each other only slightly embrace upon meeting. A handshake may be held for a long time. There may be touching of hands, arms, and shoulders during the conversation, particularly if the conversation is intense or personal.

Middle Easterners—particularly Muslims—avoid casual physical contact with the opposite sex, yet people of the same sex often hug each other when meeting. A short, crisp handshake may be a virtue in the West but mildly insulting in the Middle East. You can expect a handshake to be somewhat warmer, so be careful not to jerk your hand away in apparent distaste.

A Smile Is a Signal

For Westerners, the smile sends a pleasant and unambiguous message. It means that the person smiling is happy or amused, or is just sending out a friendly signal.

In some Asian countries, smiling during a formal introduction is considered disrespectful or frivolous. The smile is a gesture appropriate to informal or casual occasions only.

In some Latin cultures, the smile can be saying "excuse me" or "please."

Memo to Myself

In the Middle East and in the Mediterranean, men holding hands is a gesture of friendship, not necessarily a signal of a homosexual relationship.

So, if your smile is not returned, don't be offended. It does not mean that the other person is hostile or aloof; it may simply mean he or she is being polite.

Eye Contact

The American practice of "look 'em right in the eye" doesn't go over well in some places—and could, in fact, be considered rude or even belligerent. In some cultures, it is deemed a sign of respect to deliberately avoid eye contact. This has led to misunderstandings in the United States: In some cities, hostilities have broken out between customers and Korean shopkeepers because the customers have interpreted the refusal to look at them as an insult. Some American teachers also have said that they at first thought some of their Asian students were chronically inattentive in class because they did not look at the teacher while he or she spoke.

So, if the other person does not respond to your offer to shake hands, or if the person responds with the barest touch, does not return your smile, and refuses to even look at you, it may very well be because of his culture, not your personality.

The Language of Gestures

Familiar and seemingly innocent gestures can offend people and get you in trouble while traveling or doing business abroad. Gestures send emphatic messages, but the language of gestures varies widely.

Americans point to their chests to indicate "me." Chinese point to their noses. In Columbia, people scratch their elbows with their fingertips to indicate that someone is stingy.

Other gestures that may be misinterpreted abroad include

➤ Pointing with your index finger

➤ Giving the "thumbs up" signal

➤ Flashing the "okay" sign by making a circle with your thumb and index finger

➤ Using the crooked index finger to beckon

Business Blunders

Keep in mind that gestures are a flawed and even dangerous means of cross–cultural communications.

In some countries, you may see customers clapping their hands or snapping their fingers to summon waiters or servants. However, you, the visitor, should not do either.

In some cultures, it is considered rude to engage in conversation with your arms akimbo or folded over your chest.

The "V for victory sign," or the sign for "two," is insulting in England and Ireland if the palm is turned inward. In fact, this is another gesture that should be avoided altogether.

Personal Space

Americans are probably most comfortable standing about 18 inches away from another person during conversation. Asians tend to stand a bit farther away, and Latinos and Mediterraneans stand a little closer.

This should not be a big problem for you. If the person speaking with you is standing too close and you find it uncomfortable, don't back off—he may either find it insulting or may pursue you until you find yourself backed into a wall. The best defense is to hold your ground but turn slightly away from the face-to-face position. If you feel that the person is standing too far away, resist the urge to move closer.

Dining Habits

To much of the world, Americans have very strange eating habits:

➤ Some find the idea of a "working breakfast" barbaric. "Brunch" is a bizarre concept and is unheard of in many places.

➤ Lunch here is an afterthought, something often snatched on the run. But, in many parts of the world, the main meal is taken at midday.

➤ Here the main meal is taken at the end of the work day and is called "dinner," a word that signifies the midday meal in other English-speaking countries.

➤ Here the evening meal begins within an hour or so of 7 P.M. Elsewhere it is lighter and later. In Spain, supper generally comes around 10 P.M.

When traveling on business abroad, you should adjust your schedule to conform with local dining customs.

Strangeness

An open mind and a sense of adventure is necessary for those Americans who would sample the cuisine of the world. Americans must be aware that others might be put off by some of our favorites dishes, such as grits, hot dogs, marshmallows, pumpkin pie, and corn on the cob (which many Europeans consider fit only for animals).

The polite traveler does not register shock or even surprise to find that the Japanese eat horse meat, that sea slugs are popular in China, that sheep eyes are eaten in the Middle East, that kidney pie is a favorite in England, or that locals eat a mixture of sheep's organs and entrails (called "haggis") in Scotland.

Happily, however, the polite traveler is not compelled to share the local enthusiasm for such delicacies.

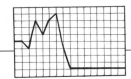

The Bottom Line

Diapers are called "nappies" in England, which could lead to some embarrassing or hilarious misunderstandings.

If you are presented with an unfamiliar dish, it may be better for your peace of mind not to ask what it is. Taste it. If you don't like it, you can cut it up and move it around on your dish. If your host asks what you think of it, don't criticize it. Say something like, "It has a very distinctive flavor. I've never had anything quite like it."

If you know what it is and you know you don't want to eat it, beg off politely. "I know this is a delicacy, but I've tried it before, and I find that it doesn't sit well with me."

Culinary Caveats

If you are the host, it is your job to know about and respect the dietary laws of others.

➤ Vegetarianism is more widespread than ever, and some extend their restrictions to fish and dairy products.

➤ Muslims do not drink alcohol or eat foods cooked with alcohol. Neither do they eat the flesh of any animal that scavenges.

➤ Many Jews do not eat pork or shellfish. For some, meat and fowl must be kosher, which means that it must have been slaughtered, prepared, and cooked in compliance with Jewish law.

Business Blunders

Don't automatically assume that your foreign guests will be delighted to be taken to an "ethnic" restaurant serving what you consider to be "their" food.

➤ If you are invited to a Chinese banquet, remember that it consists of many courses; eat sparingly at the beginning.

➤ Never point with your chop sticks. Never stick your chop sticks upright in the rice bowl—it's bad luck.

➤ When dining in the Middle East, do not touch food with your left hand.

As you can see, it's easy to get into uncomfortable situations when it comes to eating in different cultures.

Giving Gifts: Tread Carefully

Be very careful when selecting gifts for person from other cultures. This is an area laced with land mines. Following are some cautions:

Business Blunders

When it comes to cross-cultural gift-giving, it may be wise to stay away from flowers altogether. Various flowers and colors symbolize different things in different cultures.

➤ If you admire a certain possession of someone, particularly your host, he may feel obliged to offer it to you as a gift. You must not accept, no matter how strongly you are urged to do so. Refuse politely, but firmly.

➤ In some Asian cultures, gifts are not opened in the presence of the donor, so don't wait around for them to be opened.

➤ In the Middle East, a handkerchief signifies tears and parting. And never give gifts that are representations of partially clad or nude women or representations of animals, even pets.

➤ The Chinese consider clocks to be inappropriate gifts. Cash gifts should be in even numbers and should be presented with both hands.

➤ In Korea, the name of a living person is never written in red.

➤ Gifts of knives can be considered a signal of "cutting" a relationship in some Latin cultures.

Small mistakes in the gift-giving realm are likely to be forgiven if the gifts are presented in a spirit of kindness and generosity.

Flower Talk

Giving flowers may place you in dangerous territory. For example, white flowers symbolize mourning among Chinese, and yellow flowers have similar connotations among

Latinos and Middle Easterners. In Europe, chrysanthemums are linked with death. In many places—including the United States—red roses signify romantic intentions.

If you are planning to give a gift to someone from abroad and are concerned about appropriateness, ask someone from that culture, preferably a member of the recipient's family. You may even want to contact the cultural attaché at that country's embassy.

Entertaining Spouses

If you have an international colleague who is bringing a spouse along on a business trip, it is wise to design a program of activities for that person, one that is not only entertaining but also enriching. First, try to learn something about the visitor's interests, age, and education. Is the person a fan of sports, classical music, or gardening? Places to visit could include tourist attractions in your city, botanical gardens, museums, a cutting-edge computer center, a colorful or exquisite restaurant, or an interesting or challenging golf course. Never underestimate the importance of having the good will of your client's spouse.

While it will be helpful for you to be aware of the many cautions and tips in this chapter, don't let worry about possible social blunders make your relations with persons from other cultures overly stiff, excessively mannered, and cautious.

Even the most well-intentioned and well-informed business executive or traveler is bound to make mistakes while navigating the sea of customs, traditions, and attitudes that gives our world such richness and wonder.

A willingness to confess ignorance and ask for help, the ability to apologize sincerely and gracefully, an open and friendly attitude, and a genuine desire to learn will see you through just about any episode of cultural confusion.

Relating to the Disabled Worker

The American business scene has been enriched in recent years as a result of the Americans with Disabilities Act, which has removed so many physical, social, and psychological barriers.

That's the good news. The bad news is that many people, even the most self-possessed and confident people, feel awkward or uncertain in the presence of the disabled. They are hesitant, obviously uncomfortable, or overly solicitous—all of which makes the disabled person uncomfortable.

From the File Drawer

Some disabled persons refer to others as "TABS," for "temporarily able-bodied." This can be a helpful reminder to all of us.

In this next section, you will find the rules, guidelines, and insights needed to help you deal successfully and comfortably with your disabled colleagues. There is a very good chance that you will have such coworkers or supervisors in the course of your career. After all, 43 million Americans have disabilities, making them the largest and most diverse minority population in our society.

When meeting a disabled person for the first time, and when dealing with the disabled on an occasional basis, the most important thing to remember is that the disabled person is probably just as anxious to put you at ease. Remember, too, that these encounters are more difficult for the disabled than for you because that person must also deal with overcoming physical difficulties while trying to establish a comfortable working relationship.

Learn, remember, and practice the three R's of relating to the disabled:

➤ Respect

➤ Reason

➤ Relax

Let's look at each of these in turn.

Respect

Extend to the disabled the same respect you show to others. Their disability does not give others the right to become overly familiar or solicitous. The disabled person has as strong a sense of personal dignity as anyone else.

Reason

Old-fashioned common sense and common courtesy will enable you to avoid making the most frequent and most annoying mistakes and will help you to correct the mistakes you do make.

Relax

Take it easy. There is no real reason for you to be tense or anxious. In fact, getting uptight about meeting with, dealing with, or working with the disabled can only make you and those around you uncomfortable.

Once you have mastered the three R's and recognize that the disabled person is at least as committed as you are to removing any awkwardness between you, things should begin to move along nicely. To keep them moving that way, here are some important things to remember.

Guidelines

While common sense and respect will go a long way toward helping you in your dealings with the disabled, some pointers are helpful.

Memo to Myself

Check the temptation to say, "You don't look handicapped." Many people suffer serious health conditions that are not immediately apparent.

➤ Don't just go ahead and render assistance to a disabled person who seems to need help. Offer assistance, and wait until the offer is accepted. Listen to the form the assistance should take, and do not go beyond that. For example, if the other person asks you to move an object so that he can bring a wheelchair closer to a desk, don't move the object and then push the wheelchair.

➤ Always shake hands, unless this is obviously impossible or inconvenient for the other person.

➤ Don't shout, and speak directly to the disabled person, not through a third person. It is even more important to remember this when addressing a hearing-impaired person. If someone is signing for that person, resist the temptation to speak to the signer. Look at and speak to the person, and forget about the signer.

➤ Never distract a working guide dog.

➤ Always remember that you are dealing with an adult. Disabled people resent being fussed over, so don't patronize. Don't touch or pat. Don't use first names unless invited to.

Relax; there is no reason for anxiety.

Go Ahead, Say It

Sometimes you might get a little tongue-tied in the presence of the disabled. On the one hand, this is a tribute to your sensitivity and more gracious instincts. On the other, it can generate unnecessary tension and restrict the free flow of conversation.

So, don't worry about using common cliches such as

"Running around."

"Did you hear?"

"See you later."

You can talk about or bring up just about any topic. The disabled have as wide a range of interests as anyone else. But use some common sense. Movies, a common topic for conversation, is a good example. You can talk to a blind person about the ideas, conflicts or, contradictions in a movie plot. You can talk about your running regime, and a disabled person will probably be no more bored or disinterested than your other acquaintances.

And, yes, you can talk about the person's disability, or about disabilities in general. If you have a question, ask it.

However, you should avoid some expressions. Some disabled people object to the word *handicapped* because it derives from "cap in hand," which is a reference to begging. *Invalid* connotes the idea that they're somehow "not valid." Of course, words such as *dumb* (meaning "mute"), *cripple*, *afflicted*, and *deformed* are not only vulgar but also cruel.

Wheelchair Etiquette

If someone is using a wheelchair, think of it as an extension of that person's body. Don't touch it or lean on it. Don't move it without permission.

Ask if you can help if you see that the person in the chair is approaching a steep incline or an obstacle such as a curb. You can also ask if you notice that the person is working hard to traverse heavy shag carpet.

Get Down to Eye Level

Get to eye level while holding a conversation with a person in a wheelchair, if you can do so comfortably and without making a big deal out of it. It is physically uncomfortable to be looking up while conversing, and it's impossible to deal with another person on an equal basis if one of you is looking down and the other looking up.

If the owner is out of the chair, don't move it. Moving a chair or crutches can cause discomfort and even panic.

If you are giving a party or arranging a social function, think about access and obstacles.

Don't say *confined* to a wheelchair or *bound* to a wheelchair. For some, that chair is a freedom machine: It's liberating, not confining. The word to use is *uses*.

Assisting Someone Who Is Visually Impaired

Blind people want to function as independently as possible. You can render assistance in ways that allow for this. As an example, suppose that you see a blind man without a guide dog standing at an intersection.

If a blind person is stopped, waiting for assistance, you might ask him if he would like to go across the street with you. If he says yes, offer him your elbow. Having contact with your elbow means that you will be walking slightly ahead of him so that he will be able to sense any change in direction. Don't stop at the opposite curb, but hesitate and say "curb" or "step up."

Memo to Myself

You can use an imaginary clock to help a blind person locate things. In a restaurant, for example, you can say, "The mashed potatoes are at 10:00 and the chicken breast is at 7:00."

Imagine that Margaret, a visually impaired person, moves into the office next to yours, and you want to introduce yourself. First, announce your presence. If others are with you, introduce them, giving their locations: "This is Harry Glebe on my right, and Tom Finton on my left." (It will avoid confusion if Harry stays on the right and Tom on the left during the subsequent conversation.)

If Margaret extends her hand, take it. If you can't, say why. "I'd like to shake, but I'm afraid I'll drop these files." If you are the one offering to shake hands, say, "Allow me to shake your hand."

Let Margaret know when you are leaving, even if the others stay.

Here are some useful tips to remember:

➤ Don't touch, pat, or talk to a working guide dog. While in harness, they are trained to react to humans as just another object to be avoided. Don't pet the dog without permission, even when it is out of harness and resting.

➤ Don't move anything, not even a paper clip or magazine, in a blind person's work or living environment. If you do, return it to the exact spot.

➤ Watch your voice level. For some reason, people tend to raise their voices when speaking to a blind person.

➤ You are not being polite or protective when you refrain from telling a blind person that he has egg on his necktie.

➤ When giving blind persons a seat, place their hand on the back of the chair. When helping them into a car, place their hand on the inside door handle.

➤ In giving directions, make the blind person the basic reference point. "You are on First Street, facing west. Main Street is next. Turn right, and Second Street is the next intersection."

Try to imagine that you are unable to see anything; it will help you to be helpful without being annoying.

Memo to Myself

If a person does not immediately understand what you are saying, shouting is not the answer. Try speaking more slowly, more clearly, and directly to the other person.

Conversing with Someone with Hearing Loss

A new phrase has entered the language in recent years: culturally deaf. This is an expression by the deaf and hard of hearing to indicate that their situation is not so much a "disability" as a "culture," with its own language, customs, and attitudes. It is a way of saying that the deaf should not be treated as a person with a defect or a shortcoming, but simply as one who may not immediately understand what you are saying.

For instance, if you do not speak Spanish, you would not consider a Spanish person disabled simply because he does not understand what you are saying.

If there is a deaf person in your workplace, or if you expect that you may be dealing with persons with hearing loss, you can easily learn some of the basic elements of sign language.

Some deaf people depend entirely on lip reading, and some with partial hearing loss may depend on it to one degree or another. Therefore, make sure that you are facing the other person directly, preferably with the light on your face and at the same eye level. Keep your hands away from your face.

Following are some other hints:

➤ Don't raise your voice or use exaggerated lip movements.

➤ It's okay to tap the other person's shoulder to signal him to look at you, but a wave or other hand gesture is preferable.

➤ Don't get frustrated if the message doesn't get across right away. Try changing the wording. "I'd like you to read the Carter report" can become "Will you please read the Carter report." Or, "The Carter Report—please read it." If this doesn't work, write it down or get someone to use sign language.

From the File Drawer

Early records, as far back at the second century B.C.E., indicate that deaf people were treated as fools or were classified as children. It wasn't until the sixteenth century that systematic efforts were made in various parts of Western Europe to provide educational opportunities for the deaf.

For those with partial hearing loss, follow these tips:

➤ Don't speak from another room.

➤ Speak slowly and clearly, but don't shout.

➤ Turn off the radio or the television.

➤ Face the other person, and don't turn away until you have finished speaking.

➤ You can bend a little closer, but do not speak directly into the person's ear.

➤ Factors such as stress and fatigue, jet lag, or the common cold can temporarily worsen hearing impairment. Take these factors into consideration.

➤ If others in a group are laughing because of something that a hearing impaired person hasn't heard, explain it to him or indicate that you will explain later.

Listening to Someone with a Speech Impediment

The two most important things about dealing comfortably with those who have difficulty speaking are patience and attention. Give the person your complete and unhurried attention. Don't interrupt. Don't complete sentences for him or anticipate what he is going to say.

➤ When possible, ask questions that require only short answers or that can be answered with a nod or a gesture.

➤ Don't correct pronunciation.

➤ Don't pretend to understand if you do not. Repeat what you thought the person said to be sure that you understand.

Understanding Someone with a Developmental Disability

It is becoming increasingly likely that more executives and others will find themselves dealing with persons who have developmental disabilities or retardation.

Here are some basic guidelines to help you along:

➤ Treat the developmentally disabled as normally as possible, and set the same standards for them as for others.

➤ If they behave inappropriately, let them know, but in a way that is neither critical nor harsh. The idea is to be firm but nonthreatening. Use a pleasant, friendly tone of voice. Be aware that these workers may be extra sensitive to criticism.

➤ Allow plenty of time for training. Considerable repetition may be needed.

➤ Do not allow them to become too affectionate. Be careful about touching them because it may signal that such behavior is appropriate.

251

The developmentally disabled can be very useful and productive employees, but extra effort and attention will be called for.

From the File Drawer

"Pity for another implies inferiority. Pity avoids contact. It explains the man who will not employ the blind man even if he is proven as fit as the next man for the job, but instead makes out a check to the nearest blind service institution—his form of magical gesture to exorcise guilt."

—Ludwig Jekels, The Psychology of Sympathy

The Least You Need to Know

➤ Don't be put off by people who don't look you in the eye or smile, or those who seem unwilling to shake your hand—they may just be doing what they consider to be the polite thing.

➤ Many foreign business executives think that Americans are too pushy, overly friendly, and abrupt when doing business.

➤ Some commonplace gestures such as pointing and beckoning may be offensive and insulting in some places.

➤ Never be afraid to confess ignorance of customs and traditions, and to ask for help and guidance.

➤ When working with the disabled, remember the three R's: respect, relax, and reason.

➤ Disabled persons are as anxious to put you at ease as you are to put them at ease.

Sports Is Serious Play

Even if you don't like sports, exercise, or exertion that goes much beyond tickling the plastics on your computer keyboard, your business career may very well require you to do yourself the enormous favor of getting in shape to participate.

For example, you may find that the corporate culture in which you wish to swim requires the ability to play golf, which takes a considerable investment in practice time and playing time, or even racquetball, which takes a considerable investment in exertion.

And, even if sports and working out are not requirements for success in your situation, you will be healthier, more energetic, and, I firmly believe, happier if you get fit and stay fit through physical activity.

Therefore, be advised that definite rules of etiquette apply in these areas, and knowing them is every bit as important as good table manners, good grooming, and proper behavior in the boardroom.

Sportsmanship

These rules come under the general heading of sportsmanship, which has been described as etiquette with an application of perspiration.

The good sportsman plays by the rules, is considerate of everyone's safety, gives opponents the benefit of the doubt, dresses properly for every occasion, and is gracious in victory and defeat. These are the general rules. Specific rules of etiquette also apply in various circumstances—in the gym, on the slopes, on the tennis court, and on the golf links.

Gym Dandies

Some people seem to think they can leave their good manners and common sense outside when they enter places where people exercise. They get grim in the gym and become so focused on what they are doing that they lose all consideration for others. Maybe it's all those mirrors.

If anything, the opposite attitude is required. Courtesy and consideration are required to minimize distractions and to promote safety.

Memo to Myself

Never join an exercise group already in progress. It's distracting, and you may have missed important safety information delivered at the start of the session.

Workout Outfits

That pink outfit might look adorable, but it also might be inappropriate. Sexy costumes are not only inappropriate, but they're also distracting and embarrassing. It's okay if one of your reasons for going to the gym or spa is to meet the opposite sex. Just don't advertise it.

The key words are *clean* and *functional*. Avoid anything that drapes or dangles. Wearing jewelry while working out is downright stupid.

Don't walk around in bare feet or with flimsy footwear, either—you could walk into a metal plate or barbell and break a toe.

Sweaty?

It is a mortal sin to leave weight machines with sweat on the pads, and somebody is sure to call it to your attention, which is embarrassing. Carry a small towel with you, but don't leave it draped over a machine or on the floor, where people will walk on or trip over it. Also, keep your water bottle and chart out of the way of others.

In the locker room, clean up the sink area after yourself, as if you had been using the bathroom in someone else's house. Don't leave your bag or sweaty clothes on the floor, particularly in front of somebody's locker.

Weight Training

Remember these tips when pumping iron:

➤ Wait your turn for a machine or a set of free weights.

➤ Don't rest on the machine between sets of reps, particularly if the place is crowded. And don't leave things like towels on the machine to hold it while you rest. Don't chat with pals while on the machine, either; use it and move on.

➤ Shut up. Grunts and moans are unnecessary, distracting, and theatrical. And don't count out loud while doing reps; it throws off others who are counting reps to themselves.

Business Blunders

If you join a gym to meet singles, that's fine. Just don't be obvious about it. Fancy or provocative duds are out of line, and jewelry is ridiculous.

➤ Strip plates and clear your squat bars. Never leave plates or barbells where people can trip over them.

Be very careful with weights. This is the area in which so many workout injuries occur.

Personal Trainers

You may find having a personal trainer very helpful in focusing your training program and keeping you at it. Here's how to work with such a trainer:

➤ Let the trainer control the workout session. Resist the idea that you know your body better than the expert.

➤ Don't talk to the trainer while the trainer is with another client.

➤ The trainer doesn't want to hear about your emotional problems or your latest business coup.

➤ If you have to cancel, do so 24 hours in advance. If you can't give 24 hours notice, pay the trainer for the missed appointment.

The trainer's time is valuable. Respect it as you would have your working time respected.

In and Around the Pool

Whether they are lap-swimming, doing water aerobics, or just splashing around, everyone has an equal right to the water.

Lap-swimmers should stay in their lanes; if they are going to rest for more than a few minutes, they should get out of the pool.

If you can't swim, stay in the wading area. Instruct children to stay out of lap-swimmers' lanes.

If you are a guest at a pool, bring your own towel and swim attire. If you see a towel on a chair, someone is probably using it and will return. Bring your own earphones, and try not to drip on people.

Memo to Myself

If there is a question about who tees off first, don't argue. Flip a coin.

Golfing the Fair Way

It is important to know the rules and the traditions of golf. Both are taken very seriously by lovers of the sport.

The rules part is easy. Rules are published every year by the Royal and Ancient Golf Club of St. Andrews and by the United States Golfing Association, head-quartered in Princeton, New Jersey. Even experienced players keep a rule book handy, and it is a must for beginners.

Dress

Each club has its own standard; if you play at someone else's club, find out beforehand what is appropriate. In any case, showing lots of skin is generally a bad idea—so are jeans, even if they are permitted.

➤ Women wear knee-length skirts, long shorts or slacks, and often polo shirts. Long or short sleeves are acceptable.

➤ Men wear slacks or long shorts and usually polo shirts.

➤ Both men and women often wear hats to ward off the sun.

➤ Golf shoes are cleated, and pros recommend a leather golf glove.

Whatever you choose to wear, be sure your attire is comfortable.

Carts

These important cart rules have been collected from country club pros:

➤ Drive slowly.

➤ No more than two to a cart.

➤ Keep the cart out of the sightline of players in your group when they are hitting the ball.

➤ Don't leave the car near the front of the green, and keep it away from the sand traps and the greens.

➤ Never let children drive the cart.

If someone in your party is displaying bad cart manners and it's making you uncomfortable, don't hesitate to mention it.

From the File Drawer

Dress standards are generally more relaxed now in the sporting world than they have ever been. Still, dress codes continue to exist and should be followed. For example, when I was living in Cairo, one could not, under any circumstances, enter the tennis courts at the legendary Gezira Sporting Club wearing anything but white.

The Play

Remember these tips when on the links:

➤ Make sure the players in front of you are well out of the way before you swing. If in doubt, yell "fore" before you settle down to address the ball.

➤ Be ready to play when it's your turn.

➤ Don't play in groups of five or more unless authorized by the club.

➤ The player with the lowest handicap tees off first to begin. After that, it's the lowest scorer on the previous hole.

➤ Never walk on another player's line on the putting green. Never put your bag on the green.

➤ If the party behind you is on your heels, you might want to invite them to play through. You, too, can ask permission to play through if you are behind a slow party.

➤ Repair: Rake the sand. Replace the divot.

➤ It's a bad idea to plan on eating or drinking on the course, and littering is a mortal sin.

➤ Golf is a sociable sport, but keep silent when another player is hitting the ball. And "trash talk" or critical banter is frowned upon.

Remember that even when you are competing, golf is supposed to be fun. Enjoy yourself, and help others to do the same.

Business Blunders

Don't show up at courtside or on any sports outing with more equipment and accessories than you need. Extravagance is bad manners, especially in sports.

Racquet Sports

White is the safest color for all racquet sports and is required at some tennis clubs. If you are dying to wear that great-looking red outfit, call the club in advance to make sure it's all right.

No matter what you see tennis players doing on television, temper tantrums and other displays of frustration or anger are very bad form. It's generally a good idea to be quiet on the courts; verbal outbursts and banter are annoying to other players and make you look silly.

In fact, tennis is a game that relies on personal integrity to an extraordinary degree. Except for matches staffed by officials, the players call the shots. It's something like having the pitcher call balls and strikes.

You call whether the ball is in or out on your side of the net. If your opponent calls something you know is wrong on his side of the net, you say nothing. And, no, you do not "get even" by miscalling a ball on your side.

Lose gracefully, and don't blame the weather, the noise, your shoes, your spouse, or karma. You can say something like, "I had a really bad game today," as if no one had noticed.

A beginner should let the more experienced player know before the game. The experienced player should give encouragement and advice and should not try to destroy his opponent.

Memo to Myself

Saying the score out loud helps to eliminate (or at least reduce) disagreements on the tennis and racquetball courts.

Keep these points in mind as well:

➤ Say the score after every point.

➤ Show up on time, and don't hog the court.

➤ If a ball comes into your court, return it when there's a break in the play.

➤ If the serve is out, don't return it.

➤ Have two balls, not one, on hand when you begin serving.

➤ Stay in your own court, and don't walk behind another court until there's a break in the action.

It is always more fun and helpful to find opponents who play at your level or somewhat above it.

On the Slopes

The rules here are bound closely to safety concerns. Disregarding them can mean mortal danger to you and others.

Safety begins with sensible clothing. Attire must be warm and waterproof and should permit freedom of movement. Layering is needed. Goggles are safer and more durable than sunglasses. Bright colors can be more readily seen against the snow. And don't forget sun block—whatever the temperature, the sun is still the sun.

Memo to Myself

Layer for warmth while skiing. Wear thin socks under heavy ski socks, and wear long underwear under everything.

Here are some additional tips on polite and safe behavior on the slopes:

➤ Stay in your place on the lift line. Offer to ride with another single rather than break up a couple or a group. If it's your first experience, stand back a while and watch how the lift procedure works. At the top, get off promptly and move away at once to avoid causing a traffic jam.

➤ Take lessons in advance. The sport only looks easy.

➤ Don't criticize or mock beginners.

➤ Never ski alone, and never ski on a closed trail.

➤ Don't push your luck. Obey the markers: green circle for beginners, blue square for intermediates, black diamond for experts.

➤ The slow skier in front of you has the right of way. If you are going to pass, yell "track right" or "track left."

➤ If climbing up or walking down, stay well to the side of the trail.

If you come upon an injured skier, remove his skis but not his boots, and mark the spot with crossed skis. Wait for someone else to come along before you go for help. Make sure you can find your way back.

It is so easy for people to get hurt while skiing—be extra careful.

Running

Running is a great, inexpensive, and convenient form of exercise. You can do it almost anytime, almost anywhere.

Before you begin, learn how to stretch, or you will probably hurt something. Be sure to get the proper footwear as well.

It's also a good idea to find designated running paths if you are running alone. Stay out of deserted or dark areas, and don't wear jewelry or carry a wallet. Let someone know where you are running and when you expect to get back.

Run against traffic and pay attention to traffic signals. Earphones also can mask traffic noise; don't expect cars to look out for you. Carry ID and a phone card or change in case you have to make a call and don't want to tote along a cellular phone.

Biking

Your bike is a vehicle. Ride with traffic and to the side of the road, if possible. If that is not possible or is dangerous, remember that you have a right to be on the road or street, and you have a right to occupy a traffic lane. Obey all traffic laws. And wear a helmet.

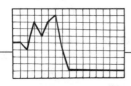

The Bottom Line

All traffic laws apply to bikers, and bikers can even be arrested for driving under the influence.

Boating

Say the executive vice president invites you for an outing on his yacht. Here are some "yachtiquette" tips:

➤ Aboard, the captain is the boss, even if he/she is not the boss at other times.

➤ If you are not helping to work the craft, stay out of the way of those who are, and offer to help out with any landlubber chores.

➤ Don't smoke below decks, particularly in the galley, where the stove may be fueled by gas.

➤ If you bring a gift aboard, make it something that can be shared: food, beer, or wine.

➤ Use fresh water sparingly.

➤ Take motion sickness medication if you think you might need it. If you get sick, stay on deck in the fresh air, and don't be embarrassed. It's not your fault.

It's okay to be a landlubber, or inexperienced sailor. But it's no excuse for bad manners.

Anchors Aweigh

For a quick cruise, wear slacks, jeans, or shorts, and a polo shirt. Avoid leather-soled shoes or high heels; sneakers are better, and nonskid Topsiders are better yet. Consider a hat to keep the sun off; women might want a scarf or bandana.

For a longer trip, you might need a swimsuit and a cover-up, as well as warmer clothes, such as turtlenecks, for night. Use soft luggage for easy stowing.

Aye, Aye, Captain

Follow these rules if you are the host:

➤ Never invite more than you can comfortably accommodate.

➤ Brief guests in advance about what to bring and what to wear.

➤ If guests will be crewing, make sure they know what they will be doing and what should be left to you. Be patient with landlubbers.

The captain must be able to exercise command without exercising his ego.

Even the greenest landlubber should be familiar with the following nautical terms.

Boating Terms

Bulkhead	Wall
Bunk	Bed
Chart	Map
Dinghy	Small rowboat
Halliard	Rope used to raise or lower a sail
Head	Toilet
Knot	A sea mile, or 6,067 feet
Ladder	Stair
Lee	The side away from the wind
Porthole	Window
Sheet or line	Rope used to work a sail
Stern	The rear of the boat
Swab	A mop, or the act of mopping

On board, you go forward toward the bow, aft toward the stern. The left side is port, and the right is starboard. You go topside and below when you go up and down.

The Least You Need to Know

➤ Getting fit and staying fit enough to compete in such sports as skiing and tennis is good strategy for business and for life.

➤ Develop a reputation as a sportsman, which means you play fair and look out for the welfare of other athletes.

➤ Don't get on the slopes until you have been trained and know how to dress and how to stay out of danger.

➤ At the health club, don't let all those mirrors make you forget the basic rules of courtesy.

➤ Don't talk to trainers while they are with clients.

➤ If invited to a tennis or golf club, find out in advance what is appropriate attire.

Rites and Passages

In the course of your career, you undoubtedly will find yourself being a guest, or even the host, at some of the ceremonial occasions that symbolize milestones or rites of passage in the lives of your colleagues, friends, and acquaintances.

The arrival of children and their maturation, along with weddings, funerals, and similar events are surrounded by and enriched by tradition and ceremony, some of it joyful, some somber. Appropriate and considerate behavior on these occasions is always much appreciated and long remembered.

Let's Start with Babies

The first invitation to be sent on the behalf of a child probably will be an invitation to his or her christening party.

Usually, baptism occurs within six weeks of birth, and sometimes within the first two weeks, in the Catholic faith. Among Protestants, baptism generally occurs within six months, although it is not unusual to have the ceremony later than that. Those who convert to a faith later in life go through the same ceremony that a baby does, except that they can select their own godparents, if they choose, and can respond to questions themselves.

Very often, the religious service is followed by a christening party. If you're invited, bring a small gift, baby clothes, or nursery items.

If you are asked to be a godparent, remember that this is a very high honor involving serious responsibilities. In most Protestant faiths, the pastor prefers that the godparents be of the same religion as the parents. In the Catholic religion, both godparents must be Catholics. The godparents are expected to oversee the spiritual education of the child, particularly if the parents are deceased. Sometimes godparents become legal guardians of a child if the parents die.

Gifts may be given jointly or separately by the godparents, and gifts to the child can take the form of a savings account in the child's name, a stroller, or a complete layette, particularly if you know that the family is going through difficult financial times. Otherwise, a silver rattle or other silver memento is appropriate.

Most often, the christening service is held in church. If the pastor agrees to have the service in the home, you should have a silver bowl to serve as a font. Ask the pastor if he requires anything else.

The form of the reception or party following the service may depend upon the time of day. If it is a morning service, there may be an informal light lunch. An early afternoon service can be followed by a tea party, and a late afternoon service can be followed by a champagne and cocktails party.

Invitations are by telephone or note, but the parents may want to have printed invitations so that they can keep some as souvenirs.

From the File Drawer

At the christening party, the baby is attired in a long white gown. The highlight of the party is the cutting of the christening cake (white with white icing and the baby's name or birth date in frosting) by the parents and a toast offered by the godparents. After the godparents have proposed their toast (or toasts), any others who have a serious, sentimental, or amusing thought may propose their own toasts to the new member of the family.

It's a good idea to tape the toast and the cake-cutting for posterity.

B'rith Milah

A Jewish baby boy is circumcised eight days after birth, is given his name, and is appointed godparents. The ceremony can take place in the home or in a special room at the hospital. Usually, only a few family members and friends are present, and gifts for the baby are sometimes presented.

A Jewish baby girl is given her name on the first Sabbath after birth in a service at the temple. The father comes forward to the Torah, recites a prayer, and says the baby's name. The rabbi recites a special blessing. Afterward, there is generally a small reception hosted by the girl's mother.

First Communion

When a Christian child reaches the age of seven or so and receives communion for the first time, it is often an occasion for a family party as well as a religious ceremony. The girls wear pretty white dresses, sometimes with veils, and the boys wear blue or gray suits. The ceremony is sometimes followed by a breakfast or brunch. Appropriate gifts include a prayer book, a rosary, or some other religious object. In Catholic churches, non-Catholics who attend the church ceremony do not receive communion.

Memo to Myself

Sometimes first communion is held in the home. Have small pieces of bread and some wine prepared for the priest to bless. The occasion is no less solemn when in the home.

Confirmation

This is usually a quiet family occasion when a child officially becomes a member of the congregation at the age of 12 or 13. Usually only family members and godparents attend the ceremony and the gathering afterward. Simple, religious gifts are appropriate. Children wear their "Sunday best" clothes, but veils are not generally worn.

Bar and Bat Mitzvah

During his bar mitzvah, the 13-year-old boy, having studied the Talmud and recited the lesson in Hebrew, is told, "You are now entering the Congregation of Israel." It is one of the most important ceremonies in the life of a Jewish man. In Reform congregations, there is a similar ceremony for 13-year-old girls, called bat or bas mitzvah.

The ceremony itself is impressive. It can last three hours in an Orthodox temple, about half that time in a Conservative temple, and about

Business Blunders

Joke gifts, no matter how innocently intended, are utterly inappropriate for ceremonial occasions such as confirmation or bar mitzvah.

an hour in a Reform temple. Often a lavish party follows the ceremony. (It is bad form to attend the party if you have not attended the ceremony.) Guests sometimes attend in formal dress. (See Chapter 6, "Business Attire and Accessories.")

Do not send or bring gifts to the temple. It is preferable to send the gifts to the home rather than take them to the party.

Funerals

At funeral services in church, dress conservatively and follow along with the rest of the congregation. At memorial services, you may say something about the deceased if you were friends or colleagues, and if you have cleared it with the family.

It is a nice gesture to bring food when visiting the home of the deceased. A letter of condolence should be handwritten; cards are a poor alternative. (See Chapter 8, "Correspondence").

If you send flowers to the funeral home, include a card saying, "To the funeral of John Smith, from Thomas Jones," or "To the funeral of John Smith, from his friends at Wilson Electronics." Some churches and temples have strict rules about flowers, so check before sending flowers there.

Don't send flowers to a Jewish family or a Muslim family.

Charity donations in the name of the deceased are always appreciated. Send the check directly to the charity, not the family, noting that it is "in memory of ...." The charity will notify the family of the donation.

If the deceased was a Catholic, you might want to send or deliver a Mass card. You can get one by calling the parish office where the deceased worshiped and making a donation in his or her name. You may send or bring the card; make sure you include your address when you sign the card.

If you visit the family at the funeral home, dress conservatively and be sure to sign the guest book when you arrive. If you are not known to the family, add something like, "I was a colleague at Wilson Electronics." Go through the receiving line, shaking hands with each family member. All you have to say is, "I'm sorry." You can, of course, add a kind remark about the deceased.

Speaking at Memorial Services

If you are asked to speak at a memorial service, follow these tips:

➤ Keep it short. Five minutes is plenty.

➤ Praise the deceased. If possible, tell a humorous story reflecting the excellent character or good humor of the deceased.

➤ Write down your remarks in advance, and practice. This is no time to ad lib or ramble.

Shiva

Shiva is the Hebrew word for "seven," and it means the week-long mourning period following the death of a family member. Close relatives visit early in the week, and friends visit later. Visit in the late afternoon or early evening, but not at mealtime. Bring a gift of food, possibly a fruit basket. Dress conservatively, and stay for about an hour. Express your sympathy when you arrive and again as you leave.

You will find that Shiva visits are not morbid occasions. Neither are they appropriate occasions for jokes or laughter. You will probably be offered food, and you should accept.

Don't let uncertainty about how to behave stop you from making the visit. You are not expected to know about all the traditions and ceremonies. The important thing is to show up and express your sympathy and support.

Catholic Mass

At a wedding or nuptial Mass, the friends and relatives of the bride and groom sit on opposite sides of the center aisle. At other Masses, you can sit anywhere.

Show up on time and dress conservatively. It is not necessary for women to wear a head covering, and men should remove hats. Follow along with what the rest of the congregation does, except when it is time for the priest to distribute Holy Communion. If you are not a Catholic, stay in your pew.

When the priest says, "Let us offer each other the sign of peace," shake hands or nod hello to those around you.

Wait until the priest leaves the altar before leaving your pew.

Memo to Myself

Guests (not members of the congregation) at a Catholic wedding, first communion, or confirmation mass shouldn't think they have to contribute if the collection basket is passed.

Seder

If you are invited to a traditional Passover seder, count on having an interesting time and on being well fed.

This occasion celebrates the exodus of the Jews from bondage in Egypt. You can send flowers in advance for the table and bring along a small gift. Passover candy is always welcome.

Call your host and ask about what to wear. If a yarmulke is needed (for men only), the host will supply one. It goes on the crown of your head.

There will be a telling of the ancient story of the exodus and a blessing of the food and the wine, which you don't have to drink if you don't care to. There also will be a

Passover plate containing such items as matzo, a roasted lamb shank, egg, green vegetables, apples, and nuts, all having symbolic significance.

It's a happy occasion, and the meal can last 90 minutes or longer.

The Wedding Guest

Being invited to a wedding is an honor, and it comes with certain responsibilities. You must observe certain formalities—for instance, you are expected to know certain things and behave in certain ways regarding seating in church, invitations, gifts, and receptions. Let's take a look at each of these topics.

Answering Invitations

First, never ask to be invited to a wedding. When invited, never ask to bring a friend. If your children are not specifically invited, leave them at home.

Answer the wedding invitation promptly. The sooner the wedding planners know how many will be attending, the better. You should reply to the invitation within a week. Also reply in the same degree of formality as is used in the invitation. If there is no address beneath the RSVP, look for it on the back of the envelope. If there is a reply card, send it with your acceptance or regrets.

If you are sending regrets to the wedding of good friends, you should write a letter explaining why you are unable to attend. If you accept and find later that you cannot attend, inform the parties promptly and with an explanation. Also, if the invitation says "reception and dinner (or supper)" and you will not be able to stay for dinner, make that clear when you accept. It is important for those planning the wedding to know how many will be having dinner at the reception.

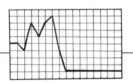

The Bottom Line

If you ask the bride what she would like, she just might suggest something that costs more than you are willing to spend.

Sending Gifts

You are not obliged to send a gift if you refuse an invitation or if you are sent a wedding announcement, as opposed to an invitation. In any case, if you know the bride or groom well, you may wish to send a gift.

If you have heard that guests have a year of grace before sending a wedding present, forget it—this is not so. In fact, it is best to send the gift prior to the wedding. Taking presents to the reception causes problems: You have to transport the gift there, and somebody else has to transport it out of there. In between, somebody has to watch over it.

Send the present to the bride in care of whomever issued the invitation, usually her parents. If you suspect that the bride might wish to have the gift sent directly to her, ask her or her parents. If you must send the gift after the wedding, send it to the bride and groom at home.

For many people, it is a common practice—and perfectly proper—to give a gift of money. You can put a check into an envelope and take it to the reception, or you can send it to the bride at home. At the reception, hand the envelope to the bride or groom as you go through the receiving line or just before you leave. Before the wedding, make the check out to the bride, "June Webling." If given at the reception, make it out to "June Smith" or to "June and Henry Smith," if the bride is taking the name of her husband.

Don't send a present bought on sale unless you know it can be returned. And don't have it mono-grammed, which will make it unreturnable. The store can include a card saying, "The customer requests that you bring this gift to the store if you wish it to be monogrammed."

Memo to Myself

If you are going to buy a gift through a store registry department, do so as soon as the invitation is received. You will have a wider range of gifts, with a wider range of prices, to select from.

You can use your personal calling card (*not* your business card) as an enclosure card. Simply strike a line through your name, and write a brief message above it: "Best wishes and every happiness to you and Henry, Love ...."

No Thanks?

If two months have passed since the wedding and your gift has not been acknowledged, it is entirely appropriate for you to contact the bride to make sure the present was received. It's probably best to write, and the tone of the letter should be warm and friendly:

> "Dear June: Since I haven't heard from you, I'm worried that you may not have received the silver serving tray I sent from Caldwell's on June 3. I know how busy you must be. Still, it would relieve my mind to know that the tray had been received. I hope you and Henry had a wonderful honeymoon in Paris, and I look forward to getting together with you both. Love, Aunt Agnes."

If you get together with the bride and groom at the home after the honeymoon and your gift tray is not on display, don't ask where it is. That's impolite.

The Out-of-Towner

If you are invited to a wedding in a different city, you are responsible for making your own hotel reservation and paying your own hotel bill. Often the bride's parents, or whoever sends the invitation, will reserve a block of rooms at a certain hotel. You can then call that hotel and reserve or arrange for your own accommodations. Out-of-towners would be well advised to call the bride or her family for some advice on how to dress. When you arrive, don't invite yourself to the rehearsal dinner; it may be a very small affair.

Seating in Church

Arrive about 15 minutes before the ceremony. If you are to sit in one of the reserved pews at the front of the church, you will be told in advance, or you will receive a handwritten note or an engraved pew card with the pew number or the notation "Within the ribbon"—this means that you are to sit in one of the pews marked by ribbons. There is no seating arrangement within the pew itself. If you have such a card, hand it to the usher when you arrive. If not, give the usher your name and he will refer to a seating list.

If no special seating arrangement applies for you, the usher will ask you if you are a friend of the bride or the groom, and will escort you to a pew on the left side (for the bride) or the right side (for the groom). A woman generally takes the usher's arm to walk down the aisle. The groom may be from out of town, causing the distribution in the church to be dramatically out of balance. In this case, ushers may ask some of the bride's friends to sit on the right, and they should agree readily to do so. If there is congestion or a long line, guests may wish to seat themselves.

If a wife takes the usher's arm, her husband may follow or walk beside them. If there are children, the husband walks behind the children.

➤ If you see a friend, ask the usher if you may use that pew, if there is space.

➤ If a white runner is in place in the center aisle, the two side aisles are used for seating.

➤ Once seated, you may talk quietly with those around you prior to the start of the ceremony.

➤ If you secure an aisle seat, giving you a good view of the wedding procession, you don't have to give it up. Let newcomers slide past you.

➤ The mother of the bride is seated last, and ushers won't seat you after that. If you arrive late, linger in the back of the church or slip inconspicuously into one of the back pews.

➤ After the ceremony, stay in your pew until those from the reserved pews in the front have passed.

The Reception

It's bad manners to go through the reception line carrying a drink. Give it to a waiter, or put it down on a table. Say your full name to the first person in line, usually the bride's mother, who may introduce you to the next person. If not, don't hesitate to repeat your name. People tend to forget names in such situations. Speak briefly to each person, and shake hands. Kiss the bride if you are a close friend or relative. You may give a collective greeting to the bridesmaids. The main thing is to keep the line moving.

Business Blunders

It is bad form for wedding guests to skip the ceremony and show up for the reception. If that happens, an explanation and apology are in order.

➤ Sign the guest book without using titles. Couples sign "Gertrude and Randy McGuire."

➤ No one dances before the bride and groom. Their parents then join them on the dance floor, followed by wedding attendants and then the guests.

➤ At dinner, it is taboo to switch place cards because you want to sit with a friend.

➤ The best man, and perhaps the father of the bride, will propose a toast. Do not offer a toast yourself unless you are called upon to do so.

➤ Do not scramble or leap to catch the bride's bouquet. She may be throwing it to her maid of honor or one of the bridesmaids.

➤ If you must leave before the cutting of the cake, slip away quietly and later write a note to the bride's parents thanking them and saying what a good time you had. If you stay, remember that the departure of the bride and groom signals that the reception is over. Find the bride's parents, and thank them.

If you have thanked the bride's parents at the reception, it is not necessary to write a letter of thanks, although it certainly would be much appreciated.

The Least You Need to Know

➤ Considerate and courteous behavior is never more important or more appreciated than during the more solemn or happy ceremonial occasions in life.

➤ If someone asks you to be a godparent, remember that it is a high honor, and be sure you know your responsibilities before you accept.

➤ Gifts of a religious nature are appropriate for occasions such as first communion, but other gifts are also acceptable.

➤ If you wish to speak at a memorial service, clear it with the family, and be prepared, sincere, and brief.

➤ Never invite yourself to a wedding or ask to bring a friend.

➤ If you send regrets to a wedding invitation, or if you receive a wedding announcement instead of an invitation, it is not necessary to send a gift.

Index

Q

R

S

WITHDRAWN
No longer the property of the
Boston Public Library.
Sale of this material benefits the Libra